M000086530

Living Gluten and Dairy-Free with French Gourmet Food

A practical guide

By Chef Alain Braux

C.E.P.C., C.M.B.

B.S. Holistic Nutrition

Copyright © 2010 by Alain Braux International Publishing, LLC.

All rights reserved. No part of this book may be reproduced or transmitted in any forms or by any means, electronic or mechanical, including photocopying, recording or by any form of information storage and retrieval system, without the written permission of the author except where permitted by law.

ISBN-13: 978-0-9842883-1-1

ISBN-10: 0-9842883-1-7

Living Gluten and Dairy-Free with French Gourmet Food is a trademark of Alain Braux, Alain Braux International Publishing, LLC.

Disclaimer: This book has been written as an educational tool only. It is not a substitute for the informed medical recommendations of your personal physician or other qualified healthcare provider. The information within these pages is designed to help you learn about and understand what can be a very confusing illness. I hope that this book will allow you to have a better dialogue with your healthcare providers and make your life easier.

The publisher and the author of this book are not responsible for any products and services mentioned or referred to in this book, and disclaim any liability regarding the information offered in this book. They also disclaim any responsibility for any damage, loss, or expense to property arising out of, or relating to the text in this book. If you have any doubts as to the validity of the information given, please do not purchase this book. Thank you for your understanding.

Real people, who were gracious enough to share their stories with you, wrote all the stories contained in this book. They agreed to have their real names published. I thank them in the back of the book. They, as well as the author and publisher, are not legally responsible to you or anyone related to you for telling you their stories. They offer them only as a way to help you understand that you are not alone, and that you can live happily and healthfully with this difficult condition.

Before starting a new diet plan or lifestyle change, or beginning or modifying an exercise program, please check with your personal physician to make sure that the changes you plan to make are right for you. Sincerely, Alain Braux.

For information regarding this and other Alain Braux International Publishing, LLC books and speaking engagements, please contact Alain Braux through AlainBraux.com or alainbraux@gmail.com

Edited by **Kathleen Thornberry**

Cover design by **Nathan Stueve**.

Back photograph by **Athena Danoy**.

Manufactured in the United States of America. (October 2010)

TABLE OF CONTENTS

Living Gluten and Dairy-Free with French Gourmet Food............................3

FOREWORD 11

What is Happening To You? 13

    Paula T — Austin, TX..16

    Liz M — Dallas, TX...21

    Annie P - Durango, CO 25

    Jeff W — Austin, TX..30

How To Live GFCF at Home..34

    Getting Started 35

    Karen M - Austin, TX...41

Shopping and Eating GFCF in the Real World 42

How to Handle Your GFCF Social Life 47

    Can You Have a GFCF Social Life? Absolutely! 48

    Maggie T – Austin, TX 51

What is Your Responsibility as a GFCF Patient? 52

    Dawn A – Austin, TX...55

    Special Foods to Consider..55

    Other Products That Could Possibly Contain Gluten 58

Not Feeling Better Yet? Could There Be Another Cause?........................60

    Jocelyne V – Austin, TX 61

What Other Health Issues Could Be Created by Gluten Intolerance? 64

Anemia, Iron Deficiency, and Fatigue 64

    Kelly F – Austin, TX...66

Osteoporosis...69

Low Thyroid Functions (Hypothyroidism)...74

    Kim S – Austin, TX..74

Your New Gluten and Dairy-Free Diet 76

    Jessica M – Austin, TX...80

Time to Heal That Gut 81

For a Healthy Diet, All You Need is Love… and The Following Ingredients 87

Trish B – Austin, TX 94

Living With Autism 98

Kecia J – Austin, TX 100

Meagan M – Austin, TX 108

Nicole D – Austin, TX 112

Appendix A 114

Gluten Intolerance and Celiac Disease Organizations 114

Appendix B 118

Living with Autism Information 118

Information about Autism Agencies, Organizations and Foundations 118

Suggested Autism Reading List 120

Appendix C 122

Hidden Sources of Gluten and Dairy 122

First, the Good News: What You Can Still Eat 122

SAFE – Grains, Flours, Starches (Gluten-Free/Wheat-Free) 122

SAFE – Other Foods Allowed 123

A Word About Wine and Spirits 123

Alcohol Products That Are Usually Safe: 123

Products That May Contain Gluten (gliadin) and Dairy (casein) 124

The NO-NO Lists! 128

NO-NO Grains and Flours 128

NO-NO Products Made From Wheat & Flour 129

CAUTION: Suspicious Foods and Food Products 130

The Following Foods and Food Products MAY Contain Wheat or Gluten 130

The Following Foods and Food Products Contain or MAY Contain Dairy and Casein 134

Mysterious Ingredients Listed on the Nutritional Labels of Prepared Foods: What you need to know 135

Appendix D: Gluten-Free, Dairy-Free Shopping List 149

Recettes. *Recipes* 184

Recipes Introduction 185

Pains. *Breads* 193

Mélange de Farine a Pain Sans Gluten. *Gluten-Free Bread Flour Mix* 193

Boule de Pain à la Provençale. *French Provencal Boule* 194

Pain Sans Gluten a la Farine de Sarasin. *Gluten-Free Buckwheat Bread* 197

Pain au Quinoa. *Quinoa Bread* 198

Brioche au Chocolat et a l'Orange en Casserole. *Chocolate and Orange Brioche in French Oven Pot* 199

Pain de Mais aux Herbes de Provence. *Corn Bread with Provencal Herbs* ..200

Pain Brioché aux Amandes. *Brioche-Style Almond Bread* 201

Pain d'Epices de Mamie. *Mamie's Spiced Bread* 202

Petit Déjeuner. *Breakfast* 203

Mélange de Farine de Pâtisserie Sans Gluten. *Gluten-free Pastry Flour Mix* 203

Petit Déjeuner A Votre Santé. *A Votre Santé Healthy Home-made Breakfast Cereal* 204

Crêpes Petit Déjeuner au Quinoa. *Quinoa Pancakes* 206

Gaufres de Bruxelles. *Brussels Waffles* 207

Biscuits aux Canneberges et Noix. *Cranberry Walnut Scones* 208

Petits Gâteaux aux Bluets et Citron. *Blueberry Lemon Muffins* 210

Petits Gâteaux d'Automne aux Fruits Rouges. *Autumnal Red Fruit Muffins* 211

Petits Gâteaux a la Noix de Coco et Graines de Pavot. *Coconut Lemon Poppy Seed Muffins* 212

Gâteaux pour le Goûter. *Tea Time Poundcakes* 213

Gâteau Moelleux aux Bananes et Noisettes. *Moist Banana and Hazelnut Pound Cake or Muffins* 213

Quatre-Quarts au Citron. *Lemon Pound Cake or Muffins* 214

Gâteau a la Noix de Coco and aux Canneberges. *Coconut Cranberry Walnut Bread* 215

Petits Gateaux Secs. *Cookies* 216

Cookies au Chocolat et Pecans. Chocolate Chip and Pecan Cookies 216

Brownies à la Farine de Coco. *Coconut Flour Brownies* 217

Petits Gâteaux Secs à la Noix de Coco et au Citron et Citron Vert. *Lemon-Lime Coconut Flour Cookies* 218

Sablés Diamants. *Shortbread Cookies with Raspberry Dots* 219

Macarons Meringues à la Noix de Coco. *Coconut Macaroon Meringues* 220

Biscuits Croquants au Chocolat et Amandes. *Almond Butter Chocolate Chip Crisps* 221

Biscuits Quinoa aux Chocolat, Pecans et Orange. *Chocolate-Pecan-Orange Quinoa Cookies* 222

Langues de Chat. *Cat's Tongue Cookies* 223

Escargots à la Pate d'Amandes. *Almond Paste Snails* 224

Hors D'Œuvres. *Appetizers* 225

Tapenade. *Tapenade* 225

Crêpes aux Courgettes. *Zucchini Appetizer Crepes* 226

Socca de Nice. *Socca from Nice* 227

Trempette Arzu aux Epinards et Artichauts. *Arzu Spinach and Artichoke Dip* 228

Soupes. *Soups* 230

Soupe de Santé Verte d'Alain. *Alain's Healthy Green Soup* 230

Soupe Gaspacho. Gazpacho *Soup* 231

Soupe de Légumes au Bœuf. *Beef Vegetable Soup* 232

Soupe de Courgettes. *Zucchini Soup* 234

Soupe de Tomates à la Niçoise. *Niçoise-style Tomato Soup* 235

Soupe aux Lentilles et à la Tomate. *Lentil Tomato Soup* 236

Soupe de Poix Chiches à la Sauge. *Garbanzo Bean Soup with Sage* 237

Salades. *Salads* 238

Vinaigrette de Santé d'Alain. *Alain's Healthy Salad Dressing* 238

Taboulé de Quinoa. *Quinoa Tabouleh* 239

Salade Niçoise. *Niçoise Salad* 240

Salade aux Petits Poix et Poivrons. *Peas-full Egg Salad* 242

Salade de Pâtes au Thon. *Garden Pasta Tuna Salad* 243

Viandes et Œufs. *Meats and Eggs* 244

La Daube a la Niçoise. *Niçoise-style Daube* 244

Le Ragout de Porc aux Câpres. *Pork Stew with Capers* 246

Cotes d'Agneau au Romarin. *Rosemary Lamb Chops* 247

Poulet Farci aux Riz et Figues. *Roasted Chicken Stuffed with Rice and Figs*. 248

La Polenta de Ménage au Poulet. *Family-Style Polenta with Chicken* 250

Tian de Courgettes au Riz. *Zucchini and Rice Egg Dish* 251

Galettes de Sarasin Complete. *Brittany-Style Savory Crêpes* 252

Poissons et Fruits De Mer. *Fish and Seafood* 254

Ma Façon Rapide de Préparer des crevettes ou Coquilles de St. Jacques. *Alain's Quick Way to Prepare Poached Shrimp or Scallops* 254

Le Rouget a la Niçoise. *Red Mullet a la Niçoise* 255

Thon Façon Côte d'Azur. *Tuna Côte d'Azur-style* 256

Risotto aux Crevettes. *Shrimp Risotto* 258

Accompagnements. *Side Dishes* 259

Les Macaronis à La Provençale. *Provencal-Style Macaroni* 259

Ratatouille. *Ratatouille* 260

Epinards aux Raisins et aux Pignons. *Spinach with Raisins and Pine Nuts*. 262

Les Tomates au Four a la Provençale. *Oven-Baked Tomatoes Provençale* 263

Risotto de Quinoa aux Poivrons Rouges. *Quinoa Risotto with Red Bell Peppers* 264

Tomates Farcies à la Viande de Bœuf. *Beef-Stuffed Tomatoes* 265

Purée de Pommes de Terre a l'Ail. *Mashed Potatoes with Garlic* 266

Haricots Verts avec sa Vinaigrette et Amandes. *Haricots Verts in Almond-Garlic Vinaigrette* 267

Riz Sauvage au Romarin et Baies de Goji et Noix. *Rosemary Wild Rice with Goji Berries and Walnuts* 268

Desserts. *Desserts* 269

Classique Mousse au Chocolat. *Classic French Chocolate Mousse* 269

Soufflé aux Framboises Léger comme un Nuage. *Light as a Cloud Raspberry Souffle* 270

Crème Brulée à la Lavande. *Lavender Crème Brulée* 272

Ma Marquise Préférée au Chocolat. *My Favorite Chocolate Marquise*.........274

Pots de Cocos. *Coconut Pots* 275

GF Beignets aux Pommes. *Apple Fritters*..276

Ganses Légères à la Niçoise. *Light Niçoise-Style Beignets*...........................278

Crêpes a l'Orange et au Grand Marnier. *Orange Grand Marnier French Crepes* 279

Glace au Chocolat. Chocolate « Ice Cream »...280

Gateaux et Tartes. *Cakes and Tarts*...281

Clafoutis aux Cerises. *Cherry Flan* 281

Gâteau au Chocolat Sans Farine. *Flourless Chocolate Cake* 282

Gâteau Exotique Aux Carottes. *GF Exotic Carrot Cake*..............................284

Gâteau au Chocolat à la Farine de Noix de Coco et à la Ganache. *Gluten-Free Coconut Flour Chocolate Cake with Ganache Filling and Icing*.................286

Ganache au Chocolat Noir. *Dark Chocolate Ganache*.................................287

Gâteau Leger au Champagne et Cointreau. *Champagne-Cointreau Chiffon Cake* 288

Glaçage a l'Orange. *Orange Frosting*...289

Poire Bourdaloue. *Pear Tart with Almond Cream* 290

ACKNOWLEDGMENTS...292

Do you want to know more about Chef Braux? 295

FOREWORD

Bonjour and Welcome! If you have read my first book "**How to Lower your Cholesterol with French Gourmet Food**", welcome back. If not, thank you for reading this book, and if you like it, thank you for letting your friends know about it.

My name is Alain Braux. I am a gluten and dairy-free chef and nutritherapist at Peoples Pharmacy in Austin, Texas. I have been a traditionally trained French chef for the past 40 years, working as a pastry chef, baker and chef. For the past 12 years, I have been also been involved in nutrition as a nutritherapist - a term used in Europe for nutritionists that use only food as a healing medium, as opposed to nutritionists, who usually work with supplements, homeopathy and herbal medicine. Since supplements are not my area of expertise, I will only briefly mention them. If you want to know more about me and what I do, you're welcome to visit me at: **www.alainbraux.com**.

Even though I began writing this book to help my clients and others with gluten intolerance, I have recently discovered I am gluten intolerant myself. I had been feeling strange: bloated for no particular reason, feeling tired even after a good night's sleep, brain fog and dragging my feet in the afternoon. Wanting to know for sure, I went to a reputable Austin gastroenterologist and took a blood test. It turns out I, too, am sensitive to gluten. Me, a Frenchman, allergic to gluten! How could I live without my croissant for breakfast or piece of baguette with my favorite cheese? Talk about denial! So you see, I will be making the same tough culinary choices in my life that you may have to make in yours. I now have even more incentive to write this book, both for you and for myself.

In this book, I will address the issues of gluten intolerance (or allergy), celiac disease and casein intolerance. I have found from my personal contact with autistic children's parents that a gluten and casein-free (GFCF) diet has proven highly beneficial to their children. I am aware that a lot of scientists will disagree with my statement, but I trust my clients' observations when it comes to their own children. They live with them day in, day out and know their children much, much better than any scientist could, however qualified.

Since I am not a doctor or a researcher, I will not pretend that I can give you all the scientific information regarding your condition. I will endeavor to give you the best information I can, but for more specifics I will refer you to books written by experts. Two of my many GFCF heroes are **Dr. Stephen**

Wangen, author of "Healthier Without Wheat: A New Understanding of Wheat Allergies, Celiac Disease, and Non-Celiac Gluten Intolerance". The other is Jaquelyn McCandless, MD, author of "Children with Starving Brains. A Medical Treatment Guide for Autism Spectrum Disorder." Please refer to these books for more detailed scientific explanations.

I would like to take this opportunity to thank all the generous people suffering from different versions of gluten and dairy intolerance, as well as the courageous parents of autistic children, for sharing their very personal stories. These kind people are proof that you are not alone with this affliction, and that these conditions are manageable. Thank you all for sharing your experiences with us. If you are interested to know who they are, their names are listed at the back of this book.

As a self-published author, your good word helps spread this information to everyone that might benefit from it. I also would like to let you know that I pledge to donate $1.00 per book sold to the local chapters of the Gluten Intolerance Group of North America and the National Autism Association. I hope this small donation will help both organizations. Thank you for helping these organizations by purchasing this book.

As a French chef, I am used to offering my clientele tasty, delicious and attractive food. The recipes in this book are no different. There is no reason why, because you are on a special diet, you should not be allowed access to beautiful and delicious food. I never believe that being on a diet means depriving yourself of one of the most basic joys in life: good food. This is my gift to you and I hope you will enjoy these recipes.

Bon Appétit y'all!

Chef Alain Braux

What is Happening To You?

Are you having abdominal pain, indigestion, constipation or diarrhea? Do you have skin rashes? Are you feeling constantly tired and unable to think straight? Are you worried about what these symptoms could be, and confused about what to do? Is it irritable bowel syndrome, Crohn's disease, a Candida albicans (yeast) infection, or a parasite? You have so many questions, and you feel you are not getting straight answers. If you have been plagued with any of these symptoms for a while, you need to find out what is really troubling you.

Perhaps your doctor has just confirmed it: you have gluten intolerance or celiac disease. Maybe you've been aware for a while that there is something wrong with your digestive system and how your body reacts to certain foods. You may have been told that you had a psychosomatic disorder – a fancy term meaning "they" thought you were either making it up, or that it was all in your head. Or "they" may have told you that you have irritable bowel syndrome, Crohn's disease or allergies. Yet, instinctively, you knew it was more than that. To be fair with your doctors, until recently, there was no actual diagnosis for what you've been suffering. The actual realization that there is more to celiac disease than a simple allergy is only a few years old. Western medicine has recently made tremendous progress regarding the testing and diagnosis of gluten intolerance or celiac disease.

Now that you know, although you may panic at the thought of facing this affliction by yourself, please remember that you are not alone and there is plenty of help available. This book is only one example. There are many other very good guides out there and plenty of help available in your community, as well as on the Internet. Plus, now that you know what is troubling you, you probably feel relief. You are not alone. I am here to help you, and I will do my best to help you understand what is making you feel ill. I will give you practical advice, and provide a bunch of tasty, healthy and perfectly safe recipes so you can enjoy your new gluten- (and possibly dairy) free life.

Let's Go Back to Science Class: How Does Human Digestion Work?

Digestion is the mechanical and chemical process your body uses to break food down into smaller and smaller molecules so that it can be absorbed into the blood stream for nutrition.

The digestive process starts by chewing food with our teeth and mixing it with salivary digestive enzymes. For example, the enzyme amylase starts breaking down starches into sugars. Saliva also helps us soften the food to be swallowed. It then travels down our esophagus into our stomach, where hydrochloric acid kills most contaminating microorganisms and begins the mechanical breakdown of some food, and the chemical alteration of the rest. The low pH of the hydrochloric acid also allows assorted digestive enzymes to do their job of dismantling your food into smaller and smaller components. For example, pepsin breaks down protein, and gastric amylase further breaks down sugars. The resulting milky liquid, called chyme, then passes on to the small intestine where the majority of final digestion occurs: bile sent by the liver breaks down fats; maltase, lactase and sucrase finalize sugar digestion; the pancreas sends trypsin to break down proteins into amino acids, lipase to break down fatty acids and amylase to break down other carbohydrates.

These enzymes have done almost all the work of dividing protein, fats and carbohydrates into smaller molecules. But these nutrients are not fully broken down yet. They still have to be separated into digestible nutrients by additional enzymes in order to be used as cellular food. These enzymes include peptidase, which separates peptides into amino acids, and the enzyme maltase, which acts upon maltose to produce glucose. These molecules are then absorbed by the villi – finger-like protuberances - in the small intestine. According to the type of molecule, they are absorbed into our body by either the lymphatic or blood capillaries. When coming into the large intestine or colon, friendly bacteria further process the remaining matter, which extracts additional nutrients. What are left are mostly undigested fiber and other waste products. Water is absorbed into the colon walls and the leftovers, called feces, are stored in the rectum before being ejected into your toilet bowl.

What Is Making You Sick?

Protein is necessary for rebuilding your cells and muscles. But in this case, one particular protein is making you sick. Gluten is the paste created when the two proteins called gliadin and glutenin are mixed with a liquid into dough. In your case, the one making you sick is gliadin. To make things easier, the umbrella term gluten is used in place of gliadin. Gluten is found in grains like wheat (including kamut and spelt), barley, rye and some people also say oats. It can also be found in malts and triticale, as well as in an assortment of additives, thickeners and flavorings. (For a complete listing of hidden gluten sources, see Appendix C). It can create a series of baffling symptoms in people who are sensitive or allergic to it.

You may be tempted to self-diagnose and heal yourself based on the
following observed symptoms:

➤ Painful bloating that is obvious
➤ Ongoing acid reflux
➤ Flatulence
➤ Regularly occurring diarrhea
➤ Never ending fatigue
➤ Dermatitis Herpetiformis (skin rash)
➤ Mysterious vitamin deficiencies that persist despite eating balanced
   meals

It was 30 years ago that a nurse suggested to me that I had a spastic colon, when I told her about the abdominal pain I was having quite regularly. Later they called it irritable bowel syndrome, and I assumed that's what I had. If I went a long time between meals, I got painful abdominal spasms. I had bouts of diarrhea and then constipation. And I had unexplained flatulence now and then. Doctors recommended that I eat more fiber in my diet plus take fiber supplements, which did make the abdominal spasms go away once and for all, and my bowels became more regular. And whenever I went off the fiber supplements, the spasms returned, along with the bouts of diarrhea and constipation. I still had bloating and gas, but assumed it was from the fiber supplements, not to mention all the beans and vegetables in my diet. twenty years ago, I began a plant-based diet which I continue to adhere to.

Then about ten years ago, I started to have diarrhea flare-ups, bloating and gas, off and on. I was a marathon runner, and the diarrhea eventually put an end to my long-distance running. Last year, I had my first bone density scan which showed I had slight osteopenia. I started working out with a personal trainer, doing weight-bearing exercises to build bone. She suggested that my abdominal problems may be due to inflammation in my gut. My abdomen would resist any attempts she tried to give me six-pack abs! Due to her keen observation, I decided to seek the advice of a gastroenterologist.

I've was diagnosed with celiac disease. I had an endoscopy in which biopsies were taken to confirm a positive blood test I had taken six months earlier. I was rather surprised by the diagnosis, but relieved to know what was causing my problems. I've been eating gluten-free for a month now and haven't seen any changes, but I know it'll take a long time for the villi in my intestines to heal because, I was told, the damage is severe.

I've lived with the adverse symptoms of celiac disease for a long time and just got used to them, while continuing to damage my body. I thought I was living a healthy lifestyle of diet and exercise before my diagnosis, so going gluten-free has been relatively easy for me. Now I'm even more committed to being proactive about my health.

Paula T—Austin, TX

Possible Reasons Why You Are Trying to Heal Yourself on Your Own

➤ You read an article in a newspaper/magazine/online that seem to describe your health symptoms and are trying to figure it out on your own
➤ You have no health insurance
➤ You're trying to save money by doing it yourself
➤ You don't like to go to your doctor. Who does really?
➤ You don't know which doctor to see
➤ You have the habit of self-medicating
➤ You may be afraid to know the truth

How can you really find out on your own if you have gluten allergy, intolerance or celiac disease? It could be a different food allergy, or it could simply be stress. Unfortunately, you have no way to test for celiac disease on your own. You could try an elimination diet where you stop eating what you suspect is making you sick; for example, stop eating any gluten-containing or dairy foods for at least 3 months. After that, introduce the offending food back in your diet and observe how you feel. Most likely, you will notice the difference. But if you want to find out quickly or want to be sure, getting tested may be the only way.

Gluten Sensitivity, Allergy, Intolerance or Celiac Disease: Which One Is It?

In a lot of cases, these words are used interchangeably and it can be confusing. They really all have different meanings. The word "sensitivity" is a very nonspecific term that indicates you are having a mild reaction to something. Remove the culprit from your diet and you will feel better quickly.

Food Allergies versus Food Intolerances

Even as the medical establishment is realizing the effect food can have on our health, many of their number still confuse the terms *food intolerance* and *food allergy*. They seem to use both terms interchangeably, when each one describes a specific type of illness caused by entirely different physiological responses by the body.

Food Intolerances

Food intolerance typically describes a non-immune reaction to a product your digestive system cannot handle for lack of a specific digestive enzyme. One good example is lactose intolerance, where the lack of the digestive enzyme *lactase* prevents the proper digestion of a form of sugar found in milk, called lactose. If you have a hard time digesting meat because your body does not produce enough *protease*, you may have a meat intolerance. The same could happen if you cannot digest a particular fruit or vegetable. Some people have an intolerance to the fruit sugar called fructose. For the vast majority of the population, eating fruit is not a problem, but the people lacking the enzymes *amylase* or *sucrase* will suffer from fructose intolerance. The term intolerance is also used loosely to describe any form of reaction by the body to any food or spice: you could get heartburn from eating spicy food, for instance, which is a type of intolerance. There can be other intolerances to artificial colors, to chemical preservatives like sulfites in some wines, and to nitrites in some processed meats. The important factor to remember is that food intolerance is not an immune reaction.

Food Allergies

How is a food allergy different than food intolerance? A food allergy, as with other types of allergies, is a series of reactions created by your immune system in the presence of allergens, typically environmental allergens. The reactions are similar to hay fever or similar type of allergy, like hives, swelling of lips, tongue and throat or similar symptoms. They mostly involved histamines and although possibly dangerous, they typically do not involve the digestive system. Think of your immune system as your own personal posse of bodyguards. In this case, they are antibodies called immunoglobulins (Ig for short). Their job is to look out for any suspicious characters called allergens. Allergens can be anything from pollen to mold to any kind of food.

Why our immune systems are reacting to food is not fully understood at this time. In a perfect world, our bodies would not view food as an allergen.

After all, we have survived for millennia thanks to food. Is it due to all the additional environmental stresses on our bodies? Is it due to the chemical products added to our food these days: artificial colorings and preservatives? Possibly. Our bodies are aggressed from all sides and have become sensitive to what they perceive to be yet another aggressor: food. We can be allergic to a wide assortment of foods, but the ones we are mostly concerned with in this book are gluten and dairy-containing foods. If, for whatever reasons, your Ig bodyguards have been given instructions to watch out for gliadin and casein, they will attack these invaders and create all sorts of health problems for you: inflammation, mucus, sneezing and all sorts of digestive problems. Unfortunately, villi inflammation, the worst consequence for celiac disease sufferers, will cause the progressive destruction of the small intestine villi, the same villi that allow your body to absorb all the good nutrients, vitamins and minerals it needs to thrive.

Gluten Intolerance or Allergy?

Unfortunately, the descriptor "gluten intolerance" is a term used by many doctors to describe people with a gluten allergy, especially when it affects their digestive system. I know, this is confusing and I'm sorry for that. Lately, scientists are also discovering that it can affect much more than the digestive system. There are many symptoms attached to gluten intolerance. It can create severe skin disorders, attack the nervous system, muscle and skeleton system, even joints and teeth. Most of the time, it is used to describe the milder form of gluten allergy. The more severe version of gluten intolerance is usually described in the medical world as coeliac or celiac disease.

Celiac Disease

What makes the gluten intolerance (or allergy) into celiac disease is the inflammation of the finger-like protrusions (villi) in your small intestine which are in charge of filtering food elements like nutrients, vitamins and minerals. Typically, proteins are broken down into separate amino acids by assorted enzymes in your stomach and small intestine. When the villi become inflamed they atrophy, blocking vital nutrients. It can also create a condition called "leaky gut syndrome" that allows large proteins like gliadin and casein (milk protein) to get through your intestinal walls. Since whole proteins are not usually found in your blood, they are treated as foreign and possibly dangerous matter by your immune system, which sends out the antibodies (immunoglobulins or Ig), the "bodyguards" of the immune system. According to the type of specialist you talk to, they can also you're your condition celiac sprue, non-tropical sprue, Gee-Herter's syndrome, gluten intolerance (that's the confusing part), gluten sensitivity or gluten sensitive enteropathy. Pick your choice.

Casein Intolerance

Casein is the main protein found in milk and milk products. For people sensitive to it, especially people with the autism spectrum disorder, this protein is broken down by their digestive system into an opioid called casomorphin. It appears that casomorphin acts as a histamine releaser and causes the same effects as if they were having severe hay fever or another environmental allergy. For some sufferers, the only way to avoid these side effects is to follow a casein-free (CF in short) diet. Many parents of autistic children have reported that putting their children on a gluten- and casein-free diet (GFCF or GF/CF) improves their children's cognitive and socializing abilities tremendously. I discuss this much further in the Autism section of this book.

What Do we Call These Immune Bodyguards?

There are three main characters responsible for your protection that may be creating havoc within your body.

Number One is immunoglobulin E (IgE). Typically, IgE is the antibody that will give you typical short-terms allergy reactions: watery itchy or burning eyes, runny nose, swelling and blockage of the nasal passages, swelling of the lips and tongue, hives, bloating, abdominal pain and possible diarrhea. Some of these reactions can be fatal, such as anaphylactic shock and death. So IgE is not a guy to mess with. But IgE is not the only guy involved in most food allergies.

His buddy immunoglobulin G (IgG) is standing guard right next to him. That guy is responsible for the long-term allergic reactions. Its reactions can show up hours, even days after the ingestion of the offending food. So it more difficult to figure out what food may have caused this immune response. Unfortunately, conventional allergy tests look for IgE rather than IgG. This creates a problem, in that most food allergies, including gluten intolerance, are IgG reactions, and tend to be passed over by the testing lab unless you specifically request for IgG to be tested as well. Typical reactions to IgG antibody response tend to be less dramatic, although still annoying: eczema, bloating, water retention, fatigue and the infamous twins, constipation and/or diarrhea. But don't be fooled into complacency. IgG can, in the long term, damage your intestinal villi and turn into a much graver condition: celiac disease.

The last of the gang is immunoglobulin A (IgA), the smallest one of the bunch. It is commonly used to test for gliadin reactions. To be complete, your blood should also be tested for gliadin and transglutaminase reactions. You will need the help of a qualified gastroenterologist to interpret all of these test results.

My entire adult life I have had digestive problems, but doctors ignored me when they pressed on my abdomen and I complained about how sore and tender it was. I had no idea through the years that my intestines were actually inflamed. As time passed it got worse. After a while I realized that the most severe reactions were when I ate either dairy or wheat products. When I stopped eating the office bagels and pizza, folks thought I was being snooty, but I was just trying to get well and protect myself. Unfortunately, not realizing that I was gluten-intolerant, I continued to eat large quantities of my favorite food – whole grains, believing they were the key to good health. Instead, they were only making me sicker.

Things finally came to a head one summer a few years ago when I began a rigorous walking/jogging routine of 3 miles per day. The increased physical stress resulted in some very strange and mysterious reactions. My body became covered in ferociously itching blisters which could only be relieved by scratching the skin off and allowing the fluid in the blisters to escape. That summer I was the scab lady. My general practitioner believed I had developed an allergy to air-borne poison ivy and placed me on steroids which did not help. I knew his diagnosis was incorrect, but he would not listen. That summer was a living hell. I concluded that the rash had to have something to do with what I was eating. After three unrelenting months of this rash, I placed myself on a diet of nothing but fresh fruits, vegetables, fish and lean meats. No grains, dairy, nuts, beans, legumes or anything else of any kind. Amazingly, the rash began to disappear. When I reported this to my doctor, he did not believe me. During my strict dietary regimen I lost weight and felt better than I had in a very long time. No more rashes and no more abdominal distress. But, there was still one big problem – my stomach was terribly hungry all the time. I just could not get it full. Meat and fish are very filling, but I just could not jam enough down my throat, and when I tried, I developed other symptoms. The only symptom-free diet for me was lots of greens, yellow vegetables, and fruits. So I remained hungry.

During those weeks of hunger, I saw an allergist for food testing. The tests indicated that I needed to eliminate soy, navy beans, peanuts, almonds, and barley from my diet – all foods that were supposed to be terribly healthy. Amazingly, the tests did not indicate dairy or wheat allergies – foods I knew for sure I could not tolerate. My allergist confirmed my suspicions that I likely was gluten-intolerant. She explained that the testing process involved an endoscopic biopsy of the duodenum. From my subsequent research I learned that the biopsy could render completely inaccurate results unless I was in a full-blown gluten reaction. I absolutely was not willing to place myself back into itching hell by eating the required gluten for the test.

As I continued to research, I learned that the rash I had suffered was called dermatitis herpetiformis (not to be confused with herpes which has nothing to do with it). The characteristic that made this rash distinguishable from all other rashes was the fact that it is always symmetrically distributed on the body. If an outbreak developed on the right forearm, within 12 – 24 hours there would also be an outbreak on the left forearm. Left shin, then also right shin, etc. The standard allergy tests are useless in identifying gluten intolerance because regular allergies are produced by the body's IgE system whereas gluten intolerance and its accompanying herpetiformis is an allergy of the IgA system. IgA is an antibody produced in the lining of the intestines. Gluten in the diet combines with IgA, and together they enter the blood stream and circulate, eventually clogging small blood vessels in the skin. This attracts white blood cells (neutrophils), and releases powerful chemicals called complements, which make their way to the skin surface creating the horrible herpetiformis rash. Relief comes only through scratching away the skin to release and remove the chemicals. All the while, the villi of the intestinal lining are quietly becoming atrophied, no longer able to absorb nutrients. Through research, I have also learned that these chemicals become embedded in the connective tissue that encapsulates muscle fibers. Does this explain the burning muscular inflammation I experienced after eating gluten?

Successfully adapting to a gluten-free lifestyle requires immense self-discipline and commitment as well as complete rejection of self-pity. If there is anything the world can gain from observing the austere lifestyle of the gluten-free person, it is the message of reassurance that we all have far greater reserves of strength and character than we imagine.

Liz M—Dallas, TX

What Could Be the Cause of Gluten Intolerance/Celiac Disease?

First, a short description of celiac disease: when people like you are exposed to the gliadin protein, the enzyme tissue transglutaminase (abbreviated as TG2 or tTG) modifies the protein, and your immune system cross-reacts with your small intestine tissue wall, causing an inflammatory reaction. This is called an autoimmune reaction. This inflammation leads to the truncating of the villi lining of the small intestine (called villous atrophy). Because the intestinal villi are responsible for nutrients' absorption, this condition could lead to some nutrition deficiencies such as vitamin A, C, K, iron (anemia), calcium and vitamin D (possibly leading to osteopenia and osteoporosis). Another result of celiac disease is lactose intolerance. Finally, most patients develop bacterial and fungi (often Candida yeast) overgrowth.

One reason why gluten intolerance and celiac disease have been largely ignored until recently is that the symptoms resemble other diseases such as irritable bowel syndrome (IBS), Crohn's disease and colitis. So when you went to your doctor to complain about your symptoms, they automatically tended to look in that direction. When they could not find anything related to these diseases, they would just assume you were inventing your symptoms for one reason or another. (As a matter of fact, if you have been diagnosed with any of these well-known diseases, some gastroenterologists suggest that you get tested for gluten intolerance.)

Genetics

Almost all celiac patients have the genetic variant HLA-DQ2 allele (one of two forms of the DNA sequence of a gene) in their DNA chromosome 6. HLA-DQ2 is an antigen molecule in the intestines. In the process of digestion, the gliadin protein chains are being altered by the tTG enzyme mentioned earlier. This alerts your immune system, and in self-defense, it begins to destroy healthy cells. Unfortunately, to make things more complicated, about 5% of those people who do develop celiac disease do not have the HLA-DQ2 gene. This suggests additional environmental factors are needed for celiac disease to develop. What could these environmental factors be?

Breast Feeding or lack of it

A 2005 study suggests that infants fed gluten before their immune systems were fully mature were more likely to develop gluten intolerance. Two scenarios were studied: in one, the infants were not breastfed, and gluten was introduced into their diets early. This path is the most likely to help develop an intolerance to gluten, for not only is the child's immune system unable to protect itself until fully developed, the child is not getting any additional protection from the mother's milk. The mother's colostrum contains natural antibodies designed to protect her child. In the second group, the infants were breastfed, but still introduced to gluten early. Even though the mother's milk affords her child some protection, because her child's immune system is not fully functional, it may not be able to protect the child from the early introduction of foreign proteins. So, if at all possible, the solution would be to breastfeed children for about six months to offer protection and allow his/her immune system to develop, and to not introduce gluten-containing products too early. More research is needed, but there is a strong correlation between breastfeeding, the age at which gluten is introduced in the child's diet, and the chances of developing gluten intolerance.

Exposure to Heavy Metals

Another possible environmental factor affecting the child's tendency to develop intolerance to gluten could be early exposure to heavy metals. Most likely, that exposure would come through the mother. The metal most accused of damage is mercury. It can come from two sources: fish and dental fillings. Some fish, especially large ones on top of the food chain, are more likely to contain enough mercury in their meat to affect an unborn baby. Additionally, most "silver" dental filling contain mercury, which is known to leach out and affect any healthy person. A pregnant mom with such fillings could in effect poison her own child through no fault of her own. Two suggestions: One, avoid eating tuna, swordfish, king mackerel, shark and tilefish during pregnancy. These long-lived fish are known to be the highest source of mercury contamination. Eat other fresh fish only once a week. Don't blame them for the pollution; you know who's at fault here and it's not the fish. Two, avoid mercury-loaded fillings altogether, but if you have had them for a long time, do not have them removed during pregnancy. Either have them removed at least 6 months before you plan to get pregnant and follow a good detoxifying program, or wait until after you wean your baby.

Antibiotics Overuse

Typically, allopathic pediatricians tend to prescribe antibiotics too freely. While antibiotics kill harmful bacteria, they also kill the child's first line of protection, the friendly gut bacteria. Eventually, toxic bacteria and fungi will overdevelop, damage the villi lining the small intestine wall and create what is called the "leaky gut syndrome" which allows large foreign proteins to enter the child's bloodstream. These are seen by the immune system as an attack and it will defend itself, causing celiac disease.

As you can see, there could be multiple and complicated factors involved in gluten intolerance: genetics, breast feeding, early introduction of gluten and antibiotics overuse. There could be even more, but these are the ones that are referred to the most.

How Can You Find the Right Doctor?

You may have seen many doctors who diagnosed you with everything but gluten intolerance: IBS, Crohn's disease, food allergy, food poisoning or even psychosomatic disorder (it's all in your head – get over it!) You may fear a family doctor may lack the proper training or up-to-date knowledge. After all the actual diagnosis of gluten intolerance is fairly recent. How do you find the right doctor?

- Go to your pharmacist or alternative healer and ask them for referrals
- Ask your nutritionist at your local pharmacy for suggestions
- Get a referral from your local celiac disease support group
- Ask a trusted friend that has a celiac disease diagnosis

Don't believe people that tell you that celiac disease is not a disease for wimps! Although it is different than many diseases, in that it cannot be healed and is a lifetime condition, I would take it anytime over many other life-threatening diseases. If you had the choice, would you prefer to have cancer or celiac disease? I thought so. In very simple terms gluten and dairy intolerance and celiac disease are easy to deal with: **Stop eating the offending food for the rest of your life.** At first it will not be easy, and you may relapse, but the return of painful symptoms will set you straight, and you will be back on the road to recovery. Happily, it is much easier nowadays is to find out where gluten and casein are hiding.

If you met me today, you would think I was a pretty healthy person, and relatively speaking, I am.

If you met me five years ago, you would think I was nearly dead, because I nearly was. At least I felt nearly dead. I was hypothyroid (low thyroid levels) and my adrenal glands were nearly kaput. I kept dragging a three-page list of symptoms to a well-known endocrinologist in Austin, and the best he could do was shrug his Big-Pharma-backed shoulders and offer me zero solutions, while refusing to give me the thyroid medications I so desperately needed.

As a layperson, when I look back over my long and pathetic list of more than sixty symptoms, I am aghast that so many doctors offered me no help at all. By doing so, they guaranteed that I would get sicker and sicker. I became so ill that I spent most of 2005 bedridden. My story is the same, chorus and verse, for so many others who suffer from gluten intolerance.

After I finally got some life-saving advice from very wise women on-line, I found a true thyroid expert and he put me on desiccated (dried) thyroid medicine, adrenal support, and most importantly, he told me to quit ingesting gluten and caseins. I began to get my life back. It has been a slow, uphill battle that one nationally known health expert says is the equivalent of becoming an Olympic athlete. I climbed up and over that Olympic-sized health hurdle and if I can do it, others can do . . . but you have to have the knowledge first of the harm that gluten can cause you.

How do you begin to heal? Find a truly caring doctor who listens to how you feel and one who works as your health care partner to get you back on your feet. The doctor who healed me does not accept insurance and the money I have spent with him was worth every penny. Join on-line, patient-advocacy support groups on Yahoo and then read, read, read relevant health books.

And then get ready to thrive, not just barely survive.

I have not caught so much as a cold in more than four years. I walk our 5 dogs every day and most days, I ride my horses. I work as a professional dog trainer and writer. ALL SIXTY of my former symptoms are gone. The only medicines I take are hormone related (thyroid, adrenal and female hormones).

Please don't settle for feeling sick. You have options and you are sitting in the driver's seat when it comes to your own health.

Annie P - Durango, CO

Keeping a Food Journal

I used to provide forms for my clients to fill out, where they were to list exactly what they ate every day. But my clients found them too large and difficult to carry around, so they never used them. My new suggestion is to find a small and beautiful diary you can fit in your purse or carry with you at all times. On every page, write Breakfast, Morning Snack, Lunch, Afternoon Snack and Dinner. Under each category write all the foods you have eaten. Leave space afterward for comments. Pay attention and listen to your body after each meal or snack, and write down anything out of the ordinary: indigestion, bloating, acid reflux, gas, constipation or diarrhea, etc. Are you feeling tired, foggy, and sleepy after a particular meal? Do you suspect a particular food? Write it down. Did you sleep well or not? Write it down. Write down every detail you feel could help your doctor figure out what is making you sick. This is the best partnership you can have with your doctor, actually offering input and insight.

Your food journal is your window to your GFCF soul; your confidant, the holder of your most intimate secrets. It has always amazed me how some of my clients would rather tell me about *anything* other than their food habits. They feel it's too private an issue to discuss with anyone else, even one's own nutritherapist. This is a sign of the amount of shame put on food in this country. Unlike the French, Americans seems to be ashamed of their food habits. I'm not sure if it relates to some outdated Victorian shame, or if it's related to the way the media seems to shame people, especially women, into staying "in shape" or unrealistically skinny. There would not be any money to be made if everyone in this country felt comfortable with themselves and the food they eat. Strangely enough, French people that attach so much importance to good long meals and rich food don't seem to care as much about how thin they are and yet (frustratingly for most Americans) most French people are thin. It's called the French paradox.

In any case, your food diary is your friend. This is what will help you tell your doctor or nutritionist what you are eating and when. You should note everything you're eating at all times of the day, from dragging yourself out of bed to sleepy time. Make sure to note the time you eat each particular food. It will also help you and your doctor if you note any unexpected digestive reaction and how you feel after eating certain foods: tired, hazy-minded, energized, itchy skin, or any symptoms you feel may relate to the food you just ate. In the beginning it will not be easy to discern this feeling from that one. But after a few days doing it you will learn to listen closely to your body. You should write down any questions that come up in order to discuss them with your doctor. This diary is an invaluable tool on your road to better health. Please take it seriously.

Learning About Your Condition

The simplest way to learn about your condition is to ask your doctor, but let's face it; there is just not enough time for your doctor to answer all of your questions. Join local groups of national organizations. If you don't have the time or the energy to go to meetings, go online; look up the many web sites available for your education and join forums.

What to Talk About at Doctor's Appointments

You finally found the right doctor. He knows what ails you and knows how to help you deal with it. Ask him/her a lot of questions. If they don't know, they can probably send you to the right person. Your lifestyle questions need to be answered so you can live a healthy GFCF life. These are some of the questions you should ask:

- Tell him/her about your history of symptoms.
- Tell him/her about the kind of medications you currently are taking for your affliction or for any other health issues. It's very important.
- Tell him/her about other symptoms that could be symptoms of other allergies or illnesses.
- Tell him/her about your journal. Explain some reactions. Ask the questions you wrote down.
- Ask him/her what tests will be done and why? As the patient, you have the right to know and decide what feels right for you. If you don't feel emotionally strong enough to ask these questions, bring someone you trust to ask these questions. Sometimes that's the best way to do it.
- Ask how long it will be for your results to come back. When they are back, make sure to ask for a copy for your own records. They typically don't offer them, so you may have to ask. Don't be shy; you're paying for it.
- When the tests are back, ask for a recommended plan of action.
- If they provide this service, ask for a nutritional plan, or go see a trained nutritionist or certified dietician.
- If needed, ask him/her to clarify or explain some terms you have found while educating yourself. If it's still not clear, ask again until you get a clear answer.

Testing for Gluten Intolerance, Celiac Disease and Dairy Intolerance

First, you need to know that in the world of lab testing, a positive result means you HAVE an allergy to the food tested. A negative result means you are NOT allergic to that food. Most doctors are not trained to find gluten, dairy and other food allergies. If you can, go to one that specialize in food allergies and ask for:

Blood Tests or Serology

The most common tests will look for: IgA tissue transglutaminase (tTG), IgA tissue endomysial antibodies (EMA), IgG tissue transglutaminase, IgA antibodies and IgC antibodies levels.

Please keep in mind that before you take these blood tests, you will have to go back to eating gluten-containing foods, otherwise the test will not do what it is supposed to do: find out if your blood shows these Ig levels. I know, it's annoying and possibly downright painful to go back, but it is the only way the test will prove if you are allergic or not.

Here Comes ELISA

Who is this ELISA? No, it's not the name of your lab technician, although it is a pretty name. ELISA stands for Enzyme Linked Immunosorbent Assay. No wonder they decided to call it ELISA. Who would remember such a barbaric name? In any case, ELISA has been used in the medical world for decades to measure the levels of antibodies for a variety of medical conditions. Why are we so interested in ELISA in our case? Because it measures the levels of the most likely suspects: the immunoglobulin bodyguards: IgE and IgG. Unfortunately, this test is not used in most cases of food allergy. Why? I don't know. But make sure to ask your doctor for it by name.

A well-administered blood panel will test for about 100 of the most common foods in the American diet: wheat and gluten-containing grains like barley, rye, spelt, kamut, as well as dairy products (casein), eggs, corn, soy, almond, peanut, garlic, bananas, beef, baker's and brewer's yeast, coffee, chocolate and many more. This could be a very eye-opening test for you. You may not only be allergic to gluten and dairy, but you may also find out other foods that are bothering you. By the way, the beauty of this test is that it is not affected by the food you ate today. If you're not allergic to these foods, no antibodies will show up on this test. However, if there is a chance you are allergic to gluten, it is also very possible you are allergic to other foods. Sorry! But finding that out is actually twice as good: that you now know which food(s) are bothering you and what to remove from your diet.

Biopsy and Endoscopy — Is It Really the Definitive Test?

Some doctors believe that the ELISA test is sufficient to decide if you're allergic or not. Some don't. They want to know if your villi are damaged as well, which would confirm a diagnosis of celiac disease. They think the blood test is only a precursor to the final proof, an intestinal biopsy done through endoscopy. A tube containing a tiny camera is slid down your throat, through your stomach into your small intestine. The doctor will look to see if your intestinal villi are damaged or flattened, which is a sign of celiac disease. To make sure, he/she will cut a small sample of your villi for further analysis. Don't worry: the whole procedure is painless. So much so that some doctors don't even put you under anesthesia. If you feel that a positive blood result is enough for you and are nervous about the biopsy, you do not have to get the biopsy.

There's one more point that should be made about the biopsy. Flattened villi do not always indicate celiac disease. Other diseases can damage villa too, including HIV, Crohn's disease and gastroenteritis. It's up to the doctor to narrow the diagnosis to celiac disease.

Skin Biopsy

One of the symptoms of celiac disease is a skin rash called dermatitis herpetiformis. If a skin biopsy tests positive for dermatitis herpetiformis, you have celiac disease. A stool test is also available.

Time for Me to Jump on my Soapbox Again

Since you're the paying customer, don't be shy about asking for the tests you want done and request to be given the results in case you want a second opinion. If your physician resists doing them, there are plenty of other health providers happy to get your business. Please, do not let yourself be intimidated by some of these God-like know-it-all doctors. Their business is not only to heal you, but also to please you. You've done your homework and read books on your condition. It's time to regain control of your health and take charge (even on a credit card if you have to!) After all, it is your health we're talking about here.

Handling the Diagnosis

You found the right doctor, got all the suggested tests and now you have to face the truth. Yes, you have gluten intolerance or celiac disease. How do you feel? On one hand, you probably feel relieved that you finally know what has made you feel sick for so long. On the other, you also probably feel overwhelmed. I understand. There is so much to learn: where do you start? What to do? What to buy? What to eat? Where to eat? What a nightmare! But at least you know. Now you have to educate yourself and face this challenge. It won't be easy, but it's by no means impossible. A lot of people already live perfectly happy, gluten-free lives.

I don't mean to scare you, but there are consequences for ignoring your diagnosis. If you choose to bury your head in the sand, you may be faced with a higher mortality rate. There is a higher rate of colon cancer in celiac disease patients. You may also develop osteoporosis due to lack of calcium absorption. Additional infections and autoimmune diseases may develop. Other possible consequences are failure to thrive and delayed puberty in children; recurrent miscarriage and infertility problems; diabetes mellitus type 2; low thyroid functions (hypothyroidism); some researchers also blame some psychiatric issues like schizophrenia on gluten intolerance; and finally, there is a suspected correlation between autism and gluten intolerance.

In September of 2003, I was diagnosed with NK lymphoma of the gut. At the time, I had just finished the world's first off-road ironman triathlon. I was incredibly fit and felt great. I had no symptoms.

So then how was I diagnosed? My family has a history of colon cancer. So I went in for a very early screening in August of 2003. They found red lesions throughout my GI tract. A pathologist at Methodist in Houston looking at the biopsies thought there were enough indications this was a malignant process but not quite certain.

So I ended up at the NIH in Maryland. Dr. Elaine Jaffe, one of the world's leading lymphoma pathologists reviewed the pathology and concluded I did not have a malignant process and so we started a "watch and wait" form of treatment.

"Watch and wait" did not sit well for a very active person like me. So I continued to seek out differing opinions on my health. Some places we visited thought with certainty that I had cancer and needed to start treatment immediately. Treatment would have been a bone marrow transplant and six-months of chemotherapy. However, I decided not to start any form of treatment.

In March of 2004, I met with Dr. Glen Luepnitz in Austin. He ran a food antibody assay test and determined I had strong antibody reactions to gluten and dairy. I immediately went on a gluten and dairy free diet and have been on it ever since.

To the amazement of a worldwide group of doctors following my case, all the lesions in my GI tract started clearing up. Over the past 6 years with each colonoscopy and endoscopy, I continue to show improvement. In fact at my last check in, I had only a few spots that looked questionable. However, the pathology has even shown improvement in these areas.

My case continues to be discussed at lymphoma conferences all over the world. Today, gastroenterologists and pathologists are screening patients for gluten sensitivities because of the awareness my case has brought to the industry.

I'm incredibly happy to have changed the course of my disease process through a gluten and dairy free diet.

Jeff W—Austin, TX

Am I Going to Get Better Soon or Ever?

I don't want to make you feel worse, but at this time it seems that once your body has shown signs of being allergic to gluten and dairy, there's no going back to the good old days of being innocent and free of intolerance symptoms. The current state of science gives us no way out of this predicament. The only way to feel healthy and not experience the nasty side effects of gluten and dairy allergies are to abstain from eating gluten and casein. No more, nada, nyet. Once your body's immune system has learned to defend itself from what it sees as a foreign invader, the guards (antibodies) may fall asleep while you stop eating gluten and dairy, but they will wake up as soon as you reintroduce them in your diet. You see, the antibodies created by your immune system to protect you have a memory like an elephant. They never forget. You may try to sneak a cookie here and there after you've been off the wagon for a few weeks and, if you're lucky, you defense system's guards will pretend to be still asleep, but don't believe for a minute they have forgotten. If you insist on getting into old gluten and dairy habits, they will wake up with a vengeance and make you suffer again, just like in the bad old days. So I suggest you don't risk it and stay off.

Some scientist do believe that after a long time, if you take good care of your digestive system and help it heal, you will be allowed to splurge once in a while. It may be possible, but I would not recommend it and would suggest you get tested again before you try, keeping in mind that since you have been good about avoiding gluten and dairy for a long time, your level of antibodies may be so low that you may get a negative result. That does not necessarily mean you are cured. Besides, it's so easy now to get a decent-tasting GFCF cookie that it's not worth tempting the devil sleeping in your gut.

How Long Will It Take Before I Get Better?

It all depends on how long you have been intolerant and how severe your case is. If you're lucky and caught it early, you should better within a few weeks. If it's be going on for a long time, because your allergies started years ago and no one knew how to test for it, it will take longer. For some people who have been afflicted with celiac disease for years, it may take up to two years for their intestinal villi to heal and re-grow. Typically, the older the patient, the longer it takes to heal.

Obviously, every case is different. Only you can tell. If you're in touch with your body, you will be able to tell very quickly as soon as you're free of those nasty symptoms. If not, you can get another blood test in a few months to test for antibodies levels and have proof that you're better now. At this time I don't suggest you have another biopsy done. A blood test should be plenty of proof you're in better health. If you do not show signs of healing after a while, you may suffer from another form of intestinal disease and will have to go back to your doctor and ask them for more thorough tests. Only you can feel the discomfort and only you can tell the doctor what you're feeling. If they think it's all in your head, get a second opinion. You are in charge. You are the paying customer and you should get what you ask for.

What Current and Future Treatments are Available?

At this time, the only known treatment is to eliminate all offending foods from your diet. That's that! However, in the future, there may be products created to help you with your pain and discomfort. They do not exist at this time, but at the rate science is progressing, don't rule it out. There are talks about drugs in the pipeline to help you deal with your affliction. But remember an important factor: as is typical in the western mode of healing, these drugs will only help reduce your symptoms, but not the cause of them. Don't get fooled. You need to face the truth. The only way to heal is to avoid the offending proteins. Nothing else will do. Once you wrap your head around it, make your mind up, it's really not that hard to avoid gluten and dairy in our current society. Make the jump and just plain forget about them.

Why It May Be More Difficult Than You Think to Get Off Gluten

So, as you may have realized by now, healing from gluten or casein intolerance can be both easy and complicated. Easy because if you simply avoid gluten and casein, you will be able to heal, feel better and lead an almost normal life. Complicated because, although avoiding gluten and casein sound like a simple solution, as you soon will find out, there are many, many products out there containing gluten. The simple solution to this problem is to avoid processed food, but that's easier said than done.

Why? Because of our *emotions*. Whether we realize it or not, food and emotions are tied together in our minds. Some foods are called comfort foods for a reason; they make us feel better emotionally, because they remind us of happy times, like when your mom baked that special dessert just for you. Every time you eat that dessert, it makes you feel good emotionally. Maybe not physically, but nevertheless our emotions are very powerful and need to be fed too.

Also, because of *habit*. As you know, we are creatures of habit. Habits create a safe environment for us, whether they are good for us physically or not. Nobody likes to change his or her habits and get out of their comfort zone. Changes are stressful and we are already surrounded with stress as it is. So we take refuge in our habits as a safety mechanism. When you combine emotions and habits, change can be extremely difficult. I can only encourage you to trust how your body feels when you ingest foods that make you sick. You must make an effort to overcome your fear of change. Some people will wait until they are deathly ill before they can face change. Only when they have overcome their fears can they feel better physically and emotionally. I can only suggest and encourage you to take this whole new experience one step at a time. Courage!

How To Live GFCF at Home

Home, Sweet GFCF Home

Home is where the gluten is… lurking in the cabinets, pots and pans, china and silverware, oven, toaster and other unsuspected kitchen appliances. Unless you live alone or have managed to convince your whole family to go GF with you - a tough one I must tell you - you will have to be careful how you and other people handle food around you. If you happen to be the cook, great! Then you will have some control (I said some, not total control!)

Is a Little Bit of Gluten OK?

There is no doubt that, if you have celiac disease, you must avoid all and any source of gluten. But what about people that are "only" allergic or sensitive to wheat or gluten? How much is acceptable? How much is too much? Honestly, only you can answer that question. Of all people around you, including your doctor, your nutritionist or myself, you know your body's reactions to wheat or gluten best. For example, you may be aware that one cookie once in a rare while will not make you sick or uncomfortable. But you may also know that eating a sandwich made with wheat bread will make you sick. Only YOU know how your body and digestive system will feel after gulping down that cookie or sandwich. Please keep in mind that some people never show symptoms.

Another aspect to consider is how you look at this situation. Don't only look at it from the point of view of "What amount will make me sick". We are all tempted to cheat; I'll be the first to confess to that. But what if we switched our way of thinking to "I will feel a lot better overall if I do not cheat at all". I don't expect you to be perfect (I know I'm not), but I would suggest you consider the whole picture before you dip that hand in the cookie jar while no one is looking. You're a grown-up. I know you can do it, and if you can't, you already know the consequences. If you're going to do it, do it with gusto and without guilt (the worst part next to the digestive distress). Enjoy your slight infraction knowing you will go back to your healthy behavior tomorrow.

Another thing to consider is how long you have been allergic or sensitive to wheat/gluten. If you have been allergic for a long time, your body will have accumulated a long history with this toxic (for you) substance. It will take a while for it to heal and become healthy again. Because of that history, your body is now very sensitive to wheat and any infraction will delay your healing. If your goal is complete healing and feeling good again in your body, I would suggest you go cold turkey. There are plenty of healthier food alternatives available these days to make your new gluten/wheat-free life easier. It is much easier than it was even just a few years ago.

What if You're Only Sensitive to Wheat and Not to Gluten?

Your life will be a little easier as the list of foods difficult for you to digest will be shorter. Grains containing wheat are wheat, cracked wheat and wheat germ of course, as well as other denominations such as couscous, tabouleh, kamut, semolina and triticale. Although some people are safe with spelt grain, I would suggest caution if you never had it before. Spelt is an ancient form of wheat and contains much less gluten, but could still make you sick. Test it with a taco wrap or half sandwich made with spelt grain and see how you feel. I'm not suggesting avoiding it outright, just being aware. Other grains such as barley, rye and oats should be safe for you. Keep in mind, you know your body best. Test different grains and see what works for you. Of course, all other non-gluten grains are perfectly safe for you.

Getting Started

Changing Your Kitchen and Pantry

- First, clean your kitchen from floor to ceiling (or hire a cleaning service with strict instructions to use hypoallergenic cleaning products).

- You can start with the pantry: identify anything with gluten in it and set it aside

- You should clean out the refrigerator and freezer and toss all suspect leftovers and opened containers

- You should empty the cupboards and rewash all dishes, pots, pans and utensils

- You should wipe down all cupboards inside and out

- You should wipe down all countertops, sinks and tables and chairs

- You should identify the gluten free refrigerator shelf, drawer, countertop and cupboard that will be off limits to anyone else.

Pots and Pans

If you are mildly allergic, you do not have to have separate pots, pans and eating utensils. A good wash through the dishwasher will be sufficient. Otherwise, I would suggest you have your own pots and pans and even possibly eating and serving utensils and dinnerware. You should purchase or set aside clearly marked gluten free storage containers, utensils, cutting boards and baking items such as cookie sheets and cake pans. One trick is to use colored tape or a touch of heat-proof colored paint on your own equipment and store them in separate cabinets. For your cooking equipment, aluminum being porous, I would suggest you get rid of it. Teflon is better, but it can be scratched and contaminated; the best is either stainless steel pots with a copper bottom (any good brand will do) or my own favorite, ceramic-coated cast iron cookware such as Le Creuset. I have owned my set for 30 years and still use it today. It's a little expensive, but it will last forever and cook very evenly. (Fair warning: Le Creuset pot and pans are a little heavy to lift.)

Oven, Toaster Oven or Bread Toaster

Your oven should be pretty safe for your normal cooking, as long as you do not cook a gluten-containing dish and your favorite GF dish at the same time. For a toaster oven or toaster, I would suggest you get your own and keep it in a separate area of your kitchen to avoid confusion and potential cross-contamination. They are cheap enough that you can afford to get your own in your favorite color and feel safe. Besides, most GF sandwich breads taste a lot better when toasted. The way I handle mine is: I place my sliced GF bread in a plastic freezer box or bag, keep my GF bread frozen and toast only as many slices as I need. It's tastier that way.

Simple Food Allergy/Celiac Disease Meal preparation

If you have a simple food allergy you can, if you have the time and energy, cook two separate meals: one GFCF for you, and a regular meal for the rest of your family. Of course, the simplest choice for you would be to have the whole family on the GFCF diet. Most likely one or more of them will be allergic too.

If you have celiac disease, however, you do not have a choice. You are so sensitive to ANY possible trace of gluten or dairy that you have to put the whole family on the same diet as you. Even one-eighth of a teaspoon of gluten or dairy-containing food can make you sick. Even if you cleaned your kitchen up and down every day after cooking or baking regular food, there will be flour or other offending particles floating around in your house through your central AC system. So you (and they) don't have a choice. A treat for them would be to eat out at a restaurant once in a while, as long as that restaurant has GFCF choices for you.

Cross Contamination and Celiac Disease

Cross contamination is a serious issue for those of you with celiac disease. It comes about in two possible ways:

- A food or ingredient containing gluten or dairy could get mixed with your food. You know the result. For example, in the old days, oats were considered to be unsafe for celiac disease sufferers. Further studies confirmed them to be safe. But, most of the time, oats and wheat are handled in the same warehouses or processed with the same equipment. Thus, there is cross contamination. Solution: buy oats only for certified GF facilities or kitchen.

- Your GFCF food is cooked in a pot or pan already contaminated with gluten or dairy. Oops! You will be sick.

The first step is to get rid of ALL products containing the offending foods. From now on, any food kept in your pantry should either have no gluten-containing ingredients, or should be labeled "gluten free".

What Should Be Tossed

In the beginning, converting to a gluten free life can involve some expense. You can be practical and keep food that you can't eat to be used by the rest of the family. If you do, you should make sure it is stored separately from the food you will be eating. Also, don't forget to wipe down all of the containers themselves to remove any gluten dust that has settled on the food packages over time. You should toss any storage containers that are scratched and have been used to store gluten-containing foods (old plastic containers for example). You should toss any food without labels.

Gluten Free Meal Preparation

You have two main choices when it comes to preparing your new GFCF meals:

1. Make gluten-free substitutions with available GF and CF products

2. Cook all your food from scratch. Yes, you will have to spend more time in your kitchen or spend a lot of money buying GFCF prepared meals. If you can afford it, you should consider hiring a private chef trained in preparing such meals. Or hire a nutritherapist to help you create a customized diet taking into account all your food allergies.

Filling your Pantry. Manufactured and processed foods

When it comes to these kinds of foods, never let your guard down. You must make a habit of reading the nutrition label as well as the ingredient list on each package. Even then, a minute amount of gluten may have snuck in through some additive or flavoring, or even by being processed in a plant that handles other products containing gluten, causing cross contamination.

In appendix D I offer you a list of the gluten-free commercial products currently available. Please keep in mind that this list is constantly evolving.

Also, be aware that, if you are extremely sensitive to gluten, the denomination "gluten-free" on a package only means that this particular product contains less than 0.5% gluten. It is not a 100% gluten-free guarantee. If you want to feel confident you are buying absolutely gluten-free products, two certification programs are available. First is the Celiac Sprue Association, offering the CSA Recognition Seal. The CSA Recognition Seal certifies that this products is 100% gluten-free, which means that it contains less than 5 parts per million of gluten. The logo looks like a wheat chaff crossed by a stop sign. For more information and a list of products, please check the CSA web site at:
http://www.csaceliacs.org/CSASealofRecognition.php.

Another reputable organization offering a GF labeling certification is the Gluten Free Certification Organization at **www.gfco.org**. Their Gluten-Free Certification label offers the same standard, and shows the GF symbol in capital letters surrounded by a black circle, with the words Certified above and Gluten Free below.

To avoid possible temptation to fall off the GFCF wagon, I suggest you fill up your GFCF cupboard with the following *gluten free* items to be kept on hand:

➢ GF Crackers
➢ GF Soups
➢ GF Cookies
➢ GF Pretzels

- ➤ GF Sauce mixes
- ➤ GF Peanut butter
- ➤ GF Dips
- ➤ GF Boxed meals
- ➤ Rice
- ➤ Non wheat, GF cereals
- ➤ GF Pasta
- ➤ Unflavored ground coffee
- ➤ GF Chips
- ➤ Plain nuts
- ➤ Alternative milks: rice, soy, almond, hazelnut, coconut, hemp
- ➤ Soy yogurts
- ➤ Non-hydrogenated soy margarine
- ➤ Fresh fruits and vegetables
- ➤ Grass-fed meat
- ➤ Fish and shellfish (if coated with crumbs, make sure they are GF)
- ➤ Grass-fed or free-range eggs

The goal is to resupply your pantry, refrigerator and freezer well enough so that you have these special items on hand when you're ready to cook, and are not tempted to eat unsafe foods.

Then you should also resupply your cupboard with *gluten free* baking items.

- ➤ Gluten free flours or flour mixes
- ➤ GF Baking powder and baking soda
- ➤ GF Cake mixes
- ➤ Xanthan gum
- ➤ GF Vanilla extract
- ➤ GF Yeast

The best approach is to pick only products that are certified as processed in a gluten-free facility. Nothing else will do. Federal labeling mandates that any potential allergen like fish, shellfish, nuts and gluten be mentioned if they are processed in the same facility as the product you're about to buy. Your best protection is to always read the label of any processed food you buy. A simpler one would be to avoid any and all processed food, but you know as well as I do how difficult this is. We all want our bread and cookies, even if they are not quite the same as the ones you used to love. I understand that even better now that I myself have to be more careful. There are plenty of high-quality, certified gluten-free products available out there. Go to your nearest health store, grocery store with a dedicated gluten-free aisle (Whole

Foods Market, Central Market, Wheatsville, Fresh Plus in Austin) and, of course, don't forget your favorite Peoples Pharmacy store, especially the Westlake store where I work. The vast majority of the products and food we serve there are gluten-free and we know how to handle your sandwich properly. Come by and say "hi!" I'll be waiting for you.

Of course, all of your GFCF ingredients and products should be stored in separate cabinets as well. That means that you will have to learn all about what foods contains gluten and dairy, and how to find the hidden allergens in prepared foods. That is one of the purposes of this book.

Making Simple Adjustments in Your Favorite Recipes

It is easy to make simple substitutions, in even your old family recipes. Nowadays, there are many gluten and dairy substitution products for you to use. For example:

➢ Replace flour in recipes with all-purpose GF flour mixes

➢ Use GF baking powder and chocolate with no additives

➢ If you like crumb-coated fish croquettes, use rice bread or GF crumbs to coat your fish before frying in GF oil

➢ You can make your own gravy or vanilla custard with corn, potato or tapioca starches and GF vanilla extract

➢ You can make your own fruit glaze by cooking fresh fruit and thickening it with apple pectin or a GF starch

You may have to make some adjustments, but once you know how each replacement product reacts differently, you will get really nice results. You can also use books like this one to help you get started.

"I used to think surrender would send me down to nothing. Now I've started believing that it can bloom me more solidly into myself." -- Mary Karr

Being diagnosed with celiac disease was my destiny. At least, in retrospect I know this to be the case, but coming to this realization took seven years and a tremendous amount of struggle. The struggle was cleverly disguised as opportunity: to surrender to my condition; to cook in France; to start my food blog, to open my online gluten-free bakery and to sell my cookbook.

At the time of my diagnosis in 2002, the available gluten-free products were so unsatisfactory, I just remember coming home, sitting on my kitchen floor with this sandy cookie crumbling out of my mouth, the graininess grinding on my teeth, causing the tears waiting to be spilt to grow to the size of great giant peas. I felt my love affair with desserts being pulled from my chest. Then I looked up at the ceiling, cursed the food gods for hexing me as they had and exclaimed, "Is this really the best anyone can do?" As those words parted my lips, it was almost as if I already knew the answer and it was a resounding "NO!"

So I set to work experimenting and avidly working daily to make the changes I wanted for myself, which was just a moist delicious dessert that would make me forget that I was eating gluten-free. After seven years of recipe development, I was able to achieve this. Now I am so proud to be gluten-free, because now I can help parents with children who suffer from Autism and even cancer patients. We must all band together and prove how vibrant and full a gluten-free life can be.

Karen M - Austin, TX

Shopping and Eating GFCF in the Real World

Eating Out

I know you may feel the food world out there is out to get you sick. And you should be cautious, but try not to be too paranoid about eating out. A few years ago, it might have been Mission Impossible for you to eat in a restaurant, but not so much anymore, unless you live in the middle of nowhere (sorry! I can't help you there!) Nowadays, in any decent sized city, you will find restaurants offering gluten-free options on their menu. Many have finally realized that a growing part of their customer base is allergic to certain foods, including gluten. More and more, I am asked by restaurateurs to evaluate their restaurant's menu to let them know which items are gluten free, and to advise them on alternative menu choices, or to provide them with gluten free recipes.

If you are already aware of what menu items usually contain, GF options are easy for you to spot. If you are new to this, make your health challenge very clear to your waiter and ask for gluten free options. If they don't know, ask for a manager to help. If the restaurant owners or managers have done their due diligence, their menu should offer clear gluten free options. They may even have a completely separate gluten-free menu.

Say yes to assorted salads (no croutons); any grilled meat or fish; dishes made with rice (a staple of Asian and Latin American cuisine), beans, quinoa, amaranth or teff (maybe a little too exotic for mainstream restaurants but very possible): fruits, fruit desserts and fruit sorbets (caution: fruit sherbets contain dairy). Sorry, but you will have to avoid cakes and other seemingly yummy treats if you want to avoid a gut-wrenching experience, unless you are expressly told they are gluten-free. On the other hand, there are more and more gluten free pastries and desserts available out there in restaurant-land. On a shameless plug side note, you should taste my Flourless Chocolate Cake (contains dairy but can be special ordered dairy0free) at all the Peoples Pharmacy stores. According to some of my customers, it's either divine or devilishly good. Pick your favorite adjective. (This recipe is given later in the recipe section.)

Your last resort would be to only go to restaurant members of the Gluten Free Restaurant Awareness Program (GFRAP). Members of this group make sure to abide to their guidelines to ensure a pleasant dinner experience for their customers. For more information and a list of member establishments, go to **www.glutenfreerestaurants.org**.

How about cross contamination from gluten-containing foods?

People with severe celiac disease are very concerned by cross contamination from other gluten-containing products processed in the same factory or processing plant. This a very valid concern, as they are sensitive to the smallest amount of gluten in their food. Contamination can happen in a number of different ways. Your gluten-free bread could have been mixed and baked after a gluten bread has been prepared. Even if the equipment is washed properly, there is still a chance that there will still be flour floating in the air and through the ventilation system. Is your favorite potato chip fried in the same oil as a pita chip? Most likely, there will be crumbs left over from the previous gluten-containing batch. Even if the oil is filtered in between, very fine flour particles will be still present. Is your gluten-free cookie baked in the same oven as regular cookies? I'm not trying to make you more paranoid, just more aware of what could happen.

For example, in most restaurants, French fries are coated with flour to make them crispier. In the vast majority of these restaurants, even if they offer gluten-free fries, they will fry them in the same fryer as the other fries. Some will tell you that they use a dedicated fryer for gluten-free products but if you had been working as long as I have been in commercial kitchens, as well-meaning as company policies might be, they may not always been followed in each unit's kitchen for lack of proper training or just plain inattention during the lunch or dinner rush. I recently consulted for a restaurant that wanted to clean up their gluten act, and although management claimed to have GF policies in place, it turned out there were plenty of mishaps going on in the kitchen. Training and supervision is very important in carrying such policies and let's face it, it's not likely that a minimum wage employee will pay a lot of attention to your gluten health. (Everything has been corrected since my visit.)

Based on my own experience, I suggest you choose a restaurant you know well and trust; let them know about your health situation; ask a lot of questions and work with them on educating them on gluten-free products and procedures. In these tighter economical times, your local restaurants will be more likely to listen to your suggestions than they would have been a couple of years ago. Plus, there is more gluten awareness out there. So don't despair, it is actually safer to eat out these days. Enjoy yourself!

Grocery Shopping

The best approach is to pick only products that are certified as processed in a gluten-free facility. Nothing else will do. Federal labeling mandates that any potential allergen like fish, shellfish, nuts and gluten be mentioned on the label if they are processed in the same facility as the product you're about to buy. Your best protection is to always read the label of any processed food you buy. A simpler one would be to avoid any and all processed food, but you know as well as I do how difficult this is. We all want our bread and cookies, even if they are not quite the same as the ones you used to love. I understand that even better now that I myself have to be more careful. There are plenty of high-quality, certified gluten-free products available out there. Go to your nearest health store or grocery store with a dedicated gluten-free aisle (Whole Foods Market, Central Market, Wheatsville, Fresh Plus in Austin) and, of course, don't forget your favorite Peoples Pharmacy store, especially the Westlake store where I work. The vast majority of the products and food we serve there are gluten-free and we know how to handle your sandwich properly. Come by and say "hi!" I'll be waiting for you.

Making Adjustments at Work

Because you are outside of your safety zone, you might be easily tempted at work. You may also feel self conscious about telling your co-workers about your health situation. Don't be. Stand up for yourself and let your office buddies know about your new food restrictions. You may want to explain your condition on a 3" x 5" card, or send a memo to all your co-workers, including your supervisors and bosses. Let them know about cross contamination. It's your well being at stake here; educating others will only improve the situation.

You will be faced with refrigerators filled with other peoples' food, birthday cakes, holiday cookies, business meetings with free breakfast pastries and vending machines loaded with forbidden foods.

A few solutions:

- Make sure your desk is cleared of all snacks containing gluten
- Mark your own cup, plate and silverware very clearly, and explain to your boss and co-workers how important it is to never cross-contaminate your food or containers with their food or utensils.
- Bring your own brown bag lunch; eat lunch at your nearest GFCF deli or restaurant.

- If possible, keep your own small refrigerator in the office break room that is strictly for your food; put a sign on it to explain why you are so privileged, to avoid hard feelings.
- Normally, you shouldn't eat foods from vending machines because most vending machine foods typically contain gluten.
- If you are given enough notice, plan for business lunches and meetings. Bring your own food/snacks or call the restaurant/hotel ahead to find out their GFCF options. With a little experience, you will be able to spot the GFCF options on the menu. Or eat your GFCF meal before you go, and eat very lightly when you get there.
- Bring enough GFCF snacks with you to stave off any possible hunger pangs.
- Why not bring some really good GFCF cookies or cakes with you to work? Let them know it can be done without depriving yourself too much. Who knows, they may order a GF cake at The People's Pharmacy for your birthday.

Making GFCF Adjustments for Travel

Travelling does not have to be a big challenge. Here are a few ideas that should help you travel:

- Even if you stay in the U. S., bring a letter from with you from your doctor explaining your condition for use at hotels or restaurants, and even at businesses you may visit.
- Use the same GFCF card you use for your co-workers or local restaurants to explain your restrictions.
- If you travel abroad, carry an English copy of these documents and a copy translated into the travel country's language.
- Always carry with you a GFCF emergency bag with snacks, medications, cosmetics, GFCF card, list of safe foods and other necessities. Remember, no liquids allowed on airplanes. Just order water or your GF wine or liquor of choice.
- Ask for a specially prepared meal ahead of time. The safest would be a "steamed only" meal so there are no sauces, coatings or food surprises on your plate.
- If you can, call ahead to hotels and restaurants where you will be staying and let them know about your food restrictions. Some hotel and restaurant chains will advertise their GFCF food options. If at all possible, use these companies as your hotel or restaurant of choice.

-   Order food at restaurants that does not come covered in sauce or gravy; often cooks forget to consider the minute amount of gluten flour used to thicken sauces.

No matter how prepared and aware you are, there are bound to be mistakes made. For your sake I hope they are not too unpleasant.

How to Handle Your GFCF Social Life

Should You Tell Others?

By now, your family and closest friends should know about your condition. So should your boss and co-workers. So how wide do you want that group of "in the know" people to be? It's up to you. Some people are secretive about their life and health conditions. Some want the rest of the world to know, and will tell anyone within hearing distance about their "gluten-war" stories, with all the gory details. You may want to stay somewhere in between. Preserve your privacy, but be sure to inform the people who *need* to know.

How Much Do You Want Others to Know?

After all, you will have to tell your waiter or server. They will have to know that you're allergic so they don't serve you the wrong food. You might want to hand them that GFCF card we already talked about. In party or family holiday situations, you may not want your condition to be the subject of discussion. You may choose to share details with someone you feel is really interested in knowing, or someone you trust, but that might be the extent of it. On the other hand, if this is a crusade for you and you feel you have to educate the whole world, by all means, be my guest. Obviously you know yourself and your environment better than I do.

Most likely, people will not want to know all the gory details unless (like me) you enjoy shocking people that annoy you. If people want to know how it makes you feel, you might say something like: "It's similar to a food allergy; it makes me sick to my stomach and makes my skin itch painfully." If pushy inquiring minds want to know, you might say with a deadpan expression: "It could cause me to have any of the following: socially unacceptable noises in public, have explosive diarrhea or I might throw up all over your Persian carpet." That way, those curious people will never importune you again!

How Should You Handle Questions About Being Gluten Free?

Most people are curious by nature. If they honestly want to know about how you handle your affliction, there are two ways to handle it: One, just say: "I'd rather not talk about it" and risk people being offended, which is your right of course. Or you could tell them honestly about your restrictive diet and a few tricks you use to avoid temptation and illness. If you can avoid it, try to sound positive and not complain, as this society does not like complainers even when they are justified. I know it's not fair, but this is the society we live in. So, unless you decided to be a GFCF hermit, you may want to prepare yourself for people wanting to know and understand.

What to Do When People Close to You Are Not Sensitive to Your Condition

If your symptoms are grave and obvious, most people will understand and abide by your special requirements. But for some of you, your symptoms will not be obvious and some people around you might think you're "sick in your head", trying to bring undue attention to yourself or make yourself "interesting". They might not believe you, nor care enough to listen to you. Some might even want to tempt you with forbidden foods to see if you are paying attention, or to "prove" it's all an act.

This will not only test your will, but might also create feelings of envy within you of other, "normal" people who are not made the object of such scrutiny; you may feel guilt over not being able to join in party fun with others; you may feel sad the you will not be able to share the same breakfast as your loved ones; or you may feel angry that you cannot enjoy the turkey stuffing at Thanksgiving.

Try not to be too hard with yourself. You deserve to feel well and healthy, and that should be your main concern; not what other people think. Stick to your diet no matter what, knowing that you are healing yourself. Who knows, maybe one day you may be able to have a little bit of that forbidden food when you are well again. But please remember that if you have celiac disease, it is a lifelong illness. There is no going back to a gluten-loaded life.

Can You Have a GFCF Social Life? Absolutely!

How to be GFCF at Friends' and Family's Homes

If you're going for an informal visit to a friend or to your mom, it's better to bring your own snacks, nuts or fruits, so that the cracker and cheese plate offered won't tempt you. If they know you well, they may even have their own GFCF snacks to offer.

What to Eat During the Holidays

As you are already cursed to know, holidays and food are almost synonyms. Not only are they extra busy times for you, but there are lots of forbidden foods in them. That goes for religious and non-religious holidays. Whether it's Valentine Day, Easter, Fourth of July, Halloween, Thanksgiving or Christmas, there is food, food and more food. I know it's discouraging, knowing that you will have to explain to your friends or family why you cannot eat their world-famous recipe. You might hurt their feelings, but you have to explain them that to you, gluten is like sugar to a diabetic – dangerous for your health.

The first year will be the hardest. You will have to train everyone about your condition, what you can and cannot eat, and why. If you want to avoid an extensive and emotionally charged conversation, you may want to keep it short and simple by saying something like: "Sorry mom (Sis, Aunt Julia, Grandma), I've just been diagnosed with celiac disease. I have to follow a strict diet. I will email you all my doctor's recommendations and we can talk about it later if you wish". This will most likely defuse the situation and you're not the bad guy, your doctor is. Good thing he does not know!

No more rolls, gravy, turkey stuffing, crumb-coated casserole, apple or pumpkin pie, and forget about that special beer you used to enjoy. A few suggestions:

- Send a list ahead of time of what you can and cannot eat and drink.
- Offer to bring some of the food you cooked in your safe kitchen. You can bring gluten-free versions of certain food or drink items you know will prevent you from being left out or appearing to be uncooperative, i.e. gluten-free beer, gluten-free candy, gluten free desert and so on.
- You can offer to provide your hosts with a recipe to prepare especially for you, but be cautious; even if they do make an effort to accommodate you, there are still strong chances of cross contamination.
- You can offer to bring GFCF snacks, beer, candies or desserts.
- If you love chocolate candies for Valentine's, you want to tell your sweetheart which ones are GFCF, or let him/her know that flowers are a lovely alternative.
- Another trap to be aware of, is that if you had a little too much of that GF alcoholic beverage, you might not be able to resist a very tempting apple pie or buche de Noël.

How to Handle Special Events

It is a good thing in your happy life that there are a lot of special events for you to enjoy: weddings, receptions, birthday parties, happy hours, family gatherings, and neighborhood parties. The bad thing is that food is involved in most of them.

If you're lucky and people around you care about your health, they may offer you a menu choice. In that case you may be able to pick something you can actually eat. Or you may be offered an all you can eat buffet. Caution: Even though you think you can pick and choose safe foods, there is a high chance for cross contamination from the utensils people use to serve themselves with, or from a careless cook. For your safety, you may want to call the hotel/restaurant, explain your situation and ask them to set aside a safe dish for you like a salad (no croutons, dressing on the side), fruit salad with no yogurt mixed in, or the like. Most likely they will accommodate you.

Food issues were nothing new to my family. My mother was allergic to onions; my mother-in-law has celiac disease and is lactose intolerant; my husband is allergic to mushrooms, my brother-in-law limits salt and I can't eat soy. What a culinary challenge we face when we are all together!

In addition to being allergic to soy, doctors have always said I have irritable bowel syndrome. They would give me some medicine to help with the symptoms of IBS, but nothing ever made me symptom-free. I would continue to get severe cramping and diarrhea regularly. I usually assumed that when I had the bouts of cramping, etc. that I had somehow eaten something with soy in it, but I couldn't figure out what or when.

About two years ago, I was meeting with a trainer at my gym to discuss an eating plan to go along with my exercise regimen. Based on the way I answered some of his questions, he suggested that I take gluten out of my diet for a while. I decided to try it, and surprise, surprise! My bowel trouble got 100 % better. I couldn't believe it! How utterly disappointing! I knew first hand the GF foods my mother-in-law had available – and I didn't like them! I love bread, cookies, pasta, and especially pie. I found myself pretty irritated and intimidated about all of the changes I was facing, and all the foods that would be off my plate forever. I would be 'good' and be gluten free for months at a time. I felt great and then would wonder if gluten really did bother me, and I would cheat. And, yes, it really bothered me – I would be sick again.

So I committed whole-heartedly to this new diet. Eating gluten-free has been really disappointing at times, but delightful at others. Much of the prepared GF food (like lasagna) that I have tried – yuck! On the other hand, I have altered many of my favorite recipes and often the entire family prefers the GF version. I felt a thrill of victory when I made a GF pie that could stand up to any traditional competitor. I found great encouragement from family and friends who helped me find new recipes. They were supportive of my GF cooking and went out of their way to understand what I could and couldn't have when they cooked for me. I must confess I still have moments when I want an "old favorite" goodie from a bakery. For the most part though, I don't miss the gluten in my diet. The foods I eat now satisfy me and keep me healthy, not sick!

Maggie T – Austin, TX

What is Your Responsibility as a GFCF Patient?

How to Spot Gluten in Foods and Other Products

Gluten is not only hiding in plain sight in all the known grain sources of gluten, but it's also hiding within commercially prepared foods, and their descriptions do not always say "contains gluten" in bright red letters. So how do you know the good from the bad?

Name that Grain

Although the new labeling laws are making easier for you to spot the harmless from the dangerous, it does not always go far enough in helping you find out the hidden truth. You know those dastardly food producers; they will try to get away with as much as possible.

Happy Grains Are Here Again

- Rice (white, brown, and wild)
- Corn
- Buckwheat (called kasha after roasting)
- Amaranth
- Quinoa
- Millet
- Sorghum
- Manioc
- Cassava
- Teff

Please keep in mind that the above grains are safe only if they are processed in a certified gluten-free plant or kitchen, or else you may be dealing with a sneaky case of cross contamination.

Bad, Bad Grains

- **Barley -** flour, pearl barley, barley grits, flakes, also used in making beer.

- **Bulgur** – a de-branned form of wheat used mostly in the Middle East and Eastern Europe.

- **Couscous** – is a round form of semolina coated with wheat flour. Used throughout the Middle East for a well-known dish by the same name.

- **Kamut** is also an ancient form of wheat, usually roasted. It tastes nutty but will still make you sick.

- **Rye** - flour, berries, or rolled; also used in rye beer, some whiskies, some vodkas.

- **Semolina** - ground wheat used to make pasta and noodles.

- **Spelt** - an ancient form of wheat; contains less gluten but still contains some.

- **Triticale** - a hybrid of wheat and rye.

- **Wheat** (grain, germ, bran, cereals and some hard liquor). Raw wheat can be powdered into flour; germinated and dried creating malt; crushed or cut into cracked wheat; parboiled (or steamed), dried, crushed and de-branned into bulgur; or processed into semolina, pasta, or used in roux. Wheat is a major ingredient in such foods as bread, porridge, crackers, biscuits, Swiss Muesli, pancakes, pies, pastries, cakes, cookies, muffins, rolls, doughnuts, gravy, boza (a fermented beverage), and an assortment of breakfast cereals. The best known are: Wheatena, Cream of Wheat, Shredded Wheat, and Wheaties. Good old wheat we love to hate.

All of the above grains are dangerous for you if you have any form of gluten intolerance. For more details, please see Appendix C Hidden Sources of Gluten and Dairy.

Where Else in your Food is Gluten Hiding?

- Citric acid
- Dextrin
- Diglycerides
- Durum flour
- Hydrolyzed plant protein
- Hydrolyzed vegetable protein
- Malt
- Maltodextrin, although in America it is supposed to be made with corn starch
- Modified food starch
- Soy Sauce
- Starch unless specified such as "corn starch"

For more details, see the **Hidden Sources of Gluten and Dairy** in Appendix C.

Other Words Indicating that Gluten is Present

These guys are trying to fool you by using foreign words, mostly French words. How dare they use French? Not nice!

- Food titles that say "thickened" without specifying which thickener
- Au Gratin (French)
- Beef Wellington (English)
- Beignet (French)
- Bisque (French)
- Bourguignonne (French)
- Crouton (French)
- Goulash (Polish)
- Quiche (French)
- Roux (French)
- Soufflé (French)
- Stroganoff (Russian)

So, your responsibility to your own well-being is to learn this industry's "jargon" that hides gluten and dairy.

I never got a real diagnosis, but instead decided to give up gluten and casein after much trial and error. Having read about what gluten and casein sensitivity looks like, it was worth the gamble of giving up those foods. And, it was so worth it! I am never going back. The irony is that, my dad grew up on a wheat farm, and so, growing up, a meal was not complete without bread or pasta. Had I known then what I know now, it would have saved me many sleepless nights, and my grades in school would have been better. I probably would have had clearer skin as a teenager as well. As a young adult, I probably would have had less sinus and ear infections, and may have avoided an auto-immune disorder. But, as they say, "Hindsight is 20/20."

What led me to a gluten and casein free lifestyle was a chronic eye infection. I had a chicken pox lesion on my eyeball as a child, and whenever I would be under a large amount of stress, that blister would break out again. It was very painful, and would distort my vision. The medicine for it cost $125.00 for a 1/4 of an ounce. So after doing some research and talking with another Certified Clinical Nutritionist, I decided to address my diet by eliminating *cow dairy and all grains containing gluten. Since I have a Middle Eastern heritage, it makes sense for me to eat like my ancestors ate. It is interesting to me that I can eat bread or pasta from Israel, Greece, or Italy, but cannot tolerate American wheat - possibly because most of the American wheat has been genetically modified. I use gluten-free grains and flours for bread, pasta, and pastries with great success. These are brown rice, tapioca, potato, amaranth, and quinoa. I use goat and sheep's milk based yogurts, cheeses and milk. I cook most of my own food from scratch, and pack a lunch whenever I go out. For the most part, I can substitute these flours and cheeses with my old recipes. When I eat out, I ask a lot of questions. I know especially to avoid condiments, sauces, and soups, as they usually have MSG (monosodium GLUTamate). I have learned to be my own personal advocate. If not, I suffer the consequences and my gut is an unhappy camper.*

I have maintained a gluten-free, casein-free lifestyle for 3 years now, and have a stronger immune system, stronger stamina, focus to stay on task and a happier tummy. I used to eat a large meal, and would end up hungry 2 hours later. Now, with different food choices, I am satisfied for longer periods of time. I have not had a breakout on my eye in over 2 1/2 years. I am gaining some much needed weight. I sleep better at night, and have better cognitive function. Plus, my intestines don't feel like they are on fire, and are "social" (if you catch my drift; pun intended!)

Dawn A – Austin, TX

Special Foods to Consider

Blue Cheese

In the old days and in the old country, wherever your ancestors came from, the mold used in the manufacturing of blue cheese came from moldy bread and was injected into the cheese during the aging process. Nowadays, the fungi used come from a perfectly safe pasteurized *Penicillium* mold. On a side note, did you know that blue cheese is the original natural source of penicillin, a known antibacterial and antiviral healing medium? You may not believe this, but in the old days, at least in France, blue cheese was used as a healing plaster on open wounds to avoid infections. I know, it stinks but if you liked cheese, you could always lick your wounds afterwards. Gross!

Although highly unlikely, it may still be possible that a very few blue cheeses are still made with bread mold, but one is never cautious enough, so once again, read the labels. Of course, if you are allergic to dairy, avoid blue cheese at all costs.

Buckwheat

Unlike what you might think, Buck is not part of the Wheat family and does not contain gluten. Feel relieved and try some of my buckwheat recipes, especially my Mamie's (Grandma's) buckwheat crepe recipe from the Brittany part of France.

Caramel Coloring

Having been a pastry chef for years, I have a hard time believing that caramel can be made with anything other than sugar; however, it appears that in some countries (I will not name names here, but you know who you are), some grains are used in the production of caramel. Suffice it to know that in the U.S and Canada, manufacturers do not use gluten in their caramel. The same cannot be said of all countries so, as usual, read the labels for country of origin.

Corn Gluten

Although this form of labeling may scare the "bejesus" out of you (why would Jesus be scary? I still don't get this colloquialism. Oh well!), it's only another way of saying starch, and starch from corn is perfectly safe if you are allergic to gluten.

Modified Food Starch

The only starches legally required to be spelled out on FDA labels are corn and potato. When a label says "modified food starch", it could be made from *any* grain source. Again, as with caramel, American and Canadian manufacturing facilities do not use gluten in their modified starch production, so you will have to figure out the country of origin. If the country of origin isn't Canada or the USA, it may contain gluten.

MSG

As Dawn mentions above, if you are allergic to gluten, you will most likely be allergic to MSG (Monosodium GLUTamate). As you can see, gluten and glutamate share the same root, GLUT. Although we have been led to believe that MSG can only be found in Chinese food, that is no longer true. MSG is now part of the vast majority of processed foods in this country. This lab-created flavor enhancer is in almost every bottled, bagged, frozen, or canned processed food on supermarket shelves. In most cases it is hidden as a component of a flavoring and is not labeled as such. If you've seen words like autolyzed yeast, hydrolyzed protein, and whey protein you should know that they all contain MSG as part of their formulation. Each of these additives contains a percentage of glutamate, the harmful component of MSG. For more information on where to find MSG, check the Hidden Source of Gluten and Dairy list in Appendix C and on **www.msgtruth.org** and **www.msgmyth.com**. This warning also applies to other excitotoxins like aspartame (in sugar-free and diet foods) and L-cysteine.

Oats

Yes, in this instance, it has been difficult to "separate the wheat from the chaff ", but here is the important information to know: if the package does not say "certified gluten free", don't buy it. Why the confusion? Oats do not contain gluten by themselves, but like good kids living in a bad neighborhood, the gluten left behind from processing, handling and packaging wheat may taint them. Make sure that the package specifies, "processed in a facility dedicated to oat processing only" or similar words, and you will be safe eating your favorite oat breakfast. If you still have an allergic reaction to these oats, your immune system is so compromised you may also be allergic to oats.

Vinegar

There are many different types of vinegars. The traditional vinegars are made with malt and beer (avoid), red and white wine and grapes (balsamic vinegar in Italy), and pretty much any fermented fruits (apple, black current, date, raspberry, etc.) and vegetables (palm, coconut, etc.). Then there are the industrial vinegars or white vinegars made with grains, like rice and wheat. While wheat contains gluten, during the distillation process the gluten is taken out of the vinegar, so white vinegar is gluten-free. If you still are concerned about it, you may want to avoid it. On the other hand, other vinegars made from grains like malt are not distilled and still contain gluten. To stay safe, stay away from any vinegar that does not specify its distilled product of origin. Lastly, it may be made synthetically from natural gas and petroleum derivatives. I should not even have to say it but will: stay away from that kind of vinegar.

What About Alcohol?

During the distillation process, even spirits made from grain become gluten free. If that's your cup of tea (so to speak), brandy and fruit brandies (like

Grand Marnier and Cointreau), gin, scotch, tequila (which has always been gluten free by the way), vodka and whiskey are free of any traces of gluten. But you're not quite out of the woods yet. The source of some additives and coloring may be suspicious, and some spirits are aged in barrels that use a gluten-based sealant. Put on your Gluten Detective hat and do additional research if you're not sure.

Other Products That Could Possibly Contain Gluten

In the Bathroom

- Toothpaste
- Acid indigestion tablets
- Cough syrup
- Laxatives
- Lip balm
- Nasal sprays
- Cosmetic products such as: lipstick, lotions and face powders.
- Unless you have dermatitis herpetiformis, foundations, lotions, creams and skin conditioners should be safe for you; the gluten molecule is too large to pass through the skin
- If you do suffer from dermatitis herpetiformis, lotions or creams containing wheat germ oil, wheatgrass or barley grass can possibly aggravate your skin condition. If you find they do, then stop using them immediately.
- Other products: Glue even on envelopes, stamps, and stickers may contain gluten. If you have children, be aware that some crayons contain gluten.
- For even more details about this, check out the Hidden Sources of Gluten and Dairy in Appendix C.

Dealing with Gluten Reactions

Accidents do happen. Denying it won't help. A waiter or a cook makes a mistake; you misread a label; you may not realize that a certain word means gluten or dairy; you can't resist a temptation. Try not to panic or beat yourself up too hard. We are all humans prone to mistake and weakness.

You already know the consequences of eating gluten or dairy. If the reaction is mild, you know what to do. If you're in public, excuse yourself and go hide in the bathroom to wait the symptoms out. It will go away as soon as you go back to abstinence. If it is grave and you feel really bad, you may have to go to the emergency room or see your doctor as soon as possible. Most of the time, taking fiber with a lot of water will scrub your digestive system and clear the offender. Diarrhea is only your body trying to get rid of what it sees as a poison. You may also try to eat lots of bananas. I do not recommend you take any laxative drugs as they irritate your intestine even more. If the symptoms are not going away, you may still be ingesting gluten without being aware. Get tested again and consult your food diary to try to find the culprit. (See, I told you it would come handy one day!)

Coping With Your Withdrawal Symptoms

I'm not going to pretend this is going to be easy. Some people will have withdrawal symptoms similar to drug and alcohol withdrawal. Remember that for your brain, gluten and casein proteins may have an opium-like effect. To get off of them will not be easy. Depending on your allergy level, you may experience digestive difficulties (diarrhea or constipation); headaches (remember that opium-like effect on your brain); fatigue (your body is trying to get rid of all this toxic sludge and it's exhausting); possible inflammation or skin rashes acting up (your skin is your largest elimination organ, even before your colon).

A few suggestions to help make your transition easier: If you can, take a few days off and pamper yourself. Drink a lot of water. To help you eliminate those pesky gluten and casein proteins faster, use digestive enzymes three times a day at mealtime.

Continually Stay Updated on Current Medical News

If you keep up with your local GFCF group, you are most likely aware of the most recent medical developments related to your intolerance. Try to stay abreast of the latest scientific news. There is still a lot of research being done, and there is so much to learn about your disease. Stay informed. Read specialized magazines, sign up for GFCF email newsletters, online news (you can subscribe to Google news related to any subject), and GFCF web sites. It will help you ask questions during your next doctor's visit.

GFCF groups are not just there to provide recipes and chit chat. They also lobby on your behalf and fund research. You may want to help them out financially, to assist them to help you. For example, thanks to GFCF groups, a gluten labeling law was enacted in 2004 and took effect in 2006. Thanks to them you now know whether there is gluten, dairy or any other allergens in your food.

Not Feeling Better Yet? Could There Be Another Cause?

You have been diagnosed, you took charge and did your homework, you're very good at avoiding gluten yet you may be one of the few that are not experiencing relief from symptoms. What could be the cause? Despite all your precautions, are you still accidentally ingesting gluten? Possible, but at this point I trust you are good at knowing what to eat and what to avoid. Besides, you probably know by now all the possible sources of hidden gluten. But no one is perfect and those hidden gluten sources can be sneaky. Even if you trust your favorite waiter for guiding you through the menu's minefield, something they don't even suspect might slip through. Even with your best detective efforts accidents do happen.

So you might think: "What's wrong with me?" If you have been affected for a long time, it is very possible that you may take longer to heal than someone else in your situation. Another possibility is that something else is affecting you. What could it be?

Other Food Allergens

Even though you have been clearly diagnosed with gluten intolerance or celiac disease, it is still possible you might be allergic to another food. Have you done a complete food allergy panel? Maybe you should go back to your food allergy expert and ask to get that done just to make sure. Obviously something else is bothering you. It might be a good idea to get to the bottom of this and find out if there might be other culprits. After all, if your immune system is already sensitive to one allergen, it might also be allergic to others.

About 10 years ago, I started to notice problems with my balance, and very slowly over the years it got worse. Standing and talking to people, shopping, and standing in line became a nightmare. The first thing I think about in a new setting is to spot a seat, or a place where I can lean against something.

A neurologist gave me the diagnostic of "orthostatic tremors", a very rare disease. I got medicated with very addictive drugs, but I chose to abandon this route. I did not return to see doctors because I felt they did not have much to offer me. I pursued endlessly what could be causing my condition and never stopped learning about nutrition and health. For a couple of years I also pursued chiropractic care, and one chiropractor convinced me that my cerebellum was the culprit. Unfortunately, knowing this did not resolve my problem either.

About 3 months ago, I needed to lose some weight and decided to eliminate bread from my diet. After listening to a friend of mine telling me that she was back on her gluten-free diet, I decided that maybe I should also try it. After all I already eliminated bread; why not going a step further? After only three days, I was astonished at the improvement: I was able to stand far longer. I started to get relief from my chronic fatigue syndrome, started to sleep better and much less. I was also becoming stronger.

I started to research the Internet about balance and gluten intolerance, and lo and behold, I learned that the cerebellum is very often a target with gluten intolerant people. After a couple of months the improvements stopped: I had reached a plateau, and felt that maybe there was still something else affecting me. I decided to take an allergy test and the results came back indicating I was allergic to corn, eggs, cheese, brewer's yeast and mushrooms. It confirmed what I already knew: gluten intolerance does major damage to the upper colon, which in turn creates new problems, such as sensitivities to other foods and nutrient malabsorption.

I am not completely recovered, but I know that I need to give my body some time to heal. By stopping the damage done by gluten and stopping the intake of allergens, I can heal my digestive system. The drastic change that I experienced after eliminating gluten from my diet for only three days was enough to tell me that I must avoid gluten for the rest of my life. I am now convinced that gluten has been, literally, a poison to my body.

Jocelyne V – Austin, TX

What Else Could Be Bothering You?

As you probably know, there are many well-known allergens ready to give you a hard time. Any food could be an allergen to you depending on your genetic make up. After all, some of the most serious food companies make sure that their production facilities are also dairy, nut, soy, shellfish, egg, corn-free. Most doctors also know that if you are allergic to gluten, there is a strong possibility that you have other food allergies. More detective work is needed.

Some of the better known allergens are:

- Baker's yeast
- Bananas
- Brewer's yeast
- Cane sugar

- Eggs
- Garlic
- Goat's milk
- Gluten (wheat, spelt, barley and rye)
- Milk and dairy products including butter, yogurt and my favorite: cheese
- Nutmeg
- Peanuts and other nuts like almonds
- Pineapple
- Soy
- Vanilla

As you can see on this list, dairy and eggs are by far the most common food allergens in the US, even more than gluten. But remember, your food enemy might not even be on the above list. You could be allergic to ANY food out there. For example, one my most difficult cases involved creating a healthy diet for a family of 4 with a combined total of 140 food allergies. Can you believe that? It didn't leave a lot of foods to eat. That was a tough one, and it took me a while to create a customized diet so that the whole family could eat together and the mom did not have to prepare 4 different meals every day. Once you've found which food is affecting you, the best way to heal is to completely avoid it. You know the routine. For now let's talk about the Public Enemy Number One...

Milk and Dairy Products

Besides the obvious, milk, cream and cheese, dairy is present in many commercial products in the form of milk powder, butter, casein and whey powder. Again, you'll need to put on your detective cap to read the labels and find those sneaky milk products in your food. Until you become proficient at it, I suggest you avoid processed foods (you already know how I feel about that) and stay with simple foods. Pretty much everything I have already mentioned previously: fresh vegetables and fruits (organic and/or locally-grown if possible), good quality meat (grass-fed beef, farm-raised poultry and pork) and line-caught fish.

Lactose Intolerance

If you are like me, the older I get, the more I am intolerant to milk. It is a normal process. As we age, our body produces less and less lactase, the enzyme that allows us to digest the sugar lactase present in milk. When lactose is not broken down by lactase, you and I will experience a series of uncomfortable symptoms: bloating, gas, possible diarrhea and other potential public embarrassing moments. Lactose intolerance is the most widely known food intolerance in this the US. About 30 percent of the population is affected by it. After all, is it natural for human beings to drink the milk of another animal for the rest of their life? Do so you see any other example of this behavior in nature? Nope! Most likely, this is not news to you, as the vast majority of gluten-allergic people are also intolerant of milk. Typically, lactose intolerance symptoms do not go further than potentially and uncomfortable symptoms and do not create an immune system response like gluten intolerance will. Even though the term "intolerance" may be used in both instances, they do not create the same bodily response. Lactose intolerance is just a digestive problem, while gluten intolerance is an immune response problem. All you need to do is avoid the offending milk products, take a digestive enzyme such as Lactaid or drink lactose-free milk. In some milder cases of lactose intolerance, you might still be able to eat natural yogurt and real cheese because the fermentation process eliminates the lactose. I know that I don't have any problem with eating naturally fermented yogurt and aged cheeses. Of course, the fact that I am French may help me.

Some scientists believe that once you eliminate gluten from your diet and heal your intestinal villi, your body will be able to produce lactase again. Depending on your age, I'm not sure it makes sense, but if it does happen and you wish to continue to drink milk, more power to you.

Until then, there are many tasty non-dairy milk, yogurt and cheese alternatives on your grocery store's shelves. Instead of cow's milk, you can drink rice, almond, soy, hazelnut, hemp and coconut milk. Instead of dairy yogurt, you can now find very good quality soy yogurts. As for cheese, although I don't believe there is such a thing as a *good* cheese alternative, there are plenty of soy "cheese" choices at your health store for your enjoyment.

Could You Be Allergic to Milk?

In some cases, especially with autistic children, the protein in milk (casein) will provoke the same immune reaction that it does with gluten. In this case it is called a *dairy allergy*. Please keep in mind that although being intolerant to gluten can create an allergy to dairy because of damaged villi, they do not necessarily always go hand in hand. You can be intolerant of gluten, and not dairy. You can have dairy allergy, but not be allergic to gluten. Or you can have both.

What Other Health Issues Could Be Created by Gluten Intolerance?

As you know by now, gluten intolerance causes damage to your intestinal walls and villi. Because of the damaged villi, your body is not allowed to benefit from some very important vitamins and minerals, ones that are very important to your health and wellbeing. The lack of absorption of some of these vitamins leads to possible deficiencies, and the additional health conditions resulting from these deficiencies. Whether or not these health issues will affect you will depend on how long you have been allergic to gluten and casein. If you have been allergic to them for many years, don't be surprised if you also have one or more of these conditions. If your allergies are recent and have been discovered rapidly, the chances are smaller that you will be afflicted with these side health issues.

Your most important goal is to heal and repair your intestinal wall through gluten and casein abstinence. There is no point trying to fix any other health condition while your intestine is still damaged. Healing your digestive system is your goal number one. Your next goal is to eat a healing diet full of fresh fruits, vegetables, good quality fish and meat to strengthen your body and help heal the other conditions. I'll talk more about your food choices later in this book; meanwhile, let's look at the illnesses caused by the malabsorption of important vitamins and minerals.

Anemia, Iron Deficiency, and Fatigue

One of the most important minerals for our health is iron. Iron is important in the formation of red blood cells. Without it, your body cannot create a sufficient amount of red blood cells, or they are poorly formed and do not perform as needed. The proper amount of healthy red blood cells is necessary to carry oxygen to all your muscles and organs, the most important being your heart. So not enough iron absorbed through your intestinal walls may result in low iron levels and low red blood cells, a condition called anemia. There are different forms of anemia such as iron deficiency, vitamin B12 deficiency, and folic acid deficiency. If you suspect you have any of these forms of anemia, I would suggest you ask your doctor for more information on this subject.

My gynecologist actually diagnosed my celiac disease in August 2008. He put all the inexplicable pieces of the puzzle of my life together and got to the root of the lifelong issues I suffered from. I have always been very health conscious and tried to eat lots of fiber rich food, which included healthy whole wheat items. Little did I know, this "healthy" food was slowly killing me, and the gastrointestinal problems I lived with as "normal" were actually an autoimmune disease.

For as long as I could remember I had been anemic. I saw many different doctors regarding chronic intestinal issues. Diagnosed with depression from the age of 16, coupled with incredibly low energy, the disconnected world I lived in was hazy. I felt lethargic and never fully present.

A consequence of celiac disease was the development of both anemia and bulimia. No matter what I ate, I would feel sick after, so I went through periods of being scared to eat and would avoid eating because of the stomach pain I would feel after. Since my body didn't absorb nutrients, I would eat a full meal and I would still feel hungry. I was always uncomfortably over-stuffed, needing to open the top button on my pants and pop Gas-X and Tums likes candy. Sometimes, after I would eat food containing gluten, my stomach would be so bloated and I would feel so fat and sick I would make myself purge for relief. I received help for the eating disorders from a nutritionist who taught me intuitive eating and have been in recovery since 2007.

My undiagnosed celiac disease was also responsible for unexplained tooth decay and enamel defects. It was traced to the acid reflux disease that I also endured, but the severity of the condition of my teeth was beyond the effects of the acid.

On a subconscious level, I intuitively knew what foods didn't make me feel ill and had developed weird eating habits that incorporated these limited choices. I lived in a very small world of food. I had always loved white rice with duck sauce, Sour Patch Kids candy and steak with a baked potato and salad.

I stopped ovulating at the age of 25 due to a condition called "Premature Ovarian Failure" and began expensive hormone-replacement therapy supplements to decrease the menopausal symptoms. I also became aware that I had osteopenia as well. My gynecologist at this time said my period was probably just "on siesta." I felt like a 60 year old woman, with brittle bones, all dried up.

The day the doctor's office called me with the lab results and I found out I had celiac disease I felt both relieved and devastated. Priding myself that my severe food allergies to tree nuts and shellfish did not include gluten, I thought I would hardly be able to eat anything. I sat in my boss' office crying, grieving the years of pain and confusion. I was mad that the doctors hadn't figured it out sooner.

My boss told me my news wasn't that big of a deal, but she did let me take the rest of the day off. My boyfriend picked me up, and not knowing what else to do, we *went to get lunch at the exquisite Chez Foushee, a restaurant in Richmond, VA, where his best friend, Matt Greene, was the head chef. I managed to move my self-pity and tears aside and explained my allergies to the waiter. Matt created my first gluten-free meal as a diagnosed celiac. It was a dish that I felt safe eating and was also one of the best meals I have ever had.*

Since being diagnosed with celiac disease and eating a gluten-free diet, I feel like a completely different person. I have lost more than 15 pounds without even trying to and I no longer suffer from osteopenia or anemia. Witnessing how my body has begun to heal itself by eating gluten-free food, I was inspired to adopt a vegan diet which incorporates macrobiotic food in hopes the health benefits will reverse my premature ovarian failure, as it has with cancer. The tooth enamel decay has lessened and going to the bathroom is no longer an event that is marked by a ceremony of lighting matches.

The greatest new experience was the feeling of being full, and not bloated, after eating a meal for the first time in my life. I still feel grief and anger towards celiac disease some days: it has taken away my dream of having my own children, let me think my suffering was "normal" for so long, and left me in menopause at an early age, but I have grown to accept the disease over time. I am even grateful for it because of the unique opportunity to help other people who suffer from celiac disease. It's also inspired me to create art based on my feelings and experiences with food allergies. I love to eat now and have developed a passion for cooking. I am overwhelmed with excitement by all the delicious gluten-free options in so many restaurants and food stores.

Kelly F – Austin, TX

How Do You Know if You Have Anemia?

The most common symptoms are fatigue (a French word describing a general lack of energy) and skin pallor (your skin looks pale or whitish like a vampire that did not get his daily dose of fresh blood.)

You need to ask your doctor for a complete blood test (CBC). When looking at your results, look for either a low red blood cell count (RBC), a low hematocrit count (Hct), or a low hemoglobin level (Hgh). Another early way to find out if you are on your way to anemia is to test your ferritin levels. Ferretin is an iron-containing protein contained in your tissues, but most importantly in your liver, spleen, and bone marrow. Because ferritin levels will show up on a test earlier than on a regular iron level test, it is a good early way to see if you're on your way to iron deficiency anemia. Your ferritin levels can be checked with a simple blood test administered cheaply at any good quality pharmacy. Healthy levels should read above 50. If your level is lower than 30, it may be an indication of borderline anemia. And if your levels are lower than 20, it indicates an absence of stored iron, and you definitively need to confirm that result with a more complete blood test at your doctor's office. Be aware that these numbers may vary from lab to lab. If you want to make sure, check with your physician. Remember that in your case, your damaged intestinal walls may be the reason why you are not absorbing enough iron for a healthy body.

(Also, if you find that you have high levels of ferritin in your blood test, you may have what is called iron overload or in doctor's jargon, hemochromatosis. A small number of people have a tendency to accumulate too much iron in their blood and it could reach toxic levels. Don't panic, but do see your doctor about it if your levels are unusually high).

Food Sources of Iron

Depending on how long you have been iron deficient, your need for iron supplementation will vary. Most people will respond quickly, while for others, it may take up to 12 months. Even when your CBC panel looks normal, make sure your ferritin levels are in the normal range before lowering your intake of iron. It is important to check your iron levels regularly so you do not risk excess iron intake, which could be toxic.

But from the chef's point of view, I can help you with the possible alimentary reason for your lack of iron. If you are a strict vegetarian, most likely you are not getting enough iron from your diet, even if you are careful to eat vegetables containing iron. The heme iron contained in meat is much easier for our bodies to absorb. Without abusing red meat, I would suggest one to two servings of red meat (liver and venison are the best sources of iron) per week. Another one or two servings of red "meat" fish (salmon, tuna, and shrimp) will also help you with your ferritin levels. If you are ovo-vegetarian, eggs are a very good source of easily assimilable iron. If you are a strict vegan, I would suggest spinach, Swiss chard, basil, romaine lettuce, shiitake mushrooms, green beans, parsley, kale, broccoli, Brussels sprouts, asparagus, soybeans, olives, lentils, celery, quinoa, cabbage and kidney beans as well as the spices turmeric and cinnamon.

Iron Supplementation

If you choose the supplementation route, be aware that some lower quality iron supplements will not be absorbed by your body and will not help you. Avoid iron oxide and iron sulfate. They can cause digestive problems, upset your stomach or give you constipation. The better forms of iron are iron picolinate, iron citrate and iron glycinate, which are more easily absorbed and will not give you nasty side effects. Some of these are available in a liquid form or time-released capsules, which are less likely to upset your digestive system. Ask your pharmacist for these forms of iron. If they are not available at your local pharmacy, you can find them online at any other reputable online pharmacy under the names **Ferrasorb** by Thorne or **Liquid Iron** by NF Formulas. Our pharmacist recommends you take a daily dose of 500 mg of vitamin C with your iron to facilitate absorption.

Food Sources of Vitamins Necessary to Correct Anemia

Vitamin C

Bell peppers, parsley, broccoli, strawberries, cauliflower, lemon juice, romaine lettuce, Brussels sprouts, papaya, kale, kiwi fruit, cantaloupe, oranges, grapefruit, cabbage, tomatoes, Swiss chard, collard greens, raspberries, asparagus, celery, spinach, pineapple, green beans and summer squash.

Vitamin Bs

Because a gluten-free diet may not contain the same amount of B vitamins and folic acid usually provided with a gluten-filled diet (in bread for example), make sure your new diet contains plenty of fruits and vegetables offering these and many other vitamins in large quantities.

- **Vitamin B1 (thiamin)**
  Romaine lettuce, asparagus, crimini mushrooms, spinach, sunflower seeds, green peas, tomatoes, eggplant, Brussels sprouts, celery, cabbage, watermelon, bell peppers, carrots, summer squash, winter squash, green beans, broccoli, corn, kale, black beans oats, pineapple, oranges as well as tuna.

- **Vitamin B2 (riboflavin)**
  Crimini mushrooms, spinach, romaine lettuce, asparagus, Swiss chard, broccoli, collard greens, eggs, green beans, celery, kale, cabbage, strawberries, tomatoes, cauliflower, raspberries, Brussels sprouts, summer squash, green peas, plums as well as calf's liver and venison.

- **Vitamin B6**
  Spinach, bell peppers, garlic, cauliflower, bananas, broccoli, celery, asparagus, cabbage, crimini mushrooms, kale, collard greens, Brussels sprouts, watermelon, Swiss chard, cayenne pepper, turmeric, tomatoes, carrots, summer squash, cantaloupe, eggplant, romaine lettuce as well as tuna and cod.

- **Vitamin B12 (cobalamin)**
  Calf's liver, sardines, venison, shrimp, scallops, salmon, grass-fed beef, lamb, cod, and eggs.

In the same vein (pun injection), because vitamin B12 and folic acid are necessary for the formation of healthy red blood cells, it is suggested to supplement your diet with them. Because anemia from iron deficiency and anemia from B12 and folic acid look similar on a CBC, please make sure to ask your doctor which one may be your case. He/she will be able to make the difference.

If you or your doctor feels you need an emergency amount of B12, he/she may suggest regular injections until you reach the right levels. He/she also may suggest that you take daily doses of folic acid until your depletion is controlled. Because anemia is so common, when you discover that you are allergic to gluten, you should ask to be tested and possibly treated for anemia.

- **Folic acid or folate**
  Romaine lettuce, spinach, asparagus, collard greens, broccoli, cauliflower, beets, lentils, celery, Brussels sprouts, pinto beans, black beans, garbanzo beans, kidney beans, summer squash, navy beans, papaya, green beans, cabbage, bell peppers, green peas, lima beans, winter squash, tomatoes as well as calf's liver.

Osteoporosis

Osteoporosis could be another consequence of the damaged intestinal wall. This time, the important mineral missing from your body is calcium. Osteoporosis is low bone density caused in major part by a lack of absorbed calcium from your diet. While it is not the only cause for osteoporosis, it is the major reason. If you are afflicted with any level of gluten or casein intolerance, especially celiac disease, I would suggest you get a bone density test.

It can be done through heel and wrist tests, but these are an inferior way to test for low bone density. The absolute best tests for that potential problem are DEXA scan and specialized CT scans, which will measure bone density at the hip and lower back. I'd you have any suspicion of osteoporosis, please check with your physician.

There are Many Possible Causes for Bone Loss

- The number one reason is malabsorption, due to food allergies such as gluten intolerance and celiac disease.
- Excessive caffeine drinking (over 18 ounces per day) has a tendency to decrease bone mass.
- Smoking is a known factor in increased bone loss.
- Lack of exposure to sunlight, and its corollary: lack of vitamin D.
- Excessive drinking of alcohol.
- The long term use of steroid and corticosteroid drugs have a side effect of decreasing calcium absorption and loss of the body's ability to build new bone.
- Menopause is known to cause an approximate 3 percent bone loss per year for about ten years.
- The lack of regular weight-bearing exercises will lead to progressive bone loss.
- Excessive consumption of soft drinks, especially those containing phosphates
- Family history of osteoporosis.
- Hyperactivity of the thyroid gland (hyperthyroidism and hyperparathyroidism).

Do I Really Need Milk to Get my Calcium?

Because this book's title says "... and Dairy-free with French Gourmet Food", I feel I owe you a little explanation here. If you believe the dairy industry's "Got Milk?" persuasive campaign, we should all drink milk and plenty of it in order to be healthy and have strong bones. Don't believe a word of it. Any serious modern research - not backed by the dairy industry - on this fallacy will demonstrate that our body does not easily absorb the type of calcium found in milk. Why don't we see cows drinking milk all their lives? Most healthy cows fed on wild plants and grasses have very strong bones and do not develop osteoporosis. Why don't we eat greens like they do and see the results?

Not only we are the only creatures drinking another animal's milk, which does not make any sense, we are the only animals that continue to drink milk all its life. No other mammal does that. They are all weaned early in their life and still have strong bones. Have you ever heard of animals in the wild with osteoporosis? Also remember that there are many human beings all over the world that are not relying on cow's milk to get their needs in calcium covered. For example, the whole Indian continent abstains from drinking milk for religious reasons and its people still live healthy lives.

Other Ways to Get Your Calcium. Food sources of bone-building ingredients

Calcium, potassium and magnesium-rich foods such as: eggs; seafood like sardines (with their bones), flounder, salmon, tuna, shrimp and shellfish; vegetables like broccoli, cabbage, Brussels sprouts, summer squash, carrots, sprouts; dark leafy greens like kale, Swiss chard, spinach and collard greens; legumes and assorted beans, miso and tempeh (from fermented soy beans); seeds like sesame seeds and tahini (sesame butter); herbs like basil, lamb's quarters, rosemary, oat straw, dandelion; sea vegetables like dulse, kelp, nori, wakame, kombu. A good way to combine sea vegetables and seafood is to indulge in good quality sushi once in a while. It tastes great and is good for you; look at the general Japanese population for proof.

Vitamin D: Shrimp, sardines, cod and eggs. Sunshine, as little as 20 minutes a day will go a long way.

Vitamin K: Spinach, Brussels sprouts, Swiss chard, carrot, green beans, asparagus, bell peppers, tomatoes, green peas, avocados, as well as strawberries, apples and eggs.

Vitamin C: Bell peppers, parsley, broccoli, cauliflower, romaine lettuce, Brussels sprouts, kale, cabbage, tomatoes, Swiss chard, sweet potatoes, collard greens, asparagus, celery, spinach, green beans, summer squash as well as strawberries, papaya, kiwis, cantaloupe, oranges, lemons, limes, grapefruit and pineapple

And all other vitamins contained in the above foods are also working together to build a healthy body and strong bones.

Exercise

Weight bearing exercise is an important way to conserve bone and increase it. For your lower body, I suggest a minimum of 20 minutes of brisk walk per day. For upper body strength, light but regular weight lifting gives the best results.

How to help your bones grow again

The following suggestions are for your information only. Please check with your naturopath or nutritionist for the proper amounts.

Some of the biggest marketing hoopla coming from the dairy, and even sometimes the supplement industry, is that all you need to rebuild bones is calcium. This is a simplification. Yes, calcium can be helpful in rebuilding your bone matrix, but it is not all that is needed.

- **Vitamin D3** (cholecalciferol). Mostly beneficial during the winter months in the Northern part of this continent. Yes, that means you, our neighbors to the North, Canadians. Although, unless you live in the tropics and have daily access to at least 20 minutes of sun, I would say to all Americans, take it from October to April. Historically, vitamin D has been instrumental in eradicating rickets in malnourished children. It is most commonly found in cod liver oil. When I was a child, I was found to be lacking in calcium. I do remember (NOT fondly) having to ingest a large tablespoon of this horrible tasting concoction. But it did help strengthen my bones eventually. Nowadays, you can get it not only without the horrible taste, but flavored with orange or strawberry. Nice! Vitamin D3 is very important to facilitate the absorption of calcium.

  - **Calcium**. The most absorbable forms of calcium are calcium aspartate, citrate, gluconate and malate. Avoid calcium carbonate, which is poorly absorbed by most people. Because it is contained in our bones and is important for the proper functioning of nerves and muscles, calcium is the most abundant mineral found in our body. But because our body does not create its own calcium, it must be ingested through food or supplements. Many leafy green vegetables are a great source of calcium, as well as many of the other team members below.

- **Magnesium citrate**. Magnesium is also found in our bones and muscles. It is important in calcium uptake. It is a known muscle relaxant if you have cramps. It also relaxes you if you have trouble falling asleep at night. Usually, calcium and magnesium go hand in hand as two complementary sweethearts.

- **Phosphorus** works with calcium to increase bone strength.

- **Zinc** is very important in supporting our immune system and works synergistically with the other team members to help build strong bones.

- **Copper** also helps in the formation of bones. It is needed to complement zinc supplementation.

- **Selenium** is a very important mineral supportive of our immune system as well as a known antioxidant. It also helps with bone rebuilding.

- **Boron**. Another bone-building mineral. It improves calcium absorption.

- **Vitamin K** is a vitamin known to help reduce osteoporosis. It is also necessary for blood clotting.

- **Manganese** is one of the smallest team members but works with the others by activating enzymes important in the formation of the bone matrix. It is vital in mineral metabolism.

- **Vitamin C** is known to help the absorption of calcium. It is also important for the formation of collagen necessary for the bone matrix.

- **Silica**, usually from the plant equisetum, supplies silicon, which is good for calcium utilization and bone strength.

- **Glucosamine plus chondroitin** in combination are necessary for the development of bone and connective tissue.

- **Soy isoflavones** have an estrogenic effect on the body and estrogen promotes bone mass.

- **Vitamin B complex with added B6 and B12** provides strength to the proteins used in bone tissue.

You will find most of these bone-building team members in any well-designed bone multivitamin. If you cannot find it locally, look for a product called **Oscap** sold at many good quality online pharmacies.

Low Thyroid Functions (Hypothyroidism)

Although hypothyroidism is not caused by gluten intolerance, it is very commonly found in people that are allergic to gluten. The gluten allergy's symptoms are typically masking the symptoms of low thyroid function. Hypothyroidism is a condition in which your thyroid gland does not produce enough of the thyroid hormones called T4 and T3. These hormones determine the speed of your metabolism and how fast or slow your body functions. They regulate your energy levels and brain function. Think of your body as a car battery. Even if it is fully charged but you crank up everything in your car - radio, AC and so on - and your alternator (your thyroid gland) is not recharging it, you will run out of energy. If your alternator only provides very little recharging power (low T4 and T3 levels), you will feel fatigued (French word for tired), have brain fog and typically gain weight. So, if you do have allergies to gluten and casein, it is very possible that these symptoms may be masking the symptoms of hypothyroidism. If you suspect this is the case, I recommend you talk to your doctor about checking your thyroid hormone levels, and treating this condition as well as your food allergies.

About five years ago, I had a very severe thyroid problem and was facing surgery that involved removal of my thyroid. Yikes! It scared me to death so I decided to change my eating habits and go "gluten-free" to avoid surgery, as was recommended by my nutritionist.

Voila! .... something interesting happened. After six months of being on a gluten free diet, the changes were AMAZING! My skin cleared up, my allergies were 98% gone, my nails grew strong and healthy, my hair became healthier and shinier AND I was no longer having that bloated and cramped feeling I had attributed to getting older! And best of all, my thyroid is back to normal! My digestive system is back on track too! I FEEL GREAT! I am no longer exhausted and my energy level is that of a 25 year old!

Another thing, I did NOT go on gluten-free diet to lose weight, but I DID lose weight and kept it off without any effort

Kim S – Austin, TX

A Positive Attitude is Everything

Like most human beings would in these circumstances, you probably feel depressed about discovering your new condition. Like we all feel during any loss, you probably will go through the classic psychological consequences of such loss: anger, denial and sadness. They are normal feelings to go through. As soon as you have gone through and purged these feelings of loss, make an effort to see this challenge as an opportunity to heal and feel better physically and psychologically. This is the beginning of a better and healthier life for you. Embrace it. Work through it, and the world will be a better place for you. Try to stay positive through this experience.

The GF Buddy System

Do you have a GFCF buddy? It can be a family member, a good friend, a colleague or someone you have met at a local chapter of the national organization (see Appendix A). As with exercise, I recommend that you make a good connection with someone with the same kind of affliction. They can be so helpful and supportive, because they know exactly how you feel and what kind of distress you are in. If they have been dealing with it for a while, so much the better. They can be your mentor, guide and teacher. There is no need to fight this fight alone, because you are *not* alone. It has been estimated that about one out of one hundred people in this country suffer from one of the many forms of gluten intolerance.

Your New Gluten and Dairy-Free Diet

What Are Your GFCF Choices?

Do you feel like there is nothing left for you to eat? No big surprise here. Most people in the western world are so accustomed to eating wheat-based products that they are mostly oblivious to the fact that billions of people in our world have been and are still living without wheat. Whole Asian cultures thrive on a rice diet. Middle Eastern populations do very well with their traditional diet full of beans (yes, I meant that). The vast majority of the African continent live on grains and roots that are as nutritious as wheat: teff, cassavas, millet and manioc. Latin American cultures, going back centuries, have been living very well on a corn and beans diet, not to mention amaranth and quinoa. Russians and Eastern Europe's favorite grain is buckwheat, a hardy and warming grain that provides them a good source of protein. In my part of the world, Southern France, besides the fruits and vegetables also eaten in other parts of the world, our traditional diet contains fish, nuts and olives, all good sources of healthy proteins and fats (see my previous book.) So you see, once you take you wheat blindfold off, you realize that you can eat many, many other foods that will not only keep you strong and healthy but will also provide a variety of good alternatives.

Some of these choices are:

- Amaranth
- Arrowroot
- Beans, including Soy
- Buckwheat
- Cassava (also called yuca and manioc) and tapioca made from this root
- Dairy alternative products
- Eggs
- Fish
- Fruits - lots of choices
- Grains such as: Amaranth, Buckwheat, , Corn, Millet, Montina, Oats, Quinoa, Rice, Sorghum, Teff
- Meats
- Nuts and seeds
- Potatoes: white and sweet
- Soy and soy products
- Vegetables - lots of choices
- For more choices, please check Appendix D for the Shopping List

The Good GFCF News

If you are already used to eating healthfully, with a lot of fresh fruits, vegetables and home-cooked dishes, switching to a GFCF diet will be easy. All you will have to do is switch the few processed foods made with wheat and dairy to gluten-free and dairy-free versions. Due to the increase in people with allergies to these ingredients, a whole new industry has been more than happy to develop such products. You can now find GF versions of assorted breads, pasta, snacks, crackers, cookies and more. If you like to bake at home, all sorts of bread, pizza, cookies and flour mixes are also available to facilitate your life.

Nowadays you can find a wide assortment of GFCF packaged food at your local health food store, Whole Foods Market and Wild Oats nationally, or Central Market, Wheatsville (Oops! - not a very appropriate name if you're on a wheat-free diet), Fresh Plus, Sun Harvest and even Peoples Pharmacy in Austin. If these stores are not available in your neighborhood, you can find many products at specialized online stores such as Amazon.com. Please check the ever-growing list of stores in Appendix.

As a nutritherapist, I feel compelled to remind you that gluten-free junk food is still junk food. A lot of GFCF products on the market are refined carbohydrates that are loaded with sugar, and some unhealthy chemicals, none of which are good for your health. I hate to be the preaching voice here, but I strongly suggest you limit your intake of convenience foods and switch to more fresh foods. You will feel a lot better, possibly lose weight and it may help heal your condition faster. I'm not suggesting you go cold turkey, but reduce junk food to the occasional pizza, cake or cookie. With a little effort, it is not that hard to switch to fresh, homemade food. In this book, I offer you many simple recipes to get you started on that path.

I was a sick kid who grew into a very sick adult. I was diagnosed with asthma when I was four years old, and the medical profession determined that I was allergic to numerous airborne allergens and molds, but I was not found to be allergic to any foods. For twenty-six years of my life, I stayed on the medical path of antihistamines, steroids, weekly allergy shots, and the on-going use of antibiotics because I was so susceptible to infections. I often fluctuated between an extremely anxious and then depressed state, and often dealt with a fatigue that was unbearable. When I hit rock bottom with an acute viral infection that landed me in the hospital, I realized that I was at a fork in the road. I could continue to do what I was doing OR I could try something else.

Shortly thereafter, I went back to school to study nutrition and then herbal medicine. I started to change my diet to those foods that only exist in nature - if I can't pick it, grow it or hunt it, I don't eat it. I was eating the highest quality foods that I possibly could, including sprouted grain breads and raw dairy. Gradually, I started to feel much better, once my body adjusted to life without refined carbohydrates. My dad was vice president of a sugar company, so you can imagine how much sugar I had been eating! My digestion had always been less than desirable and my stomach hurt, I had lots of gas, and very frequent, loose bowel movements. I had dealt with this my entire life! So, as I studied nutrition and my teachers described normal, healthy digestion, I thought, well, what if I am allergic to something I am eating? My herbalist suggested that I remove wheat from my diet, so I walked out of his office and made the commitment to live life without wheat, which immediately elevated my health to a new level. Here is what I noticed:

- ✓ *I felt more calm, peaceful, and alert, less agitated and anxious.*
- ✓ *My bowels normalized to one to two bowel movements per day with much less gas and bloating.*
- ✓ *The quality of my skin improved. Many people commented that I was glowing!*
- ✓ *My experience of allergies and asthma diminished. I was less congested in my sinuses and my lungs felt clearer.*
- ✓ *I wasn't so sensitive to the smell of chemicals anymore and cold air didn't set off an asthma attack.*
- ✓ *I stopped getting hot flashes; in the past, my face would often flush for no apparent reason.*
- ✓ *I didn't realize how my muscles ached, until they stopped hurting.*
- ✓ *I stopped getting ulcerations in my mouth.*
- ✓ *I had noticeably more energy and needed less sleep.*
- ✓ *I stopped catching colds and GI bugs every month or two - I wasn't getting sick!*
- ✓ *I experienced more joy and less anger, tears, and frustration.*

Three years later, I am now also dairy-free and asthma-free, and I couldn't be more grateful for the discovery of my food allergies. I am living in a completely different, more vital body and feel that I am at the fullest expression of myself. I must also say that I have benefited greatly from some whole food supplements and herbal products; using these supplements was a key part of my healing.

I now believe that EVERY chronic disease process has an underlying food allergy that must be addressed for the person to get well. This is from both my personal and clinical experience. Food allergies typically manifest as a triangle, involving complaints in the nervous system, the digestive system, and the musculoskeletal system. If this is you, I encourage you to investigate! All I can say is that living a gluten-free, dairy-free life is a constant decision-making process. It is a decision you make each time you eat, and it is well worth every bit of effort. Conscious eating in exchange for vitality and wellness. There is no greater gift you can give to yourself and your family.

Charlotte S – Austin, TX

But It's More Expensive to Eat Gluten-Free You Say!

Yes, processed packaged food is always going to be more expensive, whether it is GF or not. You pay for the packaging. I usually recommend you buy in bulk to save money, but in your case, it is almost impossible because many GF products are not available in bulk (except some cereals), and there is the risk of cross contamination. Another reason for GFCF foods to be more expensive is the raw material is grown and processed in much smaller quantities than your average food commodity and require special processing facilities, all of which raise the end cost. What you may not be aware is that the main crops used for our "regular" food, like wheat, corn, cane and soy are heavily subsidized by governments all over the world thus making them available in larger quantities and at a lower retail price. So you think you're getting cheaper food. In reality, you are paying for this policy in two ways: one, with your taxes and two with your health. Refined food, especially white flour, white sugar, corn syrup and processed soy are dangerous to your health. During the refining process, these products are stripped of all their nutritional value, creating nutritional deficiencies in the long run. These you must counter with an additional complement of vitamins and minerals, which cost you additional money. Another reason for not eating these refined products is that, in my opinion, they are the main cause for malnutrition in this country and most developed countries. For all we know, these same refined and genetically engineered food products may have caused your current condition. Refined products cause all sorts of food allergies, because they are no longer natural by the time they reach your table. Avoid them at all costs if you can. They will end up costing you much more than eating real foods containing all the nutrition your body needs to function optimally.

Your New Happy, Happy, Joy, Joy GFCF Life

Joy is the word I would use to describe the gluten-free lifestyle. Free of stomach aches, migraines and indigestion. My whole life, that is what I battled - living on Tums and Zantac. I thought maybe I was just eating too much food or not healthfully enough. When I started working at Peoples RX as a Nutritionist in 2007,

I began learning more about the gluten-free lifestyle from my fellow co-workers. In school, they taught us Nutrition majors that celiac disease was rare, and most intestinal symptoms were caused by IBS.

After a coworker suggested that my symptoms could be related to celiac disease, I went ahead and went in for some tests. I received the Anti-endomysial Antibodies IgA and the celiac gene test, haplotype test for HLA DQ2 and DQ8. All tests came back positive. My doctor and I agreed that those tests results combined were enough to state I had celiac disease, even though the gold standard diagnosis is a biopsy.

There was a light bulb in my head that finally went off saying to me, this is why you have felt so bad all these years. Gluten is making you sick. Right then and there, I gave up gluten 100% and never looked back. I live a life now of Joy. Joy that I can eat an abundance of delicious gluten-free foods without having to worry about stomach aches and pains. I also have been able to lose 40 pounds since going gluten-free and have never felt better. I love to share my story with others and continue to help others in their gluten-free journey.

Jessica M – Austin, TX

My Goal for You: Live a Happy and Healthy Gluten and Dairy-free Life

If you have read my first book, you already know this, but for those of you new to the class, I will repeat it. A healthy diet is essential to a healthy body, brain and, in this case, digestive system. I will not repeat here all my beliefs about what a healthy diet should be, but I'll give the short version.

My goal is to provide you the information and education you need to understand how to live gluten and dairy-free; to tell you about an assortment of good foods that will help you live more healthfully and without deprivation; to explain how and where to shop for these foods; to provide you a solid shopping list to get you started on your GFCF way; and, finally, to provide you with an assortment of Mediterranean and French recipes not only good for your health, but also full of flavor. My wish for you is that this book will help you in your goal to live a happy and healthy life without the need for a cocktail of chemical healing. A Votre Santé (To Your Health) and Bonne Chance (good luck) with this program!

Time to Heal That Gut

Health Starts In the Gut; Or, That Gut Feeling

In our modern world, it seems the wisdom of the gut is lost. For centuries, it has been known that health begins and ends in the gut. Many of our modern degenerative diseases start with a damaged digestive system. How we treat our stomach, our small intestine, and our colon determines how we ultimately feel overall. Modern medicine focuses too much on the symptoms of after-the-fact health issues; I believe we need to start thinking about proper digestive system maintenance first. What's the use of "fixing" an unlimited list of symptoms after the fact, if we do not pay attention to the basics first? Heal the gut and the symptoms will eventually disappear.

It's a Jungle in There

For a lot of people, our digestive system is nothing but a pouch called a stomach, which receives and digests their food and a long tube leading the digested food to the exit. What they don't realize is that our digestive system can be compared to a jungle. It is a complex ecosystem of its own, populated with all sorts of creatures involved in a complex balance to either keep you healthy or make you sick. Like in nature around us, if you kill too many of the good creatures, it allows the bad ones to thrive, take over your digestive system and make you sick. There are three main types of creatures or microbes populating your digestive ecosystem: bacteria, yeast (including Candida) and parasites. Let's look at them separately.

Bacteria

Our soap ads have led us to believe that all bacteria are bad bacteria. Actually, there are good bacteria and bad. Did you know that an average human being carries around about three to four pounds of assorted bacteria in their gut? Sorry if it sounds gross to you, but for the most part, it's a good thing. There are hundreds of different species cohabitating with us at any time. Like all creatures large and small, microscopic in this case, they have a function and help us create enzymes to digest our food, support our immune system and create nutrients. Honestly, we could not survive without them. Although proper hygiene has helped us eliminate a lot of illnesses over the past hundred years, scientists have discovered that a completely sterile environment is not healthy for us. Like it or not, we do need these little buggers to stay healthy.

But what about the bad bacteria, like E-coli the commercials are scaring us with? Yes, they are out there too and we should be cautious, but not to the point of obsession. Our internal jungle needs to be kept in balance for the good bacteria to keep the bad ones in check. When we abuse certain medications like antibiotics that are designed to help us kill the bad bacteria, we end up killing the good ones too, which leaves us exposed to an invasion of other critters like candida yeast. Plus it is now known that strong bad bacteria like Methicillin-resistant *Staphylococcus aureus* (MRSA) are evolving and resisting antibiotics to the point that we have an epidemic of impossible to eliminate infections in our hospitals.

The Nice, the Mean and the Really Mean Bacteria

The Nice Bacteria

Calling bacteria nice might be stretching things a little, but hey, as long as they help me digest my food, I can call them anything I want. My nice bacteria and I live in harmony: I provide them with a warm home, good food and treat them right. They help me break down my food into important vitamins like B vitamins and vitamin K; help me absorb important nutrients; help me break down potentially toxic compounds, neutralize and get rid of them; break down vegetable fibers and proteins. They are even known to have a beneficial influence on eczema, asthma, hay fever and assorted allergies. These friendly bacteria are commonly known as *probiotics*. When kept happy and healthy, they take up most of our intestinal tract space and keep potential invaders at bay. They are your first line of defense and help in strengthening your immune system.

The few you are most likely to be on first name basis with are lactic acid bacteria (*Lactobacillus acidophilus, Lactobacillus bulgaricus*) and bifidobacteria (*Bifidobacterium*). They are easy to find in your dairy aisle in cow, kefir, goat and even soy yogurts. Be careful and make sure they are live and active probiotics. Tap the container gently and listen carefully: if you hear some noise, they are still alive and pretty busy. Joking aside, the best way to guarantee your product is loaded with live and happy bacteria is to look for these words: live and active probiotics.

You may think they are only available on the dairy shelves, but you can find them alive and well in naturally fermented sauerkrauts, kimchi (a spicy Korean version of fermented cabbage), and pickles, as well as in handcrafted miso and tempeh (naturally fermented soy products). If you are vegetarian, you can find them in young wheat grass (does not contain gluten), and algae such as spirulina and chlorella.

The trick in buying these products is to choose carefully. Buy only certified organic or from a provider you know and trust. For example, do not buy commercial sauerkrauts and pickles. Their sourness is not created by the natural fermentation of probiotics, but comes from commercial vinegar. A few farmers or local providers are offering great live sauerkrauts and pickles. Another subject I am sour on (yes, I know) is the amount of sugar contained in the vast majority of commercial yogurts. I don't care how live these yogurts are, if they are loaded with sugar, the benefits of hard-working probiotics will be countered by the negative effect of sugar on you and especially your kids. The best way to buy it is plain or natural. If you must add a touch of sugar, do like I do, add a little of your favorite natural fruit preserves, local honey, organic maple syrup or agave nectar. Your kids might cringe a little at first, but when they get used to the slight sourness of natural yogurt or kefir, they will want nothing else. Of course, if you are not allowed dairy products, the same advice applies to soy yogurts.

The Mean Bacteria

I compare the mean bacteria to your average school bully. Under control by your teachers, they may be annoying, but can be avoided. On the other hand, if they're allowed to grow in numbers and roam the school yard in impunity, they can make your life miserable, although not life-threatening. We all have a certain amount of mean bacteria in our digestive system and that's normal. But if we allow them to invade our gut by killing our friendly bacteria by accident or neglect, the mean bacteria will overtake our digestive system and we will suffer from gas, constipation, diarrhea and abdominal pain. If you feel constantly uncomfortable after eating food, you may have an invasion of mean bacteria. You may want to check with your doctor about getting a thorough stool test to uncover and control them.

The Really Mean Bacteria

These are the ones you must be very careful about. Unlike the school bully who can be merely annoying, I like to compare these to street gang members. If they infest your neighborhood, they are potentially deadly and very difficult to get rid of. I'm sure you have heard of some of these really mean bacteria. The major public enemies are salmonella, shigella and some strains of E. coli. They are never part of your normal intestinal flora, and if left unchecked are flesh-eaters, which usually create deadly toxins. They will make you very sick, and can even kill you. I sincerely hope you will never have to deal with them in your lifetime. Most of the time, they can come to your mouth from handling dirt (playground or gardening), bad hygiene from your average food handler (restaurant, meat packing plant), produce that has not been cleaned properly (spinach, lettuce) or worse, when commercial feedlots are feeding their animals with protein pellets coming from already sick animals. I don't want to make you paranoid, but it is a dangerous world out there. Please be careful. Fortunately, modern medicine has made tremendous advances in dealing with these deadly bacteria. If you fall severely ill, have stomach cramps and run a high temperature, please do not wait and get someone to take you to the closest emergency room to get treated. There is no waiting in this situation. They need to be handled swiftly, like gang members should be.

The Effects of Antibiotics Overuse

Although antibiotics are absolutely necessary in grave or extreme cases like food poisoning, most of the time they should not be used like candies for just any health situation. The abuse of antibiotics is the main reason for our general bacteria imbalance in this day and age. Our current society has made us paranoid of any symptoms, and our modern doctors have an unfortunate tendency to prescribe antibiotics at the drop of a hat. Yes we need them for an important illness, but not always as often as it appears. I implore you to find a common sense doctor that has not been trained by the pharmaceutical companies to overprescribe antibiotics. If we keep on killing the good bacteria that protect us, we will open the door to a mean bacteria invasion that will weaken our immune system, potentially opening the door to other, more dangerous health conditions.

Candida Yeast

Candida is part of a family of yeasts that can populate your digestive tract. They're like annoying visiting family members, whether you want them or not, they exist and there not much you can do about it. The most common yeast is called *Candida*. In normal amounts, your friendly bacteria control Candida. Unfortunately if your friendly bacteria have been decimated by excess use of antibiotics, like the annoying family members sensing a weakness, they will pounce and invade your gut, creating what is called *yeast overgrowth*. Like your visiting family, once they're installed, they are difficult to get rid of.

Candida is a single-cell fungus. It is known to create a wide range of symptoms - up to 20 different ones, some of them mimicking gluten allergy symptoms, such as digestive problems (constipation, diarrhea), abdominal pain, heartburn, mental fogginess and fatigue. Symptoms will also vary from men to women to babies. They can show up as thrush, bladder infection, vaginitis or diaper rash. Look up *Candida albicans* in your medical dictionary.

Candida, being a form of yeast, thrives on any form of sugar (white, raw, honey, agave nectar, etc) but not on stevia; any sugar-containing food like alcohol; any refined starches and processed carbohydrates (especially if they contain yeast), such as baked goods. Instead, eat a lot of fresh vegetables, fish, meat, and gluten-free grains like rice, quinoa, amaranth and millet. If you have a yeast overgrowth, you may want to ask your naturopath doctor what else you should avoid.

Other Annoying Neighbors: Parasites

Parasite infection can also create symptoms similar to gluten allergies. Parasites can be microscopic, or be as long as a few inches. They can be ingested from dirt, low quality raw or undercooked meat or fish. They can also come from produce, meat and fish imported from countries that do not have the same hygienic standards as in the US. But they can also come from US field workers not following proper hygiene standards. I told you it's a dangerous world out there.

Parasitic infection symptoms can be numerous: nausea, diarrhea, constipation, bloating and gas, cramps and abdominal pains, poor digestion, blood in the stools, rectal itching as well as overall fatigue and muscle pain. As you can see, these symptoms can be similar to Candida yeast infection as well as gluten allergy. A strong immune system can help you fight a parasitic infection, but in most cases a doctor or hospital visit may be the only way to deal with it. Some supplements can be helpful as well. You may want to ask your favorite nutritionist for advice. If you are not sure which affliction it could be, ask your physician for a complete blood and stool test.

Friendly Bacteria to the Rescue

Even though you may have received proper treatment for Candida or parasites, please remember that it is important to replenish your friendly intestinal flora. Remember our nice friends *Lactobacillus acidophilus* and *bifidobacterium*? Well, you need them more than ever to reestablish a healthy gut environment. First go for the big guns and find a good quality brand of probiotics at your friendly pharmacy or ask your nutritionist. Personally, I prefer the fresh ones you can find in the refrigerated cases. I hear that there are very good quality dehydrated brands but for me, alive and kicking is always better. This is your first step for repopulating your gut neighborhood.

Additional Food Sources of Friendly Bacteria

Like Winnie the Pooh says, it bears repeating: plain, naturally fermented cheese, buttermilk, yogurt and kefir (unless you are on a dairy-free diet) with live and active probiotics and no added sugar; naturally fermented pickles, sauerkraut and kimchi; apple cider vinegar (organic is best); handmade miso, tempeh and tofu and *umeboshi plums* (a Japanese fermented plum). All of these will be very helpful in maintaining your friendly digestive flora.

For a Healthy Diet, All You Need is Love... and The Following Ingredients

A healthy diet should NOT be a complicated diet. If I told you: Eat plenty of fresh vegetables, healthy proteins and fats, nuts, legumes, beans and fresh fruits, and avoid most grains, dairy products and all processed food, and stopped there, you'd probably throw this book back at me and demand a refund. The truth is that it should not be that much more complicated. Ideally, you should forget about all this vitamins and minerals stuff and just eat a varied diet of fresh food. Remember I said *ideally*. But in this day and age we like to complicate things and confuse people. The more confused you are about all this "stuff", the more money a lot of companies make on your back. Honestly, if it wasn't for all this confusion, I would not have a nutritherapist business and I would not need to write this book. Frankly, do you really believe that all these tribes that Dr. Weston Price studied over the years needed a manual to know what to eat or what not to eat? Interestingly, all these different tribes from all over the world had completely different diets and before the "modern" world caught up with them, they were all perfectly healthy and adapted to their environment whether they lived in the high mountains of Switzerland and the tiny Pacific islands. They ate what was available in their particular environment. They learned to store and preserve these foods for the winter, or for when times were lean, but that was mostly it. I could say that it would not be that difficult to live such a life close to the earth, but you would call me some sort of illuminated hippie. So I'm going to try to help you understand how a simple diet does not mean a boring and simplistic diet. Of course, the chef in me will poke its nose and complicate things a little here and there, but you would expect that from me anyway, right? So here it goes.

What You Need to Eat for a Healthy Diet

Vegetables

Ideally, the largest volume item on your plate should be vegetables - organic or locally grown healthy vegetables. You should have at least one fresh or lightly cooked vegetable at each meal. It is not that complicated. I will help you by offering you a few fairly simple recipes but tasty recipes to get you started and once you get the idea, I will let you loose to play with your food. Once you get the basic principles, you can create your own variations. It's really not that difficult.

Protein

Protein is crucial to the proper functioning and rebuilding of your whole body. It is commonly believed that your entire body regenerates itself every seven years, and lots of protein is needed for that rebuilding effort. Protein comes in basically two different forms: animal and vegetal. In the animal form, proteins present themselves as meat of all sorts: fish (my personal favorite, fresh and line caught if possible), grass-fed animals like beef, veal, bison, as well as happy cochons (pigs) and so on. The major point I would like to stress is that your meat should come from a trusted, local grass-fed animal supplier that does not stuff his animals with grains (bad omega-6 fatty acids), growth hormones and antibiotics. Ideally, their animals should be raised humanely and without stress and dispatched as quickly and gently as possible.

Other sources of protein are nuts and legumes. Nuts are a very healthy source of protein if you don't overdo it. They typically contain a lot of fat - good fats, but some people are nervous about eating too much fat. No need to be; our bodies are so well built that they contain a fat-controlling safety mechanism. If you are paying attention to what your body is telling you (you are listening to your body, right?) there is a satiety mechanism that actually stops you from eating too much fat. It will make you feel nauseous. If you haven't learned yet to listen to "body talk", now is a good time to start. It will help you tremendously in the future. Buy your nuts from the bulk department of a store with high volume so they do not have the time to turn rancid. Legumes are another good source of vegetable proteins and they are loaded with fiber.

Good Fats

Since we cannot address good quality fats from dairy, I will stick mostly to oils. To keep things simple, there are two major sources of fats: animal and vegetable. The fats coming from the animal world are mostly thought of as "bad" saturated fats because they supposedly are the cause for a host of illnesses, including heart attacks. The most recent research shows that this assumption has been largely false. Animal fats and cholesterol are not the main cause of heart trouble. More and more studies are debunking these claims, largely created in the 1970s by the margarine industry. They pointed their fat fingers at butter and animal fats so they could sell more of their hydrogenated and lifeless artificial product. Now look who've been blamed for aggravating heart health in this country: those same artificial fats that were supposed to be so good for us. As my macrobiotic teacher, Dawn Pallavi, always told us: "Question everything, including what I am saying now". Let me step down from my soapbox and continue: Animals fats, also called saturated fats, actually have quite a few benefits. For more information, read my first book, or read Sally Fallon's work at **www.westonaprice.org.** It will enlighten you on the many benefits of animal fats - as long as you consume them in moderation. It reminds me of an observation I made while I was living in Ukraine. I was told that Ukrainians favorite treat was to place a thick slice of farm-raised pork fat on a slice of hearty country-style bread, sprinkle it with sea salt and eat it as a pick-me-up snack. Yet, I have found the Ukrainian population in general to be much healthier and fitter than we are in this country. But they walk a lot and each smaller meals, made with food they raise on their farms, in other words: healthy living at its best. It reminded me of the way of life we still had at my grandmother's farm when I was little. It may not have been modern, but it was healthy. I'm sure some other old timers like me will have similar memories.

Another type of fat from animal sources that I feel is not talked about enough these days is the unsaturated fat called omega-3. It mostly comes from cold water sea fish like salmon, cod and sardines, but you might be surprised to find out that it is also present in pasture-fed meat. Beef raised on grass contain a respectable amount of omega-3 fatty acids. So, even though I still recommend you eat a small serving (4 ounces), you shouldn't shy away from beef.

Fats from Nuts and Seeds

They come mostly in two major families: saturated (coconut) and unsaturated (almond, hazelnut, macadamia, walnut, peanut, corn and seed oils). Within the unsaturated family there are the omega-6 and omega-3 children. Both of these types of fats are healthy for you as long as they are eaten in the proper balance. The ideal balance is three units of omega-6 to one unit of omega-3 (3:1 ratio). That is primarily the proportion of fats contained in our brains. Unfortunately, the modern world of fats is overpopulated with omega-6 children. In other words, because oils made from the most abundant and cheapest sources (corn and peanut for example), we are typically eating a diet loaded with omega-6 fatty acids. So it turns out that most people's diet oil ratio is 20:1, even up to 30:1. That is not good for two reasons:

1. We, as human animals, need our diet fat balance to be as close to the ideal 3:1 as we can. This is the ratio our brains need to be the most efficient. This is how our cell walls stay flexible and porous and allow all beneficial life exchanges to happen. When on an omega-6 diet, our cell walls are not porous and do not allow the proper nutrients to pass through and nourish them. These stiff walls also do not allow toxins to be eliminated from our cells and could potentially create all sorts of health problems, one of which could be depression.

2. Good oils turn bad. Like in any good family, some of the children will turn bad. This is the case with commercially processed oils: they are overheated to extract as much oil from the nuts and seeds as possible. Overheating any oil will turn its fatty acids from cis-fats to trans-fats and makes it toxic to our bodies. That is why it is not recommended to overheat your frying oil. Finally, most of the commercially made oils are using hexane, a component of gasoline, to extract additional oil from nuts and seeds and prevent these oils from turning rancid through normal oxidation. Even though processors claim to "wash" all hexane out of these oils, would you like to ingest gasoline as part of your daily diet? I didn't think so.

I am not saying to avoid omega-6 at all costs. If you get your omega-6 from organic nuts and seeds, it will be okay, unless you overdo it. Do not get it from commercially processed oils. If you must use vegetable oil in cooking, make sure to buy cold-processed oils and be aware that there is a chance they will oxidize rapidly and turn rancid. Keep them in your refrigerator, do not overheat them or they will turn toxic, and use them quickly. Some of the most-used sources of omega-6 oils are corn, soybean, palm, rapeseed (Canola) and sunflower oils. Other healthy sources are avocado, macadamia (half omega-6, half omega-3), evening primrose, borage, black currant and pumpkin seed oil.

Right now, to keep things simple in my life, the only oils I use are olive oil (cold-pressed, extra virgin) for all my salad dressings and vinaigrettes, and virgin coconut oil for pan-frying (it handles high heat very well). They are both very good for your health and easy to find. Macadamia oil is another good option. You should not need any other oils.

If you're interested in learning more about fats, you can read more in my first book, or I would suggest you read *"Fats That Can Save Your Life: The Critical Role of Fats and Oils in Health and Diseases"* by Robert Erdmann, Ph.D.

and Meirion Jones, a very complete presentation on how fats influence our health.

Grains

Because of our culture and that of our European ancestors, our diets tend to contain a lot of wheat. Whether your family came from Northern Europe or the Mediterranean basin, it's most likely that your family is used to eating wheat products: bread (all Anglo-Saxon cultures, but also Latin civilizations), breakfast pastries like croissants and such (France), Danish pastries (Denmark and other Northern countries), muffins and scones (England) and even some American creations like cookies. And let's not forget that favorite Italian import, pasta! As our palate becomes more and more international, we have come to appreciate pita bread, couscous and tabouleh, all made from wheat. So it is difficult to imagine we could even live without wheat in our daily life. Yet, millions and millions of people manage to live perfectly healthy lives without wheat. The vast majority of Eastern and Far Eastern countries did just fine without wheat until the white conquerors brought wheat products with them. All Asians lived perfectly healthy lives with rice as their main source of starch. In Latin America, corn was their main grain and they lived healthfully as well.

If we expand our culinary horizons, we discover that we do not have to have wheat and wheat products to survive. Most likely, the fact that our modern wheat has been crossbred over and over to create a breed that gives the largest yield has created a product that is foreign to our still ancient digestive systems. In other words, our bodies have not evolved in step with industry to digest these modern grains, and the result is that they make a lot of people with sensitive digestive systems sick. Our bodies may not recognize this new wheat as food, and our immune systems, in trying to protect us, may be making us sick. If we step back and realize that a lot of our diet is dictated by traditions handed down by our forebears, and that we are bombarded with highly suggestive marketing campaigns, we can and should wake up to the fact we can, in fact, live without wheat.

As it is, our modern diet contains way too many carbohydrates. I know, the FDA says we should eat six to eight servings of grains per day. Is it possible that the FDA has been influenced by the very powerful wheat lobby in the design of this food pyramid? I would not be surprised. Most recent diet studies confirm that we are eating way too many carbohydrates, and this is the main cause for the majority of obesity cases in this country, not fats as we were previously told. Granted, wheat is not the only culprit, all forms of sugar in our food are to blame, but excess intake of wheat products does not help. If you cannot live without carbohydrates, there are still plenty of sources out there: potatoes and sweet potatoes; rice and wild rice; legumes (beans, lentils) as well as many newly rediscovered grains that have been consumed for centuries by other cultures: quinoa, teff, millet, buckwheat, amaranth, soy and more. All these ancient grains can provide your carbohydrate needs, and bring a welcome change to your daily diet. Another advantage of these grains is that, except for corn, they have been left alone and have not been modified genetically over the years, and thus are still digestible. There are plenty of wheat alternatives available on our supermarket shelves nowadays. Go on a discovery voyage and see how many of these you can find. Later in this book, I provide you with a shopping list to help you get started (Appendix D). Please keep in mind that if you cannot find some of these products at your local store, you can find them online.

A Healthy Diet GFCF Can Be Simple

As you can see, as long as you eat a varied assortment of fresh, quality foods prepared healthy ways (which I will explain later), it should not be too difficult to follow a gluten and dairy-free diet. I am aware that if you are not used to cooking your food from scratch, the thought of switching to this lifestyle can be daunting. But honestly, you don't have much of a choice. Even if you could prepare only one meal a day from scratch, that would be an accomplishment. As long as you're careful with your choices, you could manage the rest of the day by buying prepared foods of good quality.

Another solution, if you can afford it, would be hiring a private chef to prepare meals according to your particular dietary needs. Yes, it may look expensive at first, but if you earn a good living and are a busy professional, this may be the healthiest way to eat. Keep the weekends for doing your own fresh cooking. There are more and more good chefs available that know about special dietary requirements who will be able to help you. Typically, after agreeing to your specific diet requirements, they will present you with a menu choice; you approve it or make some adjustments. They then do the shopping and cook up to 5 meals in one day. They can package them in plastic storage containers, label and date them and store them in your cooler or freezer as instructed. Voila! Some of them will use their kitchen and deliver to your house at an agreed upon time or, with your approval, will do all the work in your kitchen. If they cook in your house, please make sure you have proper insurance coverage. Personal chefs typically cost around $25.00/$30.00 an hour.

Another solution would be to pick up your special food "to-go" at your favorite health food store. For example, Whole Foods Market, Central Market, Wheatsville Market and others in Austin will offer a wide assortment of healthfully prepared foods at their salad bars, soup bars or in their "to-go" display. Just keep an eye on the labels, just in case.

I became a Personal Chef in 2002 after having a small catering business in Austin, Texas for several years. I specialized in providing healthy meals for busy families and couples.

As I was approaching 40 I began having gastrointestinal difficulties. I began cutting out foods that I thought maybe weren't agreeing with me and had started eliminating wheat from my diet as much as possible. I still had the same unpleasant and uncomfortable symptoms however, and could not identify the source.

During this time I took a trip with friends to Egypt. The food in Egypt was absolutely delicious but contained lots of wheat. I decided I couldn't avoid it on this trip, so I indulged in pita bread, kofta (skewered meat made with breadcrumbs), falafel and Egyptian beer. My symptoms just worsened. I can tell you that being in a third-world country with GI problems is a most unpleasant experience. In Egypt, it is typical to have to pay a few coins for every square of toilet paper. By the end of the nine days traveling in Egypt I was miserable. I was so uncomfortable, and was having horrific symptoms I had never before experienced. I knew that when I returned to the U.S. I would need to take my health more seriously and find out what was causing all these problems.

Upon my return, I ran into a friend who is a medical doctor at one of the minor emergency facilities in town. He asked me about my trip. I told him about how wonderful Cairo, Luxor and the Sinai Peninsula were, but that I'd had this problem that was really difficult to deal with. He suggested maybe I had "celiac sprue" and recommended I try a gluten-free diet. Since we had returned I had been eating wheat-free again, but had never tried gluten-free. I got on the internet and researched what I needed to know about eliminating gluten from my diet. I fine-tuned my meals but realized, after a week or so, that my "wheat-free" breakfast cereal contained oat flour. The day I quit eating it was the 1st day I felt better. The 2nd day was better... and the 3rd. I got better and better each day. After two weeks I was a completely different person. I had energy and wasn't spending my mornings on the toilet for a change. Within 6 months I'd signed up for my first Danskin Triathlon.

When I first realized that I was gluten intolerant I thought that I would have to give up my personal chef business. I was also a food writer and wrote restaurant reviews. I assumed that I couldn't continue in this field if I had dietary restrictions. Instead, I began experimenting with gluten-free substitutions for some of my favorite dishes including beef stroganoff, spaghetti and meat sauce, trout amandine, pancakes, etc. So, rather than giving up my chef business I began specializing in gluten-free cuisine. I started my own blog and started consulting with my favorite grocery stores in assisting in the gluten-free products they choose to put on their shelves. My business has grown and I am considered an expert in my field.

Trish B – Austin, TX

Do You Need Dietary Supplements?

As much as I am not a big fan of taking tons of dietary supplements, I do recognize the fact that you may be deficient in some of the most important nutrients, because your damaged villi will not allow them to get into your body and carry out their supportive roles. Below are some vitamins and minerals that are typically missing from those with a gluten and/or dairy intolerance. Although I believe that a diet full of healthy food should be the only way to go, I suggest that while your body is healing, you take a few of these supplements if your naturopath doctor or nutritionist suggests them.

Multivitamins

In your particular case, make sure to choose high potency and high quality supplements because you are most likely to be deficient in the important ones mentioned below. Another important point, especially for you, is to choose a product that is hypoallergenic (yes, I know... duh! But one can never be too safe).

Potency

Although a lot of companies try to make you believe they can cram all the vitamins and minerals into a one-a-day pill, as my son would say when he was little, "it's Pooh!" That's why most quality products will offer you an assortment of pills to be taken during your day to cover all your needs. Because you may be deficient in some of these nutrients, don't be concerned if they read more than 100 percent of recommended daily values. Typically, the recommended daily dosages are not sufficient for your particular needs. Besides, in this litigation-happy society, it's highly unlikely that any manufacturer will include toxic amounts of anything in their pills. The only vitamin you'd want to be aware of is excess vitamin A (no more than 10,000 IUs per day) especially if you're pregnant. On the mineral side, unless you are anemic, be careful not to overdo it with iron. Typically, women will require more iron in their diet than men because of their monthly periods, but still, unless your doctor tells you that you are iron deficient, be careful not to take too much iron.

Quality

The most important criteria to look for in a quality multi vitamin and mineral supplement are:
- Multiple capsules instead of one pill a day for all your needs.
- Hypoallergenic (containing no allergens)
- No fillers. Instead of cheap fillers used to make the pills look bigger, make sure your pills contain 99 percent of the good stuff.
- Look for the easily assimilated forms of the vitamins and minerals you need: calcium citrate, magnesium citrate and vitamin E (d alpha tocopherol). (See explanation below).

There are many potential quality issues with supplements. The most important issue for you of course is that they should be hypoallergenic - containing neither gluten nor dairy products in their formulation. Yes, it should make sense, but like in the food business, they can be hidden in there and not be listed on the label. Make sure to ask your doctor for a brand that they trust not to contain the very substances you are allergic to.

Another issue is the intrinsic quality of the vitamins and minerals contained in the pills. Some of the cheaper products will use lower quality nutrients or chemical supplements. As much as possible and if you can afford them, try to use supplements whose vitamins and minerals are extracted from food products. For example, looking at three of the major supplements you might need, calcium, magnesium and vitamin E, most cheap supplement companies use lower quality ingredients.

Calcium

The least expensive form of calcium is calcium carbonate. Yet it is one form that is not easily absorbed by your body. A better form of absorbable calcium would be calcium citrate.

Magnesium

As with calcium, magnesium comes in different forms. The cheapest form is magnesium oxide, which is poorly absorbed by your digestive system. Instead look for magnesium citrate, which is much better absorbed.

Vitamin E

Also known as alpha tocopherol, vitamin E also comes in two different chemical forms: usually they are listed on the label as *dl alpha tocopherol* or d *alpha tocopherol*. Even though they sound very similar on the label, d alpha tocopherol is the one your body will absorb more readily and keep you healthy.

Two other two food supplements that have a long and proven history in healing damaged digestive tract are L-glutamine and Fish Oil. Their benefits are backed by significant research.

L-glutamine

L-glutamine is the most abundant amino acid in our body, especially in our muscles. Amino acids are the building blocks of protein. They come from protein (meat, fish) and some vegetables like raw spinach and parsley. Because you may have been deficient for a while, you may need to take it as a supplement to help heal and rebuild your digestive tract. Please ask your trusted physician or nutritionist as to the necessary amount needed in your particular case.

Fish Oil

Another product beneficial for the accelerated healing of your digestive tract is fish oil. Since your villi are damaged and inflamed, fish oil is also very good at reducing inflammation. After all, you do want to heal your gut so it will allow all this good food to help you get stronger, right? That's the spirit! Fish oil is the best source animal-based omega 3 fatty acids. If you are vegetarian or vegan, you may consider taking flax seed oil as it also is a good source of omega 3, but be aware that its beneficial effects may not be as pronounced, as the body needs to take extra steps to convert flax seed oil into a beneficial form.

I have found that fish oil is slightly superior in quality than just cod liver oil. Cod liver oil contains less omega 3 fatty acids than the other form. I take a tablespoon of it morning and evening. Ask your health provider what the proper kind is for you.

Another concern is potential mercury pollution. Make sure to take pure, pharmaceutical grade fish oil tested for lead, mercury, PCBs, dioxin, furans and other possible heavy metals and residues from the plastic industry. I know, it sounds scary and paranoid, but we live in a scary world. Just be aware of these possibilities; I recommend the highest quality fish oil you can find. Ask your favorite pharmacist or nutritionist for additional suggestions.

Fish oil typically comes in liquid or soft gel capsules. I personally don't mind swallowing it liquid, especially since it now comes in different flavors. If you are sensitive to fish breath and don't care to burp fish oil (so I've been told), try the capsules, but know that it will take quite a few to get up to a tablespoon.

Living With Autism

What is the Autism Spectrum Disorder?

Since I started out knowing little about autism, I did some research. Please remember that this chapter is not written by a medical doctor and is offered for your information only. Besides, if you are the parent of a child with autism you already know a lot more than I do about the condition afflicting your child.

According to the Diagnostic and Statistic Manual of Mental Disorders (DSM-IV), Autism Spectrum Disorder or ASD, is a developmental behavioral disorder characterized by socialization and communication impairment. It is also described as stereotypical and restricted patterns in behaviors, interests and activities. Typically, children suffering from ASD present hypersensitivity or hyposensitivity to sensory stimulus. They might display intense reactions to loud sounds, bright lights, unwelcome touch, unknown tastes and smells. They have a hard time integrating with other kids in social situations, changes in their daily routine and adjusting to new things or environments. They also tend to repeat the same behavior and thought processes over and over. They may develop fixations on certain objects or people.

Again, according to the DSM-IV, there are five levels in the autism spectrum. At the higher levels of ability to function in a "normal" environment is Asperger syndrome. Then there is Rett's disorder, pervasive developmental disorder and childhood disintegrative disorder. On the lowest end of the functioning level (some might argue with that classification) is classic autism, also called Kanner's autism.

For reasons not yet fully understood, for the past few years the rate of ASD has increased alarmingly in children all over the world. In the U.S., about 1 in 500 children were diagnosed with autism in 1995. In 2000 that rate went up to one in 250. According to the Center of Disease Control and Prevention(CDC), the latest survey shows that about one in 120 children are afflicted with autism.

What is it about Gluten and Casein that Makes Some Children Sick and Not Others?

Although this scientific answer is not absolute, it is believed by some researchers that "leaky gut syndrome" is the cause of your child's misery. According to Dr. Karl Reichelt, M. D., director of clinical chemistry at the

Department of Pediatric Research at Riskhospitalet in Oslo, Norway, many children with ASD suffer from a leaky gut where the damaged villi lining the child's small intestine allows incompletely digested proteins (also called peptides) like gliadin and casein to pass through the intestinal wall into the bloodstream. He noticed that to these affected children, these proteins turn into opioid peptides called gliadomorphin and casomorphin. After passing through the leaky gut, these opioid peptides move through the bloodstream and into the brain where they attach themselves to opiate receptors, creating an assortment of sometimes extreme sensory reactions and behaviors, similar to how a normal person might behave under the influence of opiate drugs. Remove these peptides from your child's diet and there will be a good chance that his behavior will improve. Please know that this GFCF diet does not work for all children. Some parents still report some form of Pervasive Developmental Disorder (PDD) and other possible social difficulties. But in many cases, this diet is effective and deserves to be looked at. After being on this diet for a while, many of these children would not be diagnosed with ASD, according to the DSM IV criteria. So, talk to your local DAN! (Defeat Autism Now!) doctor and ask him/her for help with this diet.

I first found information on the gluten/casein free diet when my oldest son was six. He was not diagnosed with autism until age seven, but my husband and I knew well before the professionals did. Not only did we suspect autism, but also our son had suffered horrible gastrointestinal issues since around the age of two. We decided to consult an environmental allergist the summer he was diagnosed with autism, who suggested we give the gluten/casein free diet a trial for two weeks. If we did not see results then we could say that we tried and move on, but if behaviors, skin issues, or the gastrointestinal issues changed for the better, even if only slightly, we could keep going. I remember making the phone call back to the Environmental Allergist after two weeks to let him know that GFCF would be the life path for us after all. Within that two week trial period our son quit chewing on nonfood items, he was calmer, and had stopped interrupting people when they spoke. Family and friends that had no idea we were trying something new were asking us what we had changed in his life because even they saw results.

In the beginning the GFCF diet was not easy. Having a dairy allergy since birth, I was fully aware what products contained dairy and how to read ingredient labels for casein. Gluten on the other hand was much more difficult. Outside of wheat I had no idea what other grains contained it, and which ones were still safe for us to consume. The recipes I found for gluten free baked goods had a number of ingredients I had never heard of before, like xanthan gum, guar gum, teff, and millet. It was discouraging at first, but then it dawned on me that this probably was going to be permanent. That because of my son's severe gastrointestinal issues and autism he would probably need to be gluten/casein free for a very long time, potentially forever. I set out to purchase some gluten free cookbooks, made a long trip to Whole Foods, and joined online parenting groups for autism and diet. I started baking muffins, cookies, and cakes that my son fully enjoyed. As my baking trials succeeded, I gained more confidence in being able to feed my son nutritional meals and snacks that stayed within the gluten/casein free diet.

It has been five years now since that appointment with the Allergist. In the last five years we have seen so many gains in our son's health and behavior. Thanks to dietary intervention he no longer has rage episodes, chews on nonfood items, or has behavior issues at school. I have seen so many improvements in his health that it has inspired me to go back to college to work on a bachelor's degree in holistic nutrition so I can share my experiences with other families. This diet can change your life! Is it difficult? In the beginning, yes. Is it worth the time and effort? Absolutely!

Kecia J – Austin, TX

Why Do Some Kids Develop Leaky Gut Syndrome?

First, you need to know that I am a strong believer in breastfeeding for infants. Through their mother's milk, these babies receive a good helping of natural antibodies (IgA, Ig G and IgM - do they sound familiar to you?) through their mother's colostrum. They help create an adaptive immune system for the child. The most important bioactive components in colostrum are growth factors and antimicrobial factors. This is what protects the baby from day one. Assorted studies agree that breastfeeding helps protect babies from middle ear infections, infant diarrhea, upper respiratory tract infections and urinary tract infections. In children at risk of developing food allergies according to their family history, breastfeeding has been observed to limit infant food allergies, asthma and atopic dermatitis, a form of eczema. Long-term benefits have shown an improved IQ level and better protection against intestinal infections. Finally, a 2005 study concluded that introducing gluten while breast-feeding reduced the risk of celiac disease. Wow! Do you really believe that your baby would get the same benefits from a baby formula? Actually some formulas could foster the development of early childhood allergies to cow's milk, soy and other mother's milk substitutes.

They also receive a good amount of friendly probiotics to help keep their digesting systems strong and healthy. A mother's breast milk contains both healthy bacteria and medium-chain fatty acids, both of which are known disease fighters. According to S. K. Dash, Ph. D., a recognized authority on probiotics, these friendly bacteria are our first line of immune defense. In a healthy breastfed child, they colonize the intestinal tract, making it difficult for unhealthy bacteria, fungus and other potential health threats to thrive and grow.

What About Medium-Chain Fatty Acids?

Medium-chain fatty acids are known to be antibacterial, antiviral, antifungal and typically detoxifying. At the same time as the child's immune system is developing, the medium-chain fatty acids in breast milk effectively protect the child from potential pathogens. If you will, these medium-chain fatty acids protect babies until their own immune systems are strong enough to take over.

The final benefit of breastfeeding in my opinion, besides the fact that it's the cheapest natural food delivery in the world, is that it prevents the child from being fed industrialized baby "food" loaded with sugars, creating potential future addictions, possibly genetically engineered ingredients and all sorts of artificial preservatives and colors, known brain excitotoxins.

Common Sense Deduction? Or Not? You Decide.

So here comes what seems to be a common sense progression: breastfeeding strengthens the baby's immune system by providing friendly bacteria as well as many other beneficial elements; a strong immune system prevents infections (by the way, eliminating processed dairy products in your child's diet leads to a much lower incidence of ear infections); a lack of infections prevents the potential overuse of antibiotics possibly leading to leaky gut syndrome which could further lead to some of the gliadin and casein allergy symptoms we see in some autistic children. So, in a very simplistic way: breastfeeding could help prevent some forms of autism. I know, it can be a lot more complex than that, and I defer to higher authorities to debate this point. This is only my humble deduction from the point of view of a nutritherapist.

Should We Use Antibiotics with Infants or Small Children?

Yes we should, but only when it's really necessary, and in the proper amount for a small child. It should also not be used as a kill-all solution for every ailment that strikes a child, most of which are not bacterial in nature. Most allopathic pediatricians have fallen into the bad habit of prescribing antibiotics at the drop of a hat. To make things worse, they do not educate the parents on the benefits of recolonizing the child's gut with friendly bacteria. You see, as good as antibiotics are at killing dangerous bacteria, they are also good at killing our friendly bacteria. We should be good to our children and ourselves and get into the habit of taking friendly probiotics after a course of antibiotics in order to help our tiny friends repopulate our intestines and protect our health. The easiest way is to feed them with unsweetened organic, unpasteurized and live soy or coconut yogurt or kefir (please note that because of their most likely damaged digestive system a lot of autistic children are also allergic to soy). The "unsweetened" part is important because, once your friendly bacteria have been destroyed, the not-so-friendly Candida yeast will find a way to invade, creating additional problems such as systemic candidiasis, which could lead to the leaky gut syndrome we talked about earlier.

What About the Effects of Vaccination on Susceptible Children?

The parents said it before the scientists. The mothers of autistic children I know are convinced of the link between their children's health and behavioral changes and vaccination. See their stories included in this chapter. Another well known source of this conviction is **Jaquelyn McCandless, M. D.**, grandmother of Chelsey, a sweet autistic child. She is the author of a clear yet poignant book based on her experiences both as a doctor and with her granddaughter, *"Children with Starving Brains. A Medical Treatment Guide for Autism Spectrum Disorder"*. If you haven't already read her book, I highly recommend it for its medical and scientific approach to a very emotional subject. It will give you all the scientific explanations you need that I am not qualified to talk about.

She and other DAN! doctors believe that *"Early (even in utero or neonatally) injury to the immune systems of these children by toxins or pathogens starts a series of bio-chemical events that culminate eventually in neurocognitive deficits and behavioral challenges. Though there may be a genetic vulnerability in many autism spectrum children, increasing evidence suggest that a toxic mercury-based preservative long used in vaccinations may have been the "trigger" for a susceptible subset of children, particularly since 1991 when Hepatitis B vaccinations were mandated for every newborn. I join many autism experts and parents who believe that the current epidemic of regressive autism began with that mandate. Statistics show a progressive rise in incidence beginning in 1998 when the MMR vaccination was mandated (although does not contain any mercury itself). However, the incredibly steep rise in incidence started in 1991, coinciding with the requirement for newborns to receive the HepB vaccination, often within hours of birth. We believe that early injury by toxins -- likely preceded by genetic predisposition and augmented by allergies, illnesses, and repeated antibiotic use -- are among the factors that can initiate a cascade of problems starting with a weakened immune system and inflamed intestinal tract. A weakened immune system opens the door to bacterial and viral infections, overuse of antibiotics, intestinal yeast overgrowth, gut inflammation, and impaired nutritional status. The frequently called "leaky gut" syndrome and its various effects enable toxins to spread throughout the body including the brain. Furthermore, in a transiently or chronically vulnerable child, immunizations with live viruses such as the MMR pose another challenge. In this complex scenario of possibilities, vaccine-associated mercury, viruses and other toxins, as well as the child's own overactive immune components (autoimmunity) can attack neurons and thereby interfere with synaptic development and nerve signaling. With much variation from child to child, these factors can combine to create brain malnutrition and the cognitive impairment characteristic of ASD children."*

There you have it. In this increasingly polluted world, what a mother has been exposed to can be transmitted to her child through her umbilical cord and make that child sensitive to the additional chemical aggression of early childhood vaccination. As I mentioned earlier, whether a child is breastfed or not, his/her immune system is not fully developed for another few months. If it has been affected by a possible transmission of toxins from the mother, this baby's immune system is not strong enough to accept and fight off the live viruses given in early vaccination. It is now widely believed that ethylmercury (in the form of thimerosal) - which was used as a preservative until 2001 in multiple doses of vaccines mandated for newborns - is the cause of the drastic changes seen in susceptible children between their before and after vaccination days. Please be aware that thimerosal is still used today in some vaccines, especially the flu vaccine. Although the flu vaccine is not mandated, it is still strongly recommended by most pediatricians. You can find more information regarding this issue at **www.cdc.gov** as well as the National Vaccine Information Center website at **www.nvic.org** .

Another potential source of mercury from thimerosal is a fairly common pharmaceutical prenatal drug called RhoGAM (or other brand names). It is given to mothers with Rh-negative blood to prevent hemolytic disease of their newborn. Not all of them contain thimerosal, but enough do to be cautious. If you are Rh-negative, please ask your doctor to make sure that the drug they prescribe does not contain thimerosal. Some baby eye and ear drops may also contain thimerosal as a preservative.

On his birth day an infant with an immature immune system and liver is subjected to a mercury-containing Hepatitis B vaccine. As of today, this child will be given as many as 21 immunizations in the first 15 months of his/her life. Think about this a little bit. Does it make any sense? While there has not been a definitive link established between HepB vaccination and autism, empirical evidence supports this conclusion. Please do not misunderstand, every parent must make his or her own decision. I am not saying "do not vaccinate your child", I'm saying "listen to other parents, do your own research and make your choices regarding when to vaccinate based on the evidence, not just because the government says so". I highly recommend Dr. McCandless' book as a very well researched expose on the subject.

It is highly possible that these combinations of multiple factors lead to ASD. Some scientists will refute that assertion, but plenty of parents and supportive doctors already have noticed these changes in the health and behavior of their children. As far as I'm concerned my money is on the parents living this situation day in, day out.

Other Possible Sources of Mercury

We cannot honestly discount other sources of mercury. One well-known source is fish, especially larger fish, such as long-lived tuna, swordfish, king mackerel, shark and tilefish, because they are at the top of the food chain. They tend to absorb more mercury because they live longer and feed on smaller fish. The U. S. FDA standards consider fish safe if it contains less than 1 ppm (part per million) of methyl mercury. Canada's standard is less than 0.5 ppm. Safer fish to eat are line-caught salmon, flounder, sole, sardines, shrimp, scallops (except from Mid-Atlantic), and oysters. I would recommend that women of childbearing age, pregnant or lactating, avoid eating fish more than once a week.

Another source of leaching mercury is dental fillings. If you need dental work done, please make sure that no mercury-containing silver fillings are used. If you need to have them taken out for the safety of your coming child, do it at least 6 months before pregnancy to avoid the possibility that the leaching mercury will affect your unborn child. Heavy metal toxicity is suspected to be one the major sources of DNA susceptibility to autism in recent years.

Before 1991 mercury was used as an anti-fungal in paint. Due to demonstrated toxicity, it was taken off the market. Unfortunately, a lot of older houses were painted with this toxic material. As in lead toxicity, children may ingest these poisons through accidental ingestion. Before you buy an older house, you may want it properly inspected for this potential danger.

When Sander was born, he was almost nine pounds, happy, healthy, and amazingly strong. By the time he was two months old he was almost sleeping through the night -- miraculous after our first one!

I talked to the doctor about vaccinations. I was worried because allergies run in our family and I wanted to delay some of the shots. Fine, the pediatrician said. He has to have at least the DTaP -- Diphtheria, Pertussis and Tetanus.

So I got the shot and left.

The child didn't sleep again for two years. Neither did I.

Within a couple of hours, I knew I'd made a huge mistake.

Huge.

Sander started screaming, and didn't stop. Cried that entire night, and the next day, and the next. Started arching his head back like he was in pain, spitting out milk. Had weird, hard, rabbit poop, or black tar, or no poop at all. In the next three weeks, I was at the doctor's office five times.

I got:

"He's teething. He has an ear infection. Maybe it's colic. He's fine. You need to stop worrying. And no, there's no way it could be connected to the vaccine. Besides, that was a week ago!"

So.

I had a baby who was a sobbing, miserable mess, and he was obviously in pain. The doctors honestly didn't have a clue, and they didn't listen to me. I absolutely KNEW, from that day forward, that something was WRONG.

I went to a lactation consultant. "Maybe you're making too much milk."

Tried another one. "Maybe he has digestion issues."

Finally I went to an "alternative" doctor who gave me all sorts of weird herbs and supplements to take, since I was still nursing Sander. I took them, and within about three hours (warning: poop talk ahead) he had a diaper full of the nastiest, smelliest slime and black goop that you've ever seen. It looked like his guts just slid out of him. And within twenty minutes of that, he stopped crying for the first time in three weeks. And he went to sleep.

Well, that was that, I thought. Done. He had a bad reaction to the vaccine, the alternative doctor fixed me up, and the baby was going to be all right.

Except he wasn't.

He stopped crying, but he wasn't happy. Ever. He was as serious and miserable a little guy as you could ever imagine. Hit every milestone early, and I kid you not, walked at ten months. By one year old, he was climbing the tallest slide in the playground and going down headfirst.

He had a constant need for stimulation, and had to be entertained at all times.

He learned sign language, but no words. And he was never, ever, ever happy.

He didn't sleep at night, took tiny naps during the day, and followed me around fussing the rest of the time. He didn't like TV, except for sign language videos. Just liked to follow me around and fuss at me.

It was a high-pitched, awful, whining, moaning sound, like, "Unhhhhh, unhhhh," over and over again. But no words. No pointing. And it didn't get better.

Sander couldn't ride in the car without screaming. Hours and hours and hours of screaming, every time we left the house. His older brother was beginning to be traumatized!

I kept saying that something was wrong with him, but everyone said he would be fine.

I was convinced that there was something very wrong, and I was going to love it out of him. Whatever it was, I'd fix it.

But soon Sander was 18 months old, and then 20, and there were still no words.

And he wouldn't read books with me.

Or sit with me, even for a minute. He'd climb to the top of the swing set, and he'd run all over the yard, and he'd stay up all night. He had maybe ten words at 18 months, and they were strange ones. "Oof," for dog. "Ack," for cat. "Eh-eh," for shoes. Consistent, so they were words, but not real ones.

And he didn't play with trains, or with the cat. He didn't really play with anything. He responded to us, and hugged me, and let us carry him, so I knew he wasn't autistic (insert diabolical "Bwah-ha-ha," here....) but something was very wrong.

He wasn't, by any stretch, normal.

Our bedtime routine was to run Sander as ragged as we could. Play all day long, hard. Feed him. Then put him in the sling and then rock him. Back and forth, up and down, back and forth, for about a half an hour, while he screamed the entire time. Sometimes the screaming would stop for a while. If the sling didn't work, after an hour or so, Mark would go for a walk with Sander on his shoulders. He'd leave the house, quietly, and give us all strict instructions.

Then he'd walk for a good twenty minutes, sometimes thirty, while Sander finally fell asleep sitting up, leaning on Mark's head. When Mark got home, he'd ring the doorbell. The entire house had to be silent and dark, and Mark would sneak in and put Sander down on our bed and sneak away.

If he slept for an hour, we were lucky.

Sometimes Mark went for walks at 2 or 3 a.m.

You couldn't do car rides, because he'd scream. You couldn't lie down with him in bed, because he'd scream and run away and act like you were killing him.

There was something very wrong.

I did lots of research. I knew he wasn't autistic (insert another diabolical "Bwah-ha-ha," here....) but I thought maybe I'd give the gluten-free, dairy-free diet a try anyway. Maybe his guts hurt.

This is what I wrote to a friend 48 hours later:

"We started Sander out GFCF on Monday night.

We were getting very worried -- the speech therapist on Monday had said that he wouldn't do any motions to "The Wheels on the Bus" (whatever! Didn't she have better things to worry about?) and that she was very concerned that he wouldn't imitate any animal sounds. And he was still screaming to sleep every night, and waking up three to five times a night to nurse, and was just basically unpredictable: Some days he's great, other days he's a nightmare the whole day. So we started the diet Monday night. Last night he said "bat" and "bug" for the first time.

This morning he started doing the motions for "Wheels on the Bus" and humming so I would sing for him. Then he started woofing and quacking and baa-ing while pretending to be each animal.

He slept last night until 4 am, which is a record for him, and only got up twice (I'll take what I can get!) and went to sleep tonight for the second time in a row without any screaming.

He's cheerful, funny, playful and fun. He's happy and easy-going and hasn't thrown anything at me at all today. I'm not sure that I'm hoping that it's the diet, which might mean a lifetime of restrictions for him, but I sort of am, too, because that means that it's an easy fix. A lot easier than some of the scary stuff that's been floating around in my head.

So keep your fingers crossed. I'm going to be very sad if it's just a fluke, so I'm refusing to get my hopes up too much."

So, that was it. The beginning.

And now, Sander is almost six. He's happy, healthy and "normal," whatever that means. He loves Greek mythology and animals and wants to be a vet and work at Sea World.

His favorite animal is the platypus, "Because they make their own rules."

If he stays gluten-free, all is well. If he gets any gluten or dairy, behavior starts to break down. It doesn't revert completely, but enough that we're pretty careful.

This diet does work for some people, some of the time.

I don't think it works for everyone.

But it's free.

It's harmless if it doesn't work.

And when it does work, it's nothing short of miraculous.

Autism is treatable.

Kids do recover.

And mine is one of the lucky ones who got better.

Meagan M – Austin, TX

The Effect of the GFCF Diet on Children with Autism

Of the thousands of parents filling the Autism Research Institute's survey regarding the effect of diet on their child's behavior, 66% answered that their child improved on a gluten and casein-free (GFCF) diet. Please keep in mind that if you decide to follow this path of action, it must be followed strictly. To make it a little easier on you, this diet should be introduced gradually over a period of two weeks, but once in place, it should be followed strictly. All it takes is a few cookie crumbs to reverse your child's behavior. In most cases your child will show a return to sudden emotional outbursts and uncontrollable diarrhea. Regarding how to deal with this diet, follow the advice given in the gluten-free section, as well as dairy-free advice offered throughout this book.

In my contact with parents of autistic children, they have mentioned over and over again that their child's behavior improved markedly after they were put on a gluten- and casein-free diet. Gliadin is a protein in the gluten found in some grains. Casein is a protein found primarily in cow's milk and assorted dairy products. These proteins are known to create debilitating autoimmune reactions in autistic children, especially those with digestive tract distress. It also was shown to have an effect on their emotional behavior. Starting in the mid 1980s, Dr. Goodwin and his colleagues were among the first to prove that children with autism presented an abnormal brain response to these proteins. When they were placed on a GFCF (gluten-free and casein-free) diet, their neurological behavior improved markedly (better cognition, improved language skills and eye contact, etc.) over children were did not.

There seems to be a strong connection between food allergies and autism. In Italy, Dr. Lucarelli and his colleagues detected much higher levels of antibodies to casein and other milk proteins in children with autism compared to control children. They saw a clear improvement in behavior after they tried a dairy elimination diet. Around the same time, Dr. Jyonouchi and colleagues found that when exposed to food proteins from gluten, casein and soy, children with autism produced a higher amount of pro-inflammatory cytokines (small proteins secreted by the immune system) compared with non-autistic children. As you can read in this book, these observations are confirmed by the real life stories related by parents of local children. Mothers often do know best.

Why You Should Try the GFCF Diet with Your Child

Casein, which is found in milk and dairy products, is broken down by our digestive system into a peptide called casomorphin. As the name suggests, this peptide has morphine-like properties. In wheat and other grains containing gluten, a similar peptide called gluteomorphin is created. Both of these peptides have been shown by some researchers to affect your child the same way an illegal opium drug would affect a healthy person. To parents observing their children closely, their child appears withdrawn and "spacey" and they don't have the same reaction to pain that we would have. So it seems to make sense to put your child on a diet that does not contain these proteins. Some parents have told me that, because of their condition, their child will tend to eat very limited types of foods and will get very emotional when these foods are removed. It is also very difficult to introduce new foods into their diet. They will not touch any new foods. I can only suggest you give it a try like some other parents have, and see if it does improve your child's behavior. If you take your kid(s) off dairy it is a good idea to place them on calcium/magnesium regimen to replace the minerals in dairy. Please ask your doctor or nutritionist.

Casein tends to kill pain. Removing casein may allow your child to feel what we consider "normal" pain (burn, cut, bump). They may now experience pain from previously undetected maladies such as constipation, gastrointestinal inflammation and lesions, or dental cavities, and they will let you know by complaining or crying. Up to 50% of children on the autistic spectrum are known to have gastrointestinal inflammation.

I will not pretend this will be easy. Most DAN! doctors suggest you try this diet for at least 6 months to see some conclusive results. Sometimes, the child will improve rapidly. Sometimes it will take more time. As the parent you know your child best and can tell what works and what does not for him/her. Also know that this new diet will possibly be a daily fight until your child gets better. He or she will most likely experience withdrawal symptoms before they get better. As I mentioned before, children with autism tend to eat a very limited diet filled with their favorite drugs of choice: gluten and dairy. They will resist this change with all their pained soul. They may refuse to eat for a day or two, but try not to worry too much; they will not starve. They will eventually start to eat what is on their plate. Meanwhile, they should drink a lot of water. You may want to give up when you see your child's pain, but if you can find the strength, please hang in there as best as you can. If it works it will be well worth the trouble. I'd also like you to know that this GFCF diet does not work for all autistic children, but I've seen enough positive results to recommend it. Good luck!

My son, William, was first diagnosed with autism at 18 months; of course, I had my suspicions before then. William had all the classical signs of autism: no eye contact, no verbal utterances, no appropriate play with toys, an affinity for spinning objects and restless sleep patterns, in which he would awake screaming and writhing his body.

Upon learning of William's condition, I began on my quest to heal my son. I researched the internet, read books, spoke to other parents of autistic children, and counseled with medical professionals. The casein and gluten free diet came up over and over again. Most professionals in the medical field denied the positive benefits of such a diet, claiming that there is no scientific evidence to support it. Parents, however, had different stories to tell: after removing casein and gluten from their autistic child's diets, many of the autistic symptoms were relieved. I was desperate, and willing to try anything; however, at that time, there were only a few foods William would eat, most of them containing both casein and gluten. Therefore, I began by eliminating gluten from his diet.

Literally, within a week of consuming no gluten, William gave me eye contact for the first time; he responded to his name; he began babbling and gained interest in a few toys. He had more energy and seemed more alert. Finally, I felt some hope. For William, he seemed to be opening up to the world around him.

A few months into the gluten-free diet, my husband and I took William to see a gastrointestinal doctor. She did not support the diet and tried to convince us that his improvements could have been from occupational therapy and other factors. She encouraged us to reintroduce gluten into his diet, especially since William ate so little anyway. We decided to heed her advice – a bit relieved because following a gluten free diet proved difficult for us at the time.

Two weeks after adding gluten back into his diet, William regressed. He no longer babbled; he lost eye contact, and he seemed sluggish and irritable. My husband and I were disappointed, but at the same time, we were certain that eliminating gluten had made a significant different in William's well-being. This time, we decided to go at it full force: no gluten, no casein.

Miraculously, William regained his energy, speech, eye contact, etc. Best of all, William slept through the night for the first time. No longer did he wake in the wee hours of the morning screaming and writhing his body. He also had regular bowel movements (He had severe constipation before) for the first time in his life. William still had autism, of course; however, he felt more comfortable in his body and became more aware of the world around him.

William is now 4 ½ years old; you would not know he was autistic unless I told you. He is mainstreamed in a typical preschool; he has a best friend and is a happy, energetic kid. When people ask me what I think was the biggest contribution to his recovery, I tell them that it was relieving his hidden ailments, which I discovered came from his body not being able to process the proteins gluten and casein. Certainly, there are many other contributors – like occupational and speech therapy, ABA therapy, and the floor time approach. Yet, without the physical well-being William experienced from a casein/gluten free diet, I do not know how well these therapies would have taken.

Nicole D – Austin, TX

Suggestions from the Feingold Diet

As also suggested in the Feingold diet, there should be no artificial food dyes, artificial preservatives and sugar substitutes in your child's diet. All of these are known excitotoxins altering and poisoning your child's brain. To them, these artificial products have the same effect as some illegal drugs have on other people's behavior. Please be aware of this important fact in your child's healing diet plan. Some ASD children are also sensitive to salicylates (common aspirin derived from the bark of the willow tree) contained in an assortment of foods and fruits, especially dark-skinned berries like blackberries, blackcurrants, blueberries and so on. Please check the Feingold Association at **www.feingold.org** for more information. Salicylates can also be used as a food preservative.

MSG

If you or your children are already allergic to processed gluten and dairy, known sources of GLUTamate, then you/they most likely will be highly sensitive to MSG (Monosodium Glutamate). In people already sensitive to the opioid-like gliadin and casein proteins, glutamate will affect the same brain centers and create the same psychological and asocial results. Glutamate is part of a group of toxins called excitotoxins that are known to affect all of us, but that affect Autistic patients much more severely. This warning also applies to other excitotoxins like aspartame (in sugar-free and diet foods) and L-cysteine.

A comment about some new drugs claiming to "heal" Autism: most of them simply block the effects of glutamate and not much more. I would suggest you educate yourself on the hidden sources of glutamate and remove it from your diet. I hate to say it, but that means getting off all fast food and most processed foods, even some organic ones. As I always say, become your own label detective. If you can, eat freshly prepared food cooked at home. That is the safest way for you and your family. For more in formation on where to find MSG, check the Hidden Source of Gluten and Dairy list in Appendix C and on **www.msgtruth.org** and **www.msgmyth.com**.

Where Can You Get Help with Your Child's Diet?

If this is the case with your child, I highly recommend you consult with a physician, dietitian or nutritionist well versed in this subject to create a specific healthy diet plan for your child. My book is here to help you get started, but is not meant to be a replacement for a personalized plan created for your child only. In Austin, I highly recommend the nutrition team at Thoughtful House. They will provide you with a clear dietary plan and recommendations on nutritional supplementation to fill possible deficiencies. In other cities, check the online DAN! directory for guidance in finding the right health professional for you and your child. Please see Appendix B.

Appendix A

Gluten Intolerance and Celiac Disease Organizations

The Gluten Intolerance Group of North America

(253) 833-6655. www.gluten.net The mission of this organization, also known familiarly as GIG, is to provide support to people with any type of gluten intolerance, including celiac disease, dermatitis herpetiformis, and other gluten sensitivities, so they can live healthy lives.

They also publish a very informative quarterly newsletter called the GIG News Magazine. They also have two important programs designed to help GF consumers in their daily search for certified gluten-free products and restaurants. The first one is the critical *Gluten-Free Certification Organization* at www.GFCO.org which certifies gluten-free companies and their products through strict quality testing and on-site inspections. The other one is the very important *Gluten-Free Restaurant Awareness* Program at www.glutenfreerestaurants.org which has developed strict quality standards and education programs to help certify restaurants offering gluten-free menus and services.

Innate Health Foundation

(206)264-1111. www.InnateHealthFoundation.org This foundation is dedicated to offering help and resources for people with food allergies and intolerances. What I like the most about this organization is that it offer the only people-moderated (sort of a Wikipedia of the food allergies world) national listing of gluten-free manufacturers, restaurants and other food establishments, products, recipes, books, and other allergy resources. It allows anyone to add, update and correct any listings as new information becomes available. I really like this web site for its immense source of information for people with multiple food allergies or intolerances. Check it out.

Celiac-Specific Organizations

American Celiac Disease Alliance

(703) 622-3331. www.americanceliac.org This organization is dedicated to improving the lives of those afflicted with celiac disease through advocacy, awareness, education, and research.

Celiac Disease Foundation

(818) 990-2354. **www.celiac.org** The Celiac Disease Foundation provides support, information and assistance to people affected by celiac disease and dermatitis herpetiformis.

Celiac Sprue Association

(877) 272-4272 **www.csaceliacs.org** This association is a member-based support organization dedicated to provide education, support and research to people and their families sickened with celiac disease and dermatitis herpetiformis.

Raising Our Celiac Kids (R. O. C. K.)

No phone number could be found. **www.celiac.com** R. O. C. K. is a support group created to help kids and their parents live a healthy gluten-free lifestyle.

Canadian Celiac Association

(800) 363.7296. (905)507.6208 **www.celiac.ca** This association is dedicated to provide services to all people with celiac and dermatitis herpetiformis through education programs, awareness, advocacy and research.

Suggested Gluten Intolerance and Celiac Disease Reading List

As these lists constantly evolve and improve, they are only a current indication what books can help you understand and live with celiac disease, any form of gluten intolerance and autism. There are many more available on the internet, bookstores and your friendly local pharmacy, nutritionist or doctor's office. All lists are in alphabetical order.

On the Medical Importance of Gluten Intolerance and Celiac Disease

Celiac Disease: A Hidden Epidemic by Peter H. R. Green and Rory Jones

Dangerous Grains: Why Gluten Cereal Grains May Be Hazardous To Your Health by James Braly and Ron Hoggan

Full of It by Rodney Ford

Hidden Food Allergies: The Essential Guide to Uncovering Hidden Food Allergies and Achieving Permanent Relief by James Braly and Patrick Holfor

The Gluten Syndrome by Rodney Ford

Living with Gluten Intolerance

1000 Gluten Free Recipes by Carol Fenster

Cecilia's Marketplace Gluten-Free Grocery Shopping Guide by Mara Matison and Dainis Matison

Clan Thompson Celiac Pocket Guide to Over-the-Counter Gluten-Free Drugs 2008 by Lani K. Thompson

Cooking Free: 200 Flavorful Recipes for People with Food Allergies and Multiple Food Sensitivities by Carol Fenster

Gluten-Free 101: Easy, Basic Dishes Without Wheat by Carol Lee Fenster

Gluten-Free Cooking for Dummies by Danna Korn and Connie Sarros

Gluten-Free Diet: A Comprehensive Resource Guide by Shelley Case

Gluten-Free Girl: How I Found the Food That Loves Me Back... And How You Can Too by Shauna James Ahern

Gluten-Free Quick and Easy: From Prep to Plate Without the Fuss -- 200+ Recipes for People With Food Sensitivities by Carol Fenster

Incredible Edible Gluten-Free Food for Kids: 150 Family-Tested Recipes by Sheri L. Sanderson

Kids With Celiac Disease: A Family Guide to Raising Happy, Healthy, Gluten-Free Children by Danna Korn

Let's Eat Out!: Your Passport to Living Gluten and Allergy Free and other similar books from the same authors by Kim Koeller and Robert La France

Living Gluten-Free for Dummies by Danna Korn

The Complete Book of Gluten-Free Cooking by Jennifer Cinquepalmi

The Essential Gluten-Free Restaurant Guide by Triumph Dining

The Gluten-Free Gourmet series of books by the pioneer lady of gluten-free cooking Bette Hagman

The Gluten-Free Kitchen; Over 135 Delicious Recipes for People With Gluten Intolerance or Wheat Allergy by Robert Ryberg

Wheat-Free, Worry-Free: The Art of Happy, Healthy Gluten-Free Living by Danna Korn

You Won't Believe It's Gluten-Free! 500 Delicious, Foolproof Recipes for Healthy Living by Robert Ryberg

GF Magazines and Websites

Living Without. The Magazine for People with Allergies and Food Sensitivities. (800) 474-8614. **www.LivingWithout.com** I am very impressed by this magazine founded by Peggy Wagener. It is a well written source of current advices, stories and offers an assortment of recipes addressing a wide range of food allergies.

Gluten-Free Living Magazine

800-324-8781. **www.glutenfreeliving.com** Another well informed and well written magazine.

Delight Gluten-Free Magazine

www.delightgfmagazine.com A very attractive, appealing and informative magazine.

Appendix B

Living with Autism Information

Information about Autism Agencies, Organizations and Foundations
In central Texas we are very lucky to have an extremely qualified team of caring doctors, educators, nutritionists led by Dr. Wakefield. They offer a wide range of treatments to help you and your child. If you have any questions, they offer free monthly seminar created to help you understand and deal with your child's condition.

Thoughtful House Center for Children
3001 Bee Caves Road, suite 120. Austin, Texas 78746
(512) 732-8400 ext. 323 **www.thoughtfulhouse.org**

4-A Healing.com
(212)763-8688. **www.4ahealingfoundation.org** is a website created by Dr. Bock, a well-known doctor in the treatment of autism. It covers all of the 4-A disorders (Autism, ADHD, Asthma and Allergies) and is helpful to all parents in need of information. Other Dr. Bock's websites include: **www.rhinebeckhealth.**com and **www.healing-autism.com**

ABA Resources
No phone number found. **http://rsaffran.tripod.com/aba.html** provides information on behavioral therapies.

American College for Advancement in Medicine
No phone number found. **www.acamnet.org** ACAM is the main organization to find an integrative physician. It offers an updated doctor referral service.

Autism Network for Dietary Intervention
(609) 737-8985 **www.autismndi.com** This network was established to help parents understand, implement and maintain dietary intervention for their autistic children.

Autism Research Institute
(619) 281-7165. **www.autism.com** ARI is the sponsoring group of Defeat Autism Now. It conducts research and offers information based on this research.

Autism Speaks

(212) 252-8584. **www.autismspeaks.org** This important organization offers influential information and assistance organization with excellent resources.

Autism Society of America

(301) 657-0881. **www.autism-society.org** This is a major, long-established autism organization. It supports strong advocacy for autistic children.

Center for Autism Related Disorder (CARD)

(818) 345-2345. **www.centerforautism.com** This is one of the world's largest organization helping autistic children, especially with ABA.

Center for the Study of Autism

No phone number found. **www.autism.org** This center is associated with ARI and offers an excellent explanation of the biomedical approach to autism.

Defeat Autism Now!

(619) 281-7165. It is now grouped under the same web site as ARI at **www.autism.com** DAN! is the action branch of ARI, offers a doctor referral service, video and audio presentations and a wealth of information.

Dough Flutie Jr. Foundation for Autism

(508) 270-8855 **www.dougflutiejrfoundation.org** A caring source of help, information, and other resources.

First Signs, Inc.

(978) 346-4380 **www.firstsigns.org** First Signs focuses on early intervention. It is well informed, insightful, practical and empathetic.

Floortime Foundation

(301) 656-2667 **www.floortime.org** This foundation offers information on one of the most popular and effective behavioral therapies.

Organization for Autism Research

(703) 243-9710 **www.researchautism.org** Focuses exclusively on applied autistic research.

Parents Action for Children

(888) 447-3400 **www.parentsaction.org** Helps parents in their role during therapy.

Safe Minds

(404) 934-0777 **www.safeminds.org** Safe Minds was founded by parents of autistic children. It is well-researched and has good credibility.

The Feingold Association of the United States

(800)321-3287 **www.feingold.org** Is an organization of families and professionals founded in 1976. It is dedicated to help adults and children to apply proven dietary techniques for better behavior, learning and health and to generate public awareness of the potential role of some foods and synthetic additives in behavior, learning and health problems.

The GFCF Diet

www.gfcfdiet.com I could not find a national phone number. Each local chapter has its own phone number. The GFCF Diet believes that dietary intervention may be that one piece of the puzzle which helps a child with ASD toward the road to recovery.

Unlocking Autism

(866) 366-3361 **www.unlockingautism.org** This international organization of parents is a great networking site.

Suggested Autism Reading List

A Shot in the Dark by Harris L. Coulter and Barbara Loe Fisher. Written as an indictment of common vaccination procedures.

A Parent's Guide to Asperger's Syndrome and High-Functioning Autism by Sally Ozonoff, Ph. D., Geraldine Dawson, Ph. D. , and James McParland. Good information for parents of kids with Asperger's.

Autism: Effective Biomedical Treatments by Jon Pangborn, Ph. D. And Sidney MacDonald Baker, M. D. A highly recommended book about biomedical therapies focused on supplementation therapy for autism.

Autism Spectrum Disorders by Chantal Sicile-Kira. A well-presented account by the caring mother of an autistic child.

Children with Starving Brains by Jacquelyn McCandless, M. D. A classic. One of the first book documenting biomedical intervention. An important book for parents wanting to be involved.

Could It Be Autism? by Nancy D. Wiseman. An autistic mother's moving, helpful and inspiring story.

Diet Intervention and Autism by Marilyn LeBreton. A well-researched book on the effect of food for autistic children.

Enzymes for Autism and Other Neurological Conditions by Karen DeFelice. A well-researched book about the use of enzymes in treating autism.

Evidence of Harm by David Kirby. An extremely well scientifically and documented description of vaccination risks.

Special Diet for Special Kids by Lisa Lewis, Ph. D. Contains practical advices and menu plans for parents of autistic children.

The Autism Sourcebook by Karen Siff Exkorn. A nicely written overview to get you started.

The Defeat Now Conference Proceedings. These are the written accounts of DAN doctors as presented during their twice a year conference. To receive copies of these reports, contact DAN.

The Vaccine Guide by Randall Neustaedter, O. M. D. An extremely well researched book about the pros and cons of vaccination. Very important if you don't know what to do.

Thinking in Pictures by Temple Gardin. The classic personal story of one of America's most successful autistic person.

Unraveling the Mystery of Autism and Pervasive Development Disorder by Karyn Seroussi. A well-informed early book on autism.

What Your Doctor May Not Tell You About Children' Vaccinations by Stephanie Cave, M. D. and Deborah Mitchell. Doctor Cave was one of the first doctors to uncover harm created to some children by vaccination.

Appendix C

Hidden Sources of Gluten and Dairy

First, the Good News: What You Can Still Eat
If you've forgotten or are not sure which foods are wheat or gluten-free, here's your list!

SAFE – Grains, Flours, Starches (Gluten-Free/Wheat-Free)

- Almond flour
- Amaranth
- Arrowroot
- Bean flour
- Besan (chickpea flour)
- Brown rice and brown rice flour
- Buckwheat
- Cassava (manioc or yuca)
- Chickpea flour
- Corn, flour, meal and starch
- Cottonseed
- Dal (preparation of dried lentils, peas or beans)
- Flaxseed
- Garbanzo bean flour
- Gram (chickpea flour)
- Manioc (cassava or yuca)
- Potato
- Tapioca
- Millet
- Milo (sorghum)
- Montina (Indian rice grass)
- Polenta (ground corn meal or maize)
- Potato flour or starch
- Quinoa
- Rice and rice flour
- Sago (starch extracted from the sago palm in Africa)
- Sorghum (milo)
- Soy flour
- Tapioca flour
- Taro and flour (a root vegetable similar to yam)
- Teff (a cereal grain)

- Yuca (manioc or cassava)

SAFE – Other Foods Allowed

- Assorted GF beers
- Assorted beans
- Assorted organic fresh fruits
- Assorted organic fresh vegetables
- Assorted nuts and seeds
- Grass-fed or free-range eggs
- Fish and Shellfish
- Grass-fed beef
- <u>Other meats</u>: buffalo, chicken, duck, goat, goose, lamb, pork, rabbit, turkey, quail, veal and venison. Use the usual precautions.
- Olive and Coconut oils
- For more details, please see the master GFCF Shopping list

A Word About Wine and Spirits
Generally speaking, all wines and distilled spirits should be gluten-free. Wine is made entirely from fermented grapes, and the distilling process eliminates any gluten that may have been in the "mash" from which spirits are made. Most wines and spirits are aged in gluten-free steel or concrete tanks. However a few wines and spirits are aged in oak barrels which have been sealed with a wheat-flour-and-water paste. This paste is used primarily in Europe; American companies prefer to use food-grade paraffin. But some American companies import *used* barrels and casks from Europe to make high-end wines. The more expensive the wine, the more likely it is barrel-aged. Some wines that are not barrel-aged: Reisling, Sauvignon Blanc from New Zealand, Pinot Grigio from Italy, and all bag-in-a-box wines.

Alcohol Products That Are Usually Safe:

- Wine (organic preferable); champagne and sparkling wine;
- Brandy and fruit brandies like Cointreau and Grand Marnier; Armagnac; coffee liqueur (Kalhua); cognac; grappa; sake; single-malt Scotch; sherry; tequila; Maker's Mark bourbon; vermouth; vodka; rum; ouzo; gin.

But remember: the only way to be absolutely sure a wine or spirit has not been aged in a gluten-contaminated barrel is to contact the manufacturer, distillery, or vineyard.

Products That May Contain Gluten (gliadin) and Dairy (casein)
In Your Home

- Children's stickers and price tag stickers! Watch these!).
- Glue on stamps and envelopes (use self-adhesive stamps and envelopes).
- Art supplies for kids: clay, crayons, paint, play dough, and glue.
- Washing machine detergent (use Arm & Hammer Baking soda detergent).

In Your Bathroom

- Lipstick, lip balm, nail polish and artificial nails. Most contain wheat germ oil (use Burt's beeswax lip balm). BE careful when you kiss your GFCF kids!
- Toothpaste, mouthwash and dental floss (Tom's of Maine offers GF toothpaste).
- Some cleaning products, detergents and even bar soaps may contain gluten.
- Soap, shampoo and hair conditioner; hair gel and hairspray (try Kirkman Labs' Kleen products).
- Personal lubricants and spermicides.
- Cosmetics (I know most kids do not use make up - but make sure they do not get their hands on it!! I heard of one little girl drinking her mother's foundation to get her gluten fix!)
- Unless you suffer from dermatitis herpetiformis, lotions, foundation and powders should be safe, because gluten and casein proteins are too large to enter through healthy skin. But if your skin is broken or inflamed, stop using products that contain wheat germ oil, wheatgrass and barley grass.
- Sunscreen and suntan lotions (use Banana Boat Children's sunscreen).
- Please note: because the cosmetic industry does not have the same labeling standards as the food industry, it can be difficult to find out if a product has gluten or dairy in it. Sometimes even the manufacturer does not know, as they get their ingredients from different sources. The best way for you to find out the truth is to join an online GFCF group and either do a search on a particular product or ask the forum for their feedback.

In Your Medicine Cabinet

Most medicines contain three different types of ingredients: Active ingredients, Inactive ingredients, and Incipient ingredients. Active and

Inactive ingredients are usually listed separately, and Incipient ingredients are sometimes not listed at all. You must check to make sure that all of the ingredients of your medicines are safe for you.

Active ingredients: Any ingredient the pharmaceutical company intends to use in the manufacturing of the drug product.

Inactive ingredients: "Any component other than an active ingredient." Involves all aspects of the manufacturing process including processing, packing or holding of a drug product.

Incipients: Filler ingredients added to the active form of the drug. Examples are fillers, colorings, dextrates, malt and starches. The purpose of incipients is to add bulk, act as a lubricant for the power form of the drug or to absorb water. Both the sources and composition of the incipients must be identified.

Medicines that often contain gluten and/or casein:

- Antacid tablets and pills.
- Cough drops and syrup.
- Nasal sprays.
- Laxatives.
- Medicines and antibiotics may be coated with flour or use wheat flour as a filler.
- The same cautionary statement applies to over-the-counter drugs and supplements. Unless specifically labeled "gluten-free", you should avoid them. Ask your doctor or nutritionist for allergen-free products.
- Another option is to have your medications custom-made by a compounding pharmacy (Peoples Pharmacy in Austin).
- Latex or rubber gloves could be coated with wheat or oat flour. Ask your doctor or dentist to use non-coated gloves.
- Even if you have found a safe GFCF product, beware of "New and Improved" products, a new container or label design and change of delivery (liquid, capsules, pills).
- If you have any doubts, please follow the following steps when calling the company help line:

    1. Review the list of possible gluten sources in the main list below.
    2. Review the product label for potential offenders.
    3. Provide the Lot number and/or Batch number. This helps identify the specific products production history.

4. Ask them to verify the GF status of each ingredient including fillers, colorings and powders.

5. Inquire about the source of suspected hidden gluten as described above.

6. Ask them if the drug's formulation or processing has changed since this GF information was identified.

7. Inquire if any of the companies supplying the inactive ingredients have changed since the GF information was identified.

8. Is there a possibility for cross contamination during production and processing?

Please remember: Your successful inquiry into the GF status of a medication relies on your knowledge and ability to interpret labels and evaluate manufacturer's information. Your health and the health of your family depends on it.

In the Kitchen

- Household appliances - toaster, grill, oven, microwave, waffle iron - use separate appliances and utensils for GF foods. If you can't buy an extra set of new appliances, as with ovens and microwaves, put your GFCF foods on a plate.
- Cutting boards, knives and assorted kitchen tools: keep your own separate.
- Watch for double dipping in jams, preserves and honey. Also be careful with shared margarine and spreads.
- Some non-organic fresh fruits and vegetables coated with wax may contain gluten. Wash thoroughly or eat only organic fresh produce.
- Ground spices may contain wheat flour as a filler. Use Morton & Bassett Organic Spices, Frontier Organic Spices, and Central Market Organic Spices. McCormick's spices are also 100% pure spice, but they do not guarantee that their spice *blends* are GF, so avoid blends (such as "poultry seasoning").
- Some chocolate candies and chewing gum manufacturers may dust their conveyor belts with flour to prevent sticking.
- Some shortening may contain vitamin E derived from wheat germ.
- Some rice syrup brands may use barley enzymes during processing.
- Some yeast may be grown or dried on wheat flour.
- Wheat may be used as a thickener in ice cream, soups, gravies, yogurt, snack foods, lunch meats, sausage, and even in prepackaged ground meat. Read the label.

- Pet food and treats can also be a source of gluten. Please wash your hands after feeding your pets.
- Another confusing factor is that some companies may switch ingredients from batch to batch. For example, Cool Whip may or may not use wheat starch and contains casein; Duncan Hines may or may not use wheat starch in their Ready-to-Spread-Icing; Pringles may or may not use wheat starch on their chips, and so on, and so forth. To make sure, you should read the ingredients label every time.
- In Austin we are lucky because our major food stores are setting up exclusive gluten-free displays or are labeling gluten-free and dairy-free products clearly on their shelves. I hope it is the same in your neighborhood. If not, your only option may be to shop for your GFCF products on specific sites online. The best is **www.celiac.com GF Mall** but Amazon and EBay shops also have plenty of GF offerings.

Eating Out

- Do not eat at fast food restaurants. Their "food" is loaded with gluten, artificial colors and preservatives, not to mention MSG. Another problem is that even if they have some GF items, they do not have separate equipment to handle it, thus creating a strong possibility for cross contamination.
- Avoid: breaded food; sautéed foods; fried foods (unless they have a dedicated fryer, most likely the frying oil is contaminated. Even then, mistakes do happen); chicken-fried foods; marinated foods; pre-seasoned foods; premade and frozen foods; grilled foods (the grill may have been used to grill foods containing gluten, such as hamburger buns).
- Avoid all you can eat buffet as there is a high risk for cross contamination.
- When you go out to eat, go to your favorite GFCF restaurant and ask for their special menu. Most restaurants or chains are now aware of your condition. If not, create a card you can carry with you that explains your condition to the waiter and kitchen staff. They'll be glad to accommodate you. Another option is to go to a raw food or macrobiotic restaurant; typically, all the food is fresh and made from scratch at such places.
- Luckily for us, more and more restaurant chains and even local restaurants either have exclusive gluten-free menus or offer a few GF choices on their menus. Look online for your local GIG list of GFCF restaurants in your area.
- All of this may sound paranoid but like I always say "Better be safe than sorry".

The NO-NO Lists!

This is a list of the NO-NOes for **gluten-** and **casein-** free diets.

NO-NO Grains and Flours

- ✓ Abyssinian Hard Wheat (Triticum Duran)
- ✓ Atta flour
- ✓ Barley and barley flour
- ✓ Barley grass
- ✓ Barley Hordeum vulgare
- ✓ Barley pearls
- ✓ Bleached All-Purpose Flour
- ✓ Bran (wheat)
- ✓ Bread Flour
- ✓ Brown Flour Bulgur
- ✓ Bulgur Wheat
- ✓ Dinkle (spelt flour)
- ✓ Durum wheat (also called "hard" wheat. It is the type of wheat used in pasta and semolina)
- ✓ Durum flour
- ✓ Emmer
- ✓ Enriched Flour
- ✓ Einkorn (the name given to the wild form of wheat)
- ✓ Emmer (durum flour)
- ✓ Farina
- ✓ Farro
- ✓ Gluten Flour
- ✓ Gluten peptides
- ✓ Graham Flour
- ✓ Granary Flour
- ✓ Hard Wheat
- ✓ High protein Flour
- ✓ High Gluten Flour
- ✓ High Protein Flour
- ✓ Job's tears
- ✓ Kamut
- ✓ Maida (Indian wheat flour)
- ✓ Mir (a wheat and rye cross)
- ✓ Oats and Oat Flour (unless specified GF)
- ✓ Pasta

- ✓ Pearl Barley
- ✓ Rice Malt (contains barley or Koji)
- ✓ Rice Syrup (unless specified GF it contains barley enzymes)
- ✓ Rye
- ✓ Rye Semolina
- ✓ Semolina and Semolina Triticum
- ✓ Spelt (an ancient form of wheat. It contains less gluten, but still has it)
- ✓ Spelt Triticum
- ✓ Strong Flour
- ✓ Triticale; Triticale X triticosecale; Triticum and Hard Triticum
- ✓ Vegetable Starch
- ✓ All wheat products such as: Wheat Flour; Wheat Hard and Soft; Wheat bran; Wheat Durum triticum; Wheat germ; Wheat gluten; Wheat malt; Wheat nuts; Wheat oats; Wheat pasta; Wheat starch; Wheat Triticum aestivum; Wheat Triticum mononoccum; White Flour; Whole Wheat Berries and Whole-Meal Flour

NO-NO Products Made From Wheat & Flour

All of the items listed below usually contain gluten, and lots of it. Gluten-free versions of these food items can be found at many grocery and health food stores, and at specialized GFCF websites.

- Bagels
- Biscuits
- Bread
- Breakfast products: Muffins, scones, croissants, Danishes and so on
- Bread crumbs
- Breaded fish, meats or poultry
- Bread pudding
- Cake flour
- Cake & cake mixes
- Cereals
- Chicken nuggets
- Chow Mein noodles
- Coffee creamer (all kinds)
- Cookies and cookie mixes
- Croutons
- Crackers
- Doughnuts
- Dumplings

- Flavored prepackaged rice
- Flavored prepackaged pasta
- Flour tortillas
- Flavored instant coffee
- Flavored instant tea
- Fried vegetables (unless cooked in a Wok with GF soy Sauce)
- Graham crackers
- Hamburger buns
- Hotdog buns
- Ice cream cones
- Macaroni
- Melba toast
- Noodles
- Pancakes
- Pasta
- Pastries
- Pie crusts
- Pretzels
- Pizza
- Pretzels
- Rolls
- Spaghetti
- Stuffing
- Tabbouleh
- Waffles

In case you feel overwhelmed and think you cannot eat your favorite foods anymore, there are specialty GF and DF/CF versions of most these products on my Master GFCF Shopping List.

CAUTION: Suspicious Foods and Food Products

The Following Foods and Food Products MAY Contain Wheat or Gluten

Please read the label in all cases, and see the shopping list (Appendix D) for GFCF alternatives.

- Alcohol (malt beverages like beer and Smirnoff Ice vodka and the energy drink 3sum)
- Baby or infant formula
- Bacon (some very inexpensive brands contain gluten)

- Baking Powder (Clabber Girl and Calumet are GF)
- Baking Soda (verify ingredients)
- Battered foods
- Beer (unless it is certified gluten-free)
- Beverage mixes
- Blue cheese (if the mold is grown on bread)
- Bologna (not the city, the cold meat)
- Bouillon cubes or powder
- Bourbon liquor
- Breading or bread crumbs
- Brewer's yeast
- Bran Cereals
- Breaded foods
- Breakfast cereals (some are flavored with barley malt) (see shopping list for alternatives)
- Broth, prepackaged (see shopping list for alternatives)
- Brown rice syrup (often made with barley enzymes)
- Candy
- Canned baked beans (some may contain wheat as a thickener)
- Canned soups (see shopping list for alternatives)
- Cereal extract
- Cereal "Binders" (may contain wheat)
- Cheese spreads
- Chewing gum and mints
- Chocolate drink mixes (Ovaltine)
- Chocolate syrups
- Chorizo (Often uses wheat as a filler. Read label)
- Coffee creamer substitute (some are grain-based)
- Cold cuts
- Colorings
- Cough drops and syrups
- Couscous (a Mediterranean or Berber dish made of semolina wheat)
- Cracker meal
- Creamed foods
- Croutons
- Custards
- Curds
- Curry sauces
- Dextrin
- Dried fruits and dried dates (they are sometimes rolled in oat flour)
- Edible starch

- Egg mixes
- Emulsifiers
- Fast food restaurants: French fries, buns and chicken nuggets are made or coated with wheat flour
- Farina (also known as Cream of Wheat. It is the Italian word for flour)
- Fillers or extenders
- Flavorings
- Fried foods
- Frozen meals
- Fruit fillings
- Fu (dried wheat gluten)
- Glutamate
- Glutamic Acid
- Graham Flour (a form of whole wheat flour named after the Reverend Sylvester Graham, an early adopter of wholesome living. It is used in the famed Graham cracker and pie crusts, among other products)
- Gravy
- Gravy mixes (unless homemade with cornstarch)
- Ground Spices (some contain gluten)
- Gum Base
- Hard lemonade (may contain malt and/or barley)
- Herbs with wheat fillers
- Hot dogs
- Hydrolyzed oat starch
- Hydrolyzed Plant Protein (HPP)
- Hydrolyzed Vegetable Protein HVP
- Ice cream (wheat can be used as a thickener)
- Icings or frostings
- Imitation fish or meat
- Instant tea or coffee
- Kasha (a cereal mostly eaten in Eastern Europe. It is traditionally made of buckwheat (GF) but is commonly made from any cereal in the US)
- Ketchup (if made with malt vinegar)
- Lunch meats
- Malt. Watch out for Malt Vinegar , beer, some flavorings and even Rice Crispies; Malt Extract; Malt Syrup and Malt Flavoring
- Marinades
- Matzo (matzoh). A Jewish unleavened flat bread eaten during Passover. It is made from wheat flour and water.
- Mayonnaise (if made with malt vinegar)
- Medications: some of them use wheat as filler. Ask your pharmacist.
- Miso (some may be made with wheat)

- Modified Food Starch (source could be wheat)
- MSG
- Mustard (if made with malt vinegar)
- "Natural flavors"
- Non-dairy creamer
- Non-stick sprays
- Panko (bread crumbs)
- Pickles (if made with malt vinegar)
- Potato chips (some flavored versions may have wheat starch)
- Poultry – self-basting
- Processed foods: lots and lots of places where gluten and dairy hide; read the labels
- Processed meats
- Puddings
- Rice milk (some brands may use barley malt enzymes)
- Rice pilaf (often contains orzo pasta made of wheat)
- Root beer
- Salad dressings (read the label)
- Sauces and Sauce mixes (read labels carefully, often contain wheat)
- Sausages (may use wheat as a filler)
- Seasonings: if in doubt, please check source
- Seeds or snack mixes (see shopping list for alternatives)
- Seitan (a Japanese food made from pure gluten protein)
- Semolina (a form of pasta made with durum wheat. It is also found in breakfast cereals and puddings)
- Spices containing wheat fillers
- Starch (outside USA)
- Stilton cheese (same comment as blue cheese)
- Stock Cubes (many contain gluten)
- Shoyu or Soy sauce (unless specified GF): most of them are made with wheat. Get San-J Organic Gluten Free Tamari
- Soba Noodles
- Sour Cream (wheat can be used as a thickener)
- Soy milk (some brands may use barley malt enzymes)
- Stabilizers
- Suet in packets
- Supplements: Some vitamins and minerals contain gluten. Ask your nutritionist
- Syrups (see shopping list for alternatives)

- Tabbouleh (a Middle-Eastern salad made with bulgur wheat, tomatoes, chopped parsley and mint, and seasoned with lemon juice, olive oil, sea salt and ground black pepper)
- Teriyaki sauce
- Textured Vegetable Protein (TVP)
- Thickeners
- Toothpaste
- Udon (wheat noodles)
- Vanilla extract (McCormick and Nielsen-Massey are GF)
- Vegetables with commercially prepared sauces
- Vital Gluten
- Vitamins (some contain gluten)
- Wheat Germ (the seed of the wheat grain and the main source of gliadin)
- Wine. Some non-organic wines are aged in oak barrels put together with a gluten-containing glue.
- Wine coolers (may contain malt and/or barley)
- Worcestershire sauce from Canada (It's GF in the US)

The Following Foods and Food Products Contain or MAY Contain Dairy and Casein

Please read labels in all cases and read the shopping list for GFCF alternatives.

- Acidophilus milk
- All forms of cheeses: hard, soft, cottage, etc.
- Artificial Butter flavor
- Beta-Lactoglobulin
- Butter; Butter fat; Butter flavoring; Butter oil and Buttermilk
- Calcium Caseinate
- Caramel Color
- Casein; Caseinates; Casein hydrolysates
- Condensed milk
- Cream; Cream Cheese; Sour Cream; Cream Yogurt
- Delactosed whey; Demineralized whey
- All forms of Milk; Dry milk; Condensed Milk; Evaporated milk; Low-Fat and Nonfat Milk; Malted milk; Milk Cheese Lactose; Milk Powder; Milk Protein; Milk Solids; Slim Milk and Whole Milk
- Galactose
- Ghee (clarified butter. If you're not sure of the source, do not buy)
- Goat's milk and all Goat Cheeses

- Half & Half and Heavy Whipping Cream
- Ice cream
- Kefir
- Lactose; Lactalbumin; Lactalbumin phosphate
- Sodium lactylate (may or may not contain casein)
- Lacto globulin; Lactose; Lactulose
- Magnesium caseinate
- Margarine: A "D" on a label next to "K" or "U" indicates presence of milk protein. Some are dairy-free.
- Non-dairy creamer butter
- Pudding
- Rennet casein
- Sour Cream; Sour cream solids
- Sour milk solids
- Yogurt (including sweet, delactosed, protein concentrate)
- Whey in all forms, and Whey protein (It is hotly disputed whether whey is safe or not; technically, whey does not contain casein. Some persons advocate avoiding it in any case.)

Mysterious Ingredients Listed on the Nutritional Labels of Prepared Foods: What you need to know

Even the most experienced shopper can be stumped by mysterious ingredients like "agar agar." I hope these lists of safe and unsafe "mystery ingredients" will make label reading easier for you.

Gluten- and Casein-Free Foods and Additives

Please be aware that even when an additive is gluten or dairy-free, it still may not be healthy for you or your children.

- Agar-Agar: A binder made from red algae.
- Alcohol, distilled: Some people claim that the distillation process removes all traces of grain. If you want to make sure, check with the manufacturer.
- Algin: A gum made from brown algae.
- Annatto: A natural plant-based coloring.
- Arabic Gum: A natural gum derived from the acacia tree. It is used as a binder in a variety of products such as soft drink syrup, gum drops, hard candies, M&M's and edible glitter.
- Artificial colors FD&C (approved for Food, Drugs and Cosmetics): These synthetic colors are GFCF, although they are potentially dangerous, especially for autistic children. See the Feingold Diet.

- Artificial Flavorings: Same comment as for artificial colors. See the Feingold Diet.
- Ascorbic acid or Vitamin C. It can be synthetic or natural.
- Aspartame: An artificial sugar derived from petroleum. In my opinion, it is not a healthy product and is known as an excitotoxin. It adversely affects some people's brains, especially children. Autistic and ADD/ADHD children are highly sensitive to it. Avoid at all cost.
- Beet: A natural color source.
- Beta Carotene: A precursor to vitamin A. Usually extracted from carrots.
- Betanin: A food coloring from beets.
- BHA (Butylated hydroxyanisole): Is a food preservative and antioxidant. Banned in Europe. Avoid.
- BHT (Butylated hydroxytoluene): A food preservative and antioxidant. Banned in Europe. Avoid.
- Calcium Disodium: A form of sodium used as an additive to stabilize a food products.
- Carboxymethyl Cellulose: A cellulose gum used as a binder or thickener.
- Carnauba Wax: A wax coming from a Brazilian palm tree. It is used as a thickener in many food products.
- Carob Bean: A bean coming from the carob tree. It can be used as a sweetener or as a substitute for chocolate.
- Carrageenan: A vegetarian and vegan jellifying agent. It comes from a seaweed.
- Cellulose Gum or CMC: A thickener made from a plant-based cellulose derivative.
- Citric Acid: A natural preservative coming mostly from citrus fruits.
- Corn Gluten or Corn Gluten Meal (CGM): A byproduct of corn processing usually used as animal feed and pet food.
- Corn Syrup and High Fructose Corn Syrup: A cheap alternative sweetener to cane or beet sugar.
- Corn Syrup Solids: A dehydrated form of corn syrup.
- Cornstarch: Starch derived from corn.
- Cream of Tartar or Potassium Bitartrate: A byproduct of the wine making process. It can be found in baking powder, is used as a stabilizer for meringue, and prevents sugar from crystallizing. It also is a substitute for sodium-free salt.
- Dextrose: A form of glucose. It can be a precursor to vitamin C.
- Flax seed or Linseed: A graminae seed providing a good amount of insoluble fiber, as well as a good plant source of omega-3 fatty acid.
- Fructose: A form of sugar, usually coming from fruit. Nowadays it mostly comes from corn, a cheap source of sweetener.

- Fumaric Acid: An acidity regulator derived from a family of plants called *Fumaria*.
- Gelatin: A jelling agent and thickener derived from animal collagen (pork and horses). It is used in gummy bears, Jello desserts and many other forms of candy.
- Glucose: The simplest form of sugar (monosaccharide) used in our body for energy.
- Glucose Syrup: The liquid form of glucose.
- Glutamic Acid: One of the non essential amino acids. It is extracted from a seaweed and is the source of the flavor called *umami* (savor flavor). It is the base for the now infamous MSG (monosodium glutamate).
- Glutinous Rice: Also called sweet rice or sticky rice; a form of short-grain rice from Asia. It is called "glutinous" in the sense of being glue-like, but does not contain gluten.
- Glycerides: A combination of glycerol and fatty acids. They are derived mostly from vegetable oils and animal fat. They are used as a less expensive replacement for butter.
- Glycol: A polymer used in the food industry as a dispersant (to disperse water molecules) and to keep products moist. Not to be confused with ethylene glycol, a poisonous product used as a car antifreeze liquid.
- Guar Gum: An additive derived from the grinding of the endosperm of the guar bean. It is used as an emulsifier and thickener in salad dressings and other products.
- Gum Arabic: A natural gum derived from the acacia tree. It is used as a binder in a variety of products such as soft drink syrup, gum drops and hard candies, M&M's and edible glitter.
- Hydrolyzed Corn Protein (HCP): A corn-based source of amino acids. It is used as a cheap umami flavoring. Since it contains a large amount of glutamate, avoid it if you are allergic to MSG.
- Hydrolyzed Plant Protein (HPP): A flavor enhancer used in many foods and cigarettes. It also contains glutamate. If you are allergic to MSG, avoid it.
- Hydrolyzed Soy Protein (HSP): A soy-based source of amino acids. It is used as cheap umami flavoring. Since it contains a large amount of glutamate, avoid it if you are allergic to MSG.
- Inulin: A plant-based source of soluble fiber known as fructans. It is used as a thickener and is called a prebiotic – a beneficial plant food for probiotics, your friendly bacteria.
- Invert Sugar or Inverted Sugar: A mix of glucose and fructose. It is used as a sweetener and prevents sugar-based candies from crystallizing too

fast. It can be found in honey, jams and preserves, toffee and many other candies. It also keeps baked products moist.

- Lecithin: Originally, lecithin was derived from egg yolks. It is the emulsifier used in making mayonnaise. Nowadays, it is derived from soybean and other oils. It is also used as a lubricant in chocolate coating and bars. In baking, it can be used as a cheap replacement for butter and eggs.
- Malic Acid: Originally found in unripe fruits such as green apples, it is used as an acidifier in candies and "Sweet and Sour" products like potato chips. It can cause mouth irritation.
- Maltitol: A sugar alcohol used as a sugar substitute.
- Mannitol: Also called *manna sugar* for the flower (flowering ash) that resembles the Biblical food. It is a sugar alcohol used as a sugar substitute. Be careful to not ingest too much of it for it will make you "run" to the bathroom in a hurry.
- Molasses: The thick byproduct of the processing of cane and sugar beets into white sugar. Do not confuse with sweet sorghum syrup, which is called molasses in some parts of this country.
- Mono and Diglycerides: A form of fat consisting of one or two glycerides. They are used as additives in baked products, beverages, ice cream, chewing gum, shortening, whipped toppings, margarine, and confections. Avoid.
- Polysorbates: Emulsifiers derived from sorbitol, a sugar alcohol.
- Psyllium: The common name used for several plants whose seeds are used commercially for the production of mucilage, a known dietary fiber. It is also used as a thickener in ice cream and other frozen desserts.
- Rennet: Although rennet is used mainly for the production of cheese, it does not contain dairy. It is an enzyme derived from the stomachs of calves, used in cheese production to coagulate animal milk into cheese. There are vegan, plant based "rennets" as well.
- Rice Malt: A sugar resulting from the malting process of rice.
- Rum: A distilled alcoholic beverage made from sugarcane by-products such as molasses and sugarcane juice by a process of fermentation and distillation.
- Saccharin: A synthetic artificial sweetener (a coal derivative or toluene) used in chewing gums, diet sodas, candies, cookies, medicines and tooth paste. It is a suspected (but not yet proven) carcinogen. Either way, I strongly suggest you and your family stay away from this artificial sweetener.
- Silicon Dioxide or Silica: Another word for sand, the mineral used in chips – computer chips that is, not corn or potato. In processed food, it is

used as a "flowing" agent in powdered foods, as well as in pharmaceutical drugs and supplements.

- Sodium Benzoate: The sodium salt of benzoic acid. It is used as a preservative in salad dressings, carbonated drinks, jams and fruit juices, pickles, and condiments. Avoid.
- Sodium Nitrate: Also known under its old name of saltpeter. It has antimicrobial properties when used as a preservative. Sodium nitrate is also used as an ingredient in fertilizers, pyrotechnics, smoke bombs, and as a rocket propellant, as well as in glass and pottery enamels. It is a suspected carcinogen. I'll let you draw your own conclusions. Avoid.
- Sodium Nitrite: Is used as a preservative and color fixating agent in meat and fish production. Why do you think your deli meat is so pink? Sodium nitrite is the culprit. It is also used as an antimicrobial agent to prevent growth of Clostridium botulinum, the bacterium responsible for botulism. Unfortunately, there is concern regarding the formation of carcinogenic nitrosamines in meats containing sodium nitrite when they are exposed to high temperatures. It can be neutralized with ascorbic acid. I personally would still avoid it.
- Sodium Sulphite: A soluble compound of sodium used as a preservative to prevent dried fruit from discoloring, and for preserving meats. Avoid.
- Sorbate: It is another name for Sorbic acid. See below.
- Sorbic Acid: It is a natural organic compound used as a food preservative in food and drinks to prevent the growth of mold, yeast and fungi.
- Sorbitol: A sugar alcohol used a sugar substitute in candies and gums. In large doses, it is also known as an effective laxative. Be careful with those candies.
- Natural Colors: They are a mostly plant-based, healthier alternatives to artificial colors, especially for highly sensitive children like autistic children. At this time, they are Caramel coloring (E150), made from caramelized sugar, used in classic cola products; Yellow from Turmeric (E100); Red-orange color from Annatto (E160b), from the seed of the Achiote and from Saffron (E160a); Red from the Cochineal (E120) insect, from Paprika (E160c) and Betanin extracted from beets; Green made from chlorella algae (E140) and Pandan Pandanus amaryllifolius; Blue from Elderberry juice and the Butterfly Clitoria ternatea.
- Stevia: A natural sweetener extract from the plant species *Stevia rebaudiana*, commonly known as Sweetleaf, sweet leaf, sugarleaf, or simply stevia,. It can be up to 300 times sweeter than white sugar. Some

people don't care for its bitter after taste, but it is a safer sugar-free alternative than saccharin, aspartame or Splenda.

- Sucralose: Better known as Splenda in this country. It is 600 times sweeter than white sugar, but it is a chlorinated synthetic sweetener and you know what I think about sweeteners created in a lab. I encourage you to find out more about the effect of Splenda on one's health. Avoid.
- Sucrose: The scientific name for white sugar or table sugar. It is extracted from cane or beets. Sugar is a major element in confectionery and in desserts.
- Sulfites: Compounds used in wine production to stop fermentation. They are also used as preservatives in dried fruits and dried potato products. Many gluten and casein intolerant people are allergic to sulfites.
- Tartaric Acid: A white crystalline organic acid. It occurs naturally in many plants, particularly grapes, bananas, and tamarinds, and is one of the main acids found in wine. It is added to other foods to give a sour taste, and is used as an antioxidant.
- Vanilla Extract: Pure vanilla extract is made by macerating or percolating vanilla beans in a solution of ethyl alcohol and water.
- Vanilla Flavoring: An artificial version of vanilla extract.
- Vanillin: Vanillin is chemically created in labs to mimic the taste of vanilla.
- Vinegar (all except malt): An acidic liquid produced from the fermentation of an alcohol by a bacterium to create acetic acid. The acetic acid concentration typically ranges from 4% to 8% by volume for table vinegar and up to 18% for pickling. Natural vinegars also contain small amounts of tartaric acid, citric acid, and other acids. Vinegar has been used since ancient times and is an important element in European, Asian, and other cuisines. Use naturally fermented vinegars. My favorite is organic apple cider vinegar, which offers a wide range of health benefits in addition to its wonderful flavor. Distilled vinegar is made from corn, not from wheat, rye or barley. Caution: The Alcohol, Tobacco and Firearms Division of the Internal Revenue Service says: "Presently, we authorize the manufacturer of vinegar from ethyl alcohol synthesized from natural gas or petroleum derivatives. It is our opinion that most of the distilled spirits used in the production of vinegar are derived from natural gas and petroleum..." Do you really want to drink petroleum-based vinegar? Natural is always best.
- Xanthan Gum: A polysaccharide used as a food additive. It is produced by fermentation of glucose or sucrose by the *Xanthomonas campestris* bacterium. After a fermentation period, the polysaccharide is precipitated from a growth medium with isopropyl alcohol, dried, and ground into a fine powder. In GF baking it is used as a replacement for

gluten to add to the dough's stickiness. It is also used as a thickener and emulsifier in salad dressings, sauces, and ice cream.

- Xylitol: An alcohol sugar used as a sugar-free substitute. As other sugar alcohols, if taken in large quantities, it can cause digestive problems like gas, bloating and diarrhea. Do not give foods containing xylitol to your pets, as it is extremely toxic to them.

- Yeast (all except Brewer's Yeast): The yeast called *Saccharomyces exiguus* is a wild yeast found on plants, fruits, and grains that is occasionally used for baking sourdough bread. It is perfectly safe. The yeast used in beer-making is (*Saccharomyces cerevisiae).* Yeast in itself is a fungus and does not contain gluten, but it could contain traces of gluten when it is derived from the beer-making process, or when it is grown on wheat or barley.

Foods and Additives Containing Gluten

- Brewer's Yeast: A by-product of grain (wheat and barley) beer processing.
- Gelatinized starch: Gelatinization is used in cooking to make roux sauce, pastry and custard; the word "starch" can mean gluten.
- Hydrolyzed Vegetable Protein (HVP): A source of amino acids derived from the processing of assorted vegetables, sometimes including wheat. It is used as cheap umami flavoring. Since it contains a large amount of glutamate, avoid it if you are allergic to MSG.
- Hydrolyzed Wheat Protein (HWP): Is a wheat-based source of amino acids. It is used as cheap umami flavoring. Since it contains a large amount of glutamate, avoid it if you are allergic to MSG.
- Malt (malt extract, malt flavoring, and malt vinegar): The malting process is the combination of the sprouting and drying of a cereal. Most of the malted grains are barley and wheat. They are found in malt beer, malt whisky, malted milkshakes, and malt vinegar, some confections and some baked goods.
- Maltose: A sugar made from malt.
- Sauces: May have wheat protein, hydrolyzed wheat starch or wheat flour unless specified otherwise.

Foods and Additives Containing Dairy and/or Casein.

- ✓ Caprylic Acid: An antibacterial preservative derived from animal milk.
- ✓ Casein: The dominant protein in milk and cheese.

✓ Hydrolyzed Whey Protein: A milk-based source of amino acids. It is used as cheap umami flavoring. Since it contains a large amount of glutamate, avoid it if you are allergic to MSG.

✓ Lactic Acid: Also called milk acid. It is commercially produced from whey, cornstarch, potatoes and molasses. It is found in acidified milk products such as sour milk, sour cream, buttermilk, yogurt, kefir and some cottage cheeses. If listed on a product as an ingredient, you must verify its source.

✓ Lactalbumin: The albumin contained in milk and obtained from whey.

✓ Lactose: Also known as milk sugar.

✓ Lactulose: A synthetic sugar used in the treatment of constipation. It is a disaccharide (double-sugar) formed from one molecule each of the simple sugars fructose and galactose, a milk sugar.

✓ Potassium Caseinate: Can be used in processing cheese.

✓ Sodium Caseinate: A form of salt coming from casein.

Use caution with the following additives. They may contain gluten or casein depending on how they were produced. Please check with the manufacturer.

▪ Baking powder: Usually contains corn or potato starch as inert filler. Buy only aluminum-free baking powder, as aluminum may have a negative influence on an autistic or ADD/ADHD child.

▪ Caramel Color: Depending on the manufacturer, it could be made from any sugar such as fructose (corn), sucrose (can or beet sugar), or dextrose (corn) and molasses (cane). But it can also be made from lactose (milk sugar) or maltose (malt sugar). So if you're not sure, check with the manufacturer.

▪ Dextrimaltose: A sugar derivative that may be made from barley malt.

▪ Dextrin: A sweetener usually made from corn or potato starch. It is used as a crispness enhancer in the food industry. If you're not sure of its provenance, check with the manufacturer.

▪ Extenders or Thickeners: The vast majority of them contain gluten unless specified otherwise on the label.

▪ Maltodextrin: Even though it has the word malt in it, in the U.S. it is made from corn. In Europe wheat or barley could be used, so be careful.

▪ Modified Food Starch (MFS): If made in the U. S. it is GF. It may not be when manufactured in foreign countries. Please check with the manufacturer. Same for "Modified Starch".

▪ MSG (see below for a whole section on it)

▪ Mustard Flour: Although the mustard seed does not contain gluten, some people have reported that some brands of mustard flours "extend" their product with wheat flour. Please read the labels or use fresh mustard in jars.

- Natural flavorings: Flavoring substances obtained from plant (may contain wheat) or animal raw materials, by physical, microbiological or enzymatic processes.
- Pregelatinized Sodium Starch Slycolate: Source may be from any starch source. Verify.
- Rice Syrup or Brown Rice Syrup: A liquid sweetener derived by culturing cooked rice with enzymes. Although it does not contain gluten, it is sometimes processed using dried barley sprouts. Check with the manufacturer.
- Seasonings: Blends of spices and flavors. Most of them contain wheat as a filler. Organic spice blends are more pure. Please check the label or with the manufacturer.
- Sodium lactylate: An organic compound used as a food additive. It is produced from lactic acid. It is used as an emulsifier in processed foods. It may or may not contain casein.
- Soy Sauce: The vast majority of soy sauce brands use wheat in their fabrication. As far as I know, the only brand that is certified GF is San-J Organic Tamari sauce.
- Starch or Starch Derivatives: In food products, it usually refers to cornstarch unless specified otherwise. Starch source is usually corn or potato, but other gluten starches may be used. The safe starches for celiac patients used in medications are corn, rice, potato and tapioca.
- Textured or Texturized Vegetable Protein (TVP): A meat alternative made from defatted soy flour. It is mostly made from soy, but it could also be made from cotton seeds, wheat or oats. Please check with the manufacturer.
- Vodka: Vodka may be distilled from any starch or sugar-rich plant matter; most vodka today is produced from grains such as sorghum, corn, rye or wheat. Among grain vodkas, rye and wheat vodkas are generally considered superior. Some vodka is made from potatoes, molasses, soybeans, grapes, rice, sugar beets and even byproducts of oil refining or wood pulp processing. So, if you really are into vodka, please check the label or with the manufacturer for the source of their vodka. Some people claim that the distillation process eliminates all traces of gluten, but others disagree.
- Wheat Starch: A product made by removing the proteins from wheat flour. Until recently, it was thought that wheat starch was safe for celiac disease sufferers, but recent research has proven otherwise. If it is a common wheat starch labeled on a food product, it is not safe for you.

The only type that would be safe is the pharmaceutically pure wheat starch. That type is very expensive to produce, and is reserved for high-end pharmaceutical drugs, supplements and cosmetics.

- Whey (Whey Protein concentrate; Whey Sodium Caseinate): Whey is a co-product of cheese production. It is one of the components which separate from milk after curdling when rennet or an edible acidic substance is added. It is also an additive in many processed foods including breads, crackers and commercial pastries. There is heated debate in the CF community whether whey can be eaten on a CF diet. If you look at the chemical components of whey, it does not contain casein.
- Wine: Some non-organic wines are aged in oak barrels put together with a gluten-containing glue. Wine also contains sulfites, which many gluten and dairy-allergic people are allergic to as well.
- White Vinegar or White Grain Vinegar: Any type of vinegar may be distilled to produce a colorless solution of about 5% to 8% acetic acid. This can also be called distilled spirit, virgin vinegar, or white vinegar, and is used for medicinal, laboratory and cleaning purposes, as well as in cooking, baking, meat preserving, and pickling. The most common starting material is often malt vinegar.
- Whole grain or Grain Flour: Most likely a gluten grain. Verify.

Monosodium Glutamate (MSG)

The sodium of a non-essential amino acid. It may contain wheat protein when it is produced in foreign countries. Although MSG does not contain casein, it is a known allergen. It is used as a flavor enhancer, especially when one wants to achieve the famous umami flavor profile. It originally came from the salty crystal left on a seaweed after drying. A Japanese scientist, Kikunae Ikeda found a way to isolate it and make it commercially available to all Asian food lovers. It was once made from fermented wheat, but it is now produced in industrial labs from bacterial fermentation. Although once associated with Chinese restaurants, MSG is now used by most fast food chains and in many processed foods. If you have an autistic or ADD/ADHD child, I highly recommend you avoid all foods with MSG, as it is known to adversely affect their brain function through excitotoxicity.

o Fast food establishments: Most should be avoided - the worst offender by far is KFC. Other offenders are McDonald's, Burger King, Chick-fil-A, Taco Bell and many more. Make sure to go to their website ingredient listings.

The offending foods are chicken and sausage products, ranch dressing, parmesan, gravy and dipping sauces and any coated with any kind of seasoning other than sea salt (I would even avoid "plain" salt – use only sea salt). Any type of salted snack chips offered with your "meal" are suspect as well, especially Doritos, Cheetos and any chip with seasonings or cheese powder. Avoid all soft drinks and tap water. Drink bottled water only.

If you have to eat at a fast food establishment, the best advice I can offer you is to avoid all chicken products, all sausage products, all products covered with parmesan, all Ranch and Caesar dressings (stay with Italian or oil and vinegar), seasoned croutons, gravy and dipping sauces, and soups.

o Regular and chain restaurants: What you may not know is that ALL chain restaurants and most commercial restaurants buy the vast majority of their products from nationwide food suppliers like Sysco, US Foods and others. Since wholesale producers do not have to abide to the same stringent labeling requirements, they get away with adding suspect additives and preservatives to their products. Even if you would demand to look at their boxes, you would have a hard time finding any nutrition information. It reminds me of a recent consulting experience I had; even though the restaurant claimed in big red letters on their menu "no MSG added", when I did a little snooping in their stock room, I found a lot of ingredients containing just that, MSG. So the lesson is, don't believe everything you read. If you are going out to eat, unless you know for a fact that the food is cooked in that kitchen and you can see it done, at the very least avoid anything with parmesan (1% MSG by weight) on it, commercial soups, any coated or breaded food, Ranch and Caesar salad dressings, fish sauce, soy sauce and anything pre-frozen or canned. I know it sounds harsh, but if you care about your own health and that of your family, buyer beware! My solution: eat only at locally-owned restaurants where you know and trust the owner or the chef to prepare fresh from scratch food, or stay home.

o At the Deli: Avoid any Boar's Head deli meats. They use MSG in their "broth". Same thing for most deli meats unless certified otherwise. As in fast foods, avoid coated and seasoned chips.

o Visiting Grandma or friends: When visiting your grandma or friends, avoid anything with Accent in it. No bouillon cubes, soup bases or meat extracts unless certified MSG-free. No seasonings or spice blends such a Goya Sazon, Lawry's and other brands. Avoid any canned or frozen gravies. Skip the hot dogs and cold cuts. Anything with broth, such as canned tuna, sardines, or other canned fish. Also "self-basting" chicken and turkeys injected with a "broth". Nothing with hydrolyzed or autolyzed flavoring. No onion or mushroom soup mixes used in your favorite aunt's dip. No canned soup with or without "umami" like Campbell's or Progresso – buy organic soups. No premade casseroles. Sorry Bill Cosby, no Jell-o pudding or pudding pops either. No gelatin mold desserts. Avoid drinks or anything diet or low-sugar sweetened with aspartame under the name NutraSweet and other artificial sweeteners. The solution: provide them with a list of no-no foods and ingredients; eat safe food before you go; or bring your own food. You know it's safe, you prepared it yourself. Stick to what you know is safe for you and your family.

o   <u>At the grocery store</u>: Some food manufacturers are hiding MSG so you don't know it is there. In recent years, some food manufacturers have managed to get what they call a "clean label" by using soy sauce and other processed flavor enhancers that *already contain* MSG in the form of glutamic acid. They can then claim "no added MSG", even though the product may be full of glutamate.

The following companies are suspected of including hidden MSG in their food because they refuse to label their product clearly. Until they come clean do not buy any products from the following companies: Ajinomoto Food Ingredients, Campbell, Dairy Management Inc, Frito-Lay, Kraft, Nestle, Senomyx, The Mushroom Council, and Unilever. Be a food detective for your own sake.

For many more detailed information on where MSG is hidden, check the following web sites: **www.msgtruth.org** and **www.msgmyth.com**.

The following foods contain either MSG or its business end - the "free" amino acid glutamate - in amounts large enough to cause reactions if you are hypersensitive to it:

- Accent -this is nearly pure MSG
- Autolyzed yeast (found in many processed American foods, read labels)
- Beet juice - it is used as a coloring, but MSG is manufactured from beets and the extract may contain free glutamic acid - Yo Baby - organic baby

yogurt has just changed their formula to include beet extract
- Boar's Head cold cuts and most of their hotdogs
- Body builder drink powders containing protein
- Bouillon - any kind
- Braggs Liquid Aminos - sold at Whole Foods
- Campbell's soups - all of them
- Canned, food-service restaurant gravy
- Carrageenan
- Cosmetics and shampoos - some now contain glutamic acid
- Cup-a-soup or Cup-o-Noodles
- Doritos
- Dough conditioners
- Dry milk and whey powder
- Fish extract - made from decomposed fish protein – often used in Japanese sushi dishes - very high in free glutamate. The raw fish in sushi counteracts the glutamate to some degree.
- Flavored ramen noodles
- Gelatin
- Glutamic acid
- Gravy Master
- Hamburger Helper Microwave Singles (targeted towards children)
- Hodgson Mill Kentucky Kernel Seasoned Flour
- Hydrolyzed vegetable protein (found in many processed American foods like canned tuna and even hot dogs)
- Hydrolyzed plant protein (found in many processed American foods like canned tuna and even hot dogs)
- Instant soup mixes
- Kombu extract
- Kraft products nearly all contain some free glutamate
- Lipton Noodles and Sauce and Lipton Instant soup mix
- Malted barley
- Malted barley flour - found in many supermarket breads and all-purpose flours including: King Arthur, Heckers, and Gold Medal flour
- Marmite
- Medications in gel caps - contain free glutamic acid in the gelatin
- Most salty, powdered dry food mixes - read labels
- Mushrooms - naturally high in free glutamate
- Natural flavors - may contain up to 20% MSG
- Parmesan cheese - naturally high in free glutamate
- Potato chips - flavored
- Pringles (the flavored varieties)

- Progresso Soups - all of them
- Planters salted nuts - most of them
- Processed cheese spreads
- Restaurant soups made from food service soup base or with added MSG
- Salad dressings - many
- Sausages - most supermarkets add MSG to theirs
- Sodium caseinate
- Soy protein isolate
- Soy sauce: Fast food menu items that contain soy sauce, "natural flavors", autolyzed yeast or hydrolyzed protein, which can contain up to 20% free glutamic acid - the active part of MSG.
- Taco Bell - seasoned meat - contains autolyzed yeast - which contains free glutamate
- Tangle extract (seaweed extract) - found in sushi rolls (even at Whole Foods). Seaweed is what MSG was first isolated from. The raw fish in sushi counteracts the glutamate to some degree.
- Supermarket poultry or turkeys that are injected or "self-basting"
- Textured protein
- Tomatoes (over-ripe) - naturally high in free glutamate
- Unilever or Knorr products - often used in homemade Veggie dips.
- Yeast Food, Yeast Nutrients and Yeast extract
- Worcestershire sauce

Appendix D: Gluten-Free, Dairy-Free Shopping List

I created this list while walking through all the aisles, from produce to check out, at the Austin Central Market 40th Street store. It should be of some use to you no matter where you shop, whether it is at a grocery store, a health food store, or on the Internet. I do understand that not all people are trained chefs as I am, so I created this list to help you find convenient yet healthy products that can make your life easier. It may also give you some ideas for lunch and dinner when you do not have the time to prepare a whole meal. None of us have the time or the inclination to cook fresh food every day of the year. I hope this list will help you simplify your life.

As much as possible, shop for your fresh produce, meat and artisan products at your local farmer's market. Get to know your providers. Go visit their farm – it's a fun trip for your kids too. The more you know about the food you eat, the more confident you will feel in the quality of your food. I strongly believe your health depends on it.

Please keep in mind that this list is provided as a guide only. As hard as I have tried to be accurate and exhaustive, please read the labels **AGAIN** or check the manufacturer's web site if you have doubts. As you know, new products constantly appear on the shelves and other products disappear. Do as I do--keep a sharp eye on all product changes. You are your own best health detective.

Bonne chance and Bon Appétit!

Chef Alain Braux

PRODUCE DEPARTMENT

My General Produce Shopping Advice

When buying produce, try to buy the freshest picked, with the least impact on the environment. If you can, shop locally and in season. If you have access to it, buy from your local farmer's market, farmer's co-op, or directly from the farm. Many farmers offer weekly or monthly baskets where you receive an assortment of vegetables and fruits in season for a certain price. Eating food harvested in season from the area in which you live is the best way to ensure that your food is at the peak of its freshness. It also supports your local economy and avoids damaging the environment with long-range shipping. Typically, local farmers are too small to be able to afford to go through the "Certified Organic" certification process. To make sure they're not unloading produce from somewhere else in their own crates, talk to them at the market. Ask to visit their farm, take a tour and ask a lot of questions. Local farmers are proud of the products they sell, and will be happy to show you around their farm. In Austin, our best-known local farm is Boggy Creek Farm, but there are plenty of other high quality farms nearby. Use Google to find local farmers markets or farmers advertising their fresh wares.

When you shop at the grocery store, buy produce from farmers located in your state. It's not quite as good, but the next best solution. If possible, buy organic products.

Look for organic produce shipped from other states. The closer to your state, the better. Every mile counts.

Another good solution is to buy flash-frozen organic vegetables. They are frozen as soon as they are picked and keep most of their nutrients in the process. Only defrost what you will use. To prevent freezer burn, use containers with tight-fitting lids to store the unused portion. Do not refreeze defrosted vegetables.

If none of the above suggestions are possible for you, buy produce only in season. Wash it carefully in cold water with a few drops of organic soap or a special produce-washing solution like grape seed extract.

If possible, avoid buying from countries that may not have the same health and environmental laws we have in the United States. Their laws may be more relaxed than ours and your produce may be covered with pesticides that are banned here.

- Balsamic Vinaigrette
- Cole Slaw Dressing

BULK FOOD SECTION

Bulk Nuts and Seeds

Nuts

Assorted Bulk Nuts: Almonds, Walnuts, Brazil Nuts, Hazelnuts (Filberts), Pecans, Peanuts (if you're not allergic), and Raw Pistachio Kernels. I recommend raw, unroasted nuts, as the roasting process damages the healthy oils contained in them. If you want roasted nuts, roast your own, or buy only the dry-roasted variety. Do not buy sugar or honey-coated nuts.

They compound the bad: they are oil-roasted and coated with additional sweeteners.

Nut Butters

Assorted Nut Butters: Almond, Cashew, Hazelnut, and Peanut. A good source of protein to spread on a GF cracker, a vegetable chip or corn chip as a healthy snack. Some stores will even provide you with a grinder to make your own freshly-made nut butter.

Seeds

- Pumpkin, sesame and sunflower seeds (raw, hulled)
- Raw Pistachio Kernels

Dried Fruits

If at all possible, avoid ones that contain sulphur dioxide. Also, be aware that some dried fruits are coated with an additional layer of fruit juice to make them sweeter. If you are trying to control your sugar intake, read the labels and avoid these. Some dried fruits may be rolled in oat flour; read the bin label to avoid these, as oat flour often contains residual gluten.

Use: Zante Currants, Pitted Prunes, Medjool Dates, Monukka Raisins, Chilean Flame Raisins, Organic Seedless Raisins, Diced Pineapple, Organic Unsulphured Apricots, Dried Blueberries, Tropical Papaya Spears, Dried Cranberries, Tart Cherries, Calimura Dried Figs, and Organic Dried Mission Figs. My suggestion: Pitless dates are a very good natural sweet snack with a nut: almond, walnut or pecan.

Bulk Soup Mixes

Assorted Bulk Soup Mixes: black bean, split pea, curry lentil, instant refried beans, vegetarian chili mix. Easy to use for a quick lunch or dinner. They contain a good amount of complex carbohydrates and fibers. Buy organic if possible. Buying in bulk prevents you from paying for extra packaging.

FRESH FISH AND SHELLFISH COUNTER

Fresh fish is a very good source of protein and brain-helpful omega-3 fatty acids. Avoid large fish on the top of the food chain since they most likely contain an unhealthy amount of mercury. If you can afford it, go for line caught wild fish and shellfish. Ideally, I suggest you eat at least two-four ounce servings of fish/shellfish per week. Check out the lists below to learn what fish is safe and not safe to eat according to its provenance.

Wild Fish and Shellfish Safe to Eat

King salmon; Sockeye salmon; Coho salmon; canned wild pink salmon; Pacific flounder; Atlantic flounder in summer; Pacific sole; light canned tuna; Canned sardines; anchovies; canned mackerel (except king mackerel); squid or calamari; domestic shrimp; scallops (except from U.S. mid-Atlantic) and oysters.

Farm-Raised Fish and Shellfish Safe to Eat

Striped bass; Rainbow trout; Char (small salmon); shrimp (domestic); catfish (domestic); crayfish (domestic); sturgeon; tilapia; scallops; oysters; caviar (sturgeon); clams and mussels.

Fish and Shellfish OK to Eat Once a Week

Canned white tuna; Mahi-Mahi; Atlantic cod; Pacific cod; haddock; herring; Dungeness crab; spiny and rock lobsters; white fish and Alaskan King crab.

Fish and Shellfish OK to Eat Once a Month

Pacific halibut; Atlantic halibut; wild sea bass; wild grouper; line caught albacore/yellowfin tuna; bluefish; Pollack and Maine lobster.

Avoid the Following Fish – They Are Not Safe to Eat

Domestic swordfish; tilefish; marlin; shark; bluefin tuna; King, Ono and Wahoo mackerel.

Farm Raised Fish or Shellfish NOT recommended (unless you know the source personally)

- Salmon: they have been found to contain PCs and artificial coloring; farmed salmon are sold under the name Atlantic and Norwegian salmon.
- Imported shrimp: they are usually loaded with antibiotics and artificial preservatives.
- Imported scallops: artificial preservatives are used.

Wild Fish and Shellfish to Avoid Because They Are Either Overfished or Not Sustainable

Chilean Sea Bass and Orange Roughy (not sustainable); Pacific Snapper, Pacific Rock Cod, Rock Fish, Red Snapper (not sustainable); Wild Monkfish (overfished); Wild Catfish (overfished); Wild King Crab (overfished); Wild Caviar (overfished); Wild Atlantic Flounder (overfished); Wild Sturgeon (overfished).

FRESH MEAT COUNTER

These are my recommendations regarding assorted meats to be found at your local grocery store, meat market or farmers market. I recommend small portions of quality meats, as they are a great source of beneficial proteins, vitamins, minerals and omega-3 fatty acids – all nutrients necessary for good health. The important word here is "moderation". I suggest three to four meals a week at four ounces per serving. The rest of the meals should be fish/shellfish and bean and vegetable sources of protein.

Beef

Buy grass-fed, locally-raised or organic beef. Grass-fed beef contains a good amount of healthy fats, such as omega-3 fatty acids. Feedlot steers, in contrast, are fed corn and grains, giving their meat an excess of unhealthy omega-6 fatty acids. Additionally, feedlot steers are fed bovine growth hormones, antibiotics, and genetically engineered grains that have been doused with pesticides, all of which will disrupt you digestion and immune system.

Bison

Bison is grown in a grass-fed environment and allowed to roam freely and without stress until they are mature enough to be butchered humanely. There are more and more sources of this healthy meat available. Check your local farmer's market, ask around or check on the internet. You may even have it shipped to you.

Venison

In Texas and many other states, you can kill your own wild meat. Since deer feed only on what nature is offering, venison meat is healthier than any farm-raised meat.

Poultry – Chicken and Turkey and More

Buy free range, locally-raised chicken and turkey. You will get more usable meat per pound, and it is much tastier. You can also buy organic or "natural"; but be aware, the "natural" label is not particularly meaningful.

Eggs

I much prefer fresh eggs from my local farm. They taste so much better and make wonderfully yellow omelets; cakes made with them rise higher and all around, they are better for you. If they are grass-raised, they will also contain that good fat I already talked about – omega-3 fatty acids. Besides, eggs still are the cheapest source of complete proteins around. I eat them at least twice a week, sometimes more. If you live too far from a farm or farmers' market, choose organic eggs. What I talked about in the meat section goes the same for industrial chicken farms and egg farms.

Deli Department

Eat only certified GF (gluten-free) cold cuts. Ask your friendly deli person for the ingredient list for any sandwich meat, and avoid anything containing dairy, nitrates and nitrites. I personally love air-dried imported hams from France, Italy or Spain.

PACKAGED FOODS

Packaged Seeds, Grains, Flours and Egg Replacers

GF Flours

- Ancient Harvest Organic Quinoa Flour (wheat and gluten-free); Quinoa Flakes and Quinoa Grains.
- Arrowhead Mills: Organic Buckwheat Flour. Organic Millet Flour. Organic Brown Rice Flour. Organic White Rice Flour. Organic Blue Corn Meal.
- Arzu (high-protein grain mix. gluten-free): Original; Southwest; Chai.
- Authentic: Superfine White Rice Flour, Brown Rice Flour. Their flours are more finely milled than other brands, and are better suited for baked products. If you cannot find them at your grocery store, go to: http://authenticfoods.com/products/item/35/Superfine-Brown-Rice-Flour.
- Bob's Red Mill (gluten and dairy-free): Corn Grits; Cornmeal; Corn Flour; Brown Rice Flour; Old Fashioned Rolled Oats; Oat Flour; Steel Cut

Oats; Sweet White Sorghum Flour; Whole Grain Quinoa; Organic Coconut Flour; Whole Grain Corn; Corn Grits also known as Polenta; Arrowroot Starch; Whole Grain Sweet White Sorghum Flour; Tapioca Flour; Teff flour; Garbanzo Bean Flour; Soy Flour;

- Ener-G: Pure Potato Starch Flour; Xanthan Gum; Potato Flour; Sweet Rice Flour: Tapioca Flour.
- Salba Whole Grain and Premium Ground White Chia Seeds. (In my opinion, these seeds are overpriced. I get my chia seeds (a great vegetable source of omega-3 fatty acids by the way) from **www.NutsOnline.com**. Great product assortment, great prices and great service.

Soy Powder

- Fearn: Soya Powder

Egg Replacer

Good for people with egg allergies. You can still bake with the following substitutes.

- EnerG Egg Replacer (gluten free, wheat free) made of potato starch, tapioca flour, leavening (calcium lactate, calcium carbonate, citric acid), cellulose gum, carbohydrate gum.

Note: calcium lactate is not derived from dairy and does not contain lactose.

Gluten-Free Baking Mixes

GF All Purpose and Bread Mixes

- Arrowhead (all wheat and gluten-free): 73% Organic Gluten Free All Purpose Baking Mix; Perfect Flour Blend (all purpose).
- Bob's Red Mill (all gluten and dairy-free): Cornbread Mix; All Purpose Baking Flour Mix; Homemade Wonderful Bread Mix; Hearty Whole Grain Bread Mix; Biscuit and Baking Mix; Pizza Crust Mix.
- Chebe Gluten Free Mixes (all gluten-free, yeast-free, dairy-free): Cinnamon Roll-Up Mix; Pizza Crust Mix; All Purpose Bread Mix; Original Bread Mix; Bread Sticks Mix; Foccacia Flatbread Mix.
- Namaste Foods Gluten Free Mixes (wheat and gluten-free, soy, corn, potato, peanuts, tree nuts, dairy and casein-free): Bread Mix.

GF Bread Crumbs

- Hol Grain: GF, wheat-free Brown Rice Bread Crumbs.
- Southern Homestyle: GF Tortilla Crumbs; GF Corn Flakes Crumbs.

Other Assorted GF Mixes

- Orgran (gluten-free, wheat-free, dairy-free, egg-free, yeast-free, soy-free, nut-free and vegan): Gravy Mix; Gluten Substitute; No Egg Natural Egg Replacer; Falafel Mix.

GF Pancake Mixes

- Arrowhead Mills Organic Gluten Free Pancake and Baking mix (organic, gluten-free, contains dairy).
- Bob's Red Mill: Pancake Mix.
- Cherrybrook Kitchen Gluten Free Dreams (gluten-free, dairy-free, peanut-free, egg-free, nut-free): Pancake and Waffle Mix; Chocolate Chip Cookie Mix; Sugar Cookie Mix; Fudge Brownie Mix; Chocolate Cake Mix.
- Namaste: Waffle and Pancake Mix.
- Orgran (gluten-free, wheat-free, dairy-free, egg-free, yeast-free, soy-free, nut-free and vegan, no added cane sugar): Apple and Cinnamon Pancake Mix; Buckwheat Pancake Mix.
- Gluten-Free Cake and Pastries Mixes
- Arrowhead (all wheat and gluten-free): Organic Gluten Free Vanilla Cake Mix; Bake with Me Gluten Free Chocolate and Vanilla Cupcake Mix; Gluten Free Chocolate Chip Cookie Mix; Arrowhead Gluten Free Brownie Mix.
- Bob's Red Mill (all gluten and dairy-free): Vanilla Cake Mix; Cinnamon Raisin Bread Mix; Chocolate Chip Cookie Mix; Chocolate Cake Mix; Shortbread Cookie Mix; Mighty Tasty Hot Cereal Mix.
- Gluten Free Pantry Mixes (wheat and gluten-free): Quick Mix; Chocolate Chip and Cake Mix; Old Fashioned Cake and Cookie Mix; French Bread and Pizza Mix; Muffin and Scone Mix; Favorite Sandwich Bread Mix; Chocolate Truffle Brownie; Perfect Pie Crust Mix; Brown Rice Pancake and Waffle Mix.
- Kinnikinnick Foods Mixes (wheat and gluten-free): Pancake and Waffle Mix; Bread and Bun Mix; Muffin Mix; White Cake Mix.
- Namaste Foods Gluten Free Mixes (wheat and gluten-free, soy, corn, potato, peanuts, tree nuts, dairy and casein-free): Blondie Mix; Cookie Mix; Biscuits, Pie Crust and More; Spice Cake Mix; Muffin Mix; Brownie Mix.

- Pamela Products Mixes (wheat and gluten-free): Baking and Pancakes Mix; Gluten Free Bread Mix; Classic Vanilla Cake Mix; Chocolate Cake Mix.

GFCF Cake Frosting

- Cherrybrook Kitchen Frosting Mix (gluten, dairy, egg, nut-free): Vanilla; Chocolate.
- Pamela's Frosting Mixes (wheat and gluten-free): Vanilla Frosting Mix (same comment as above).

Please note: I mention these for your convenience, but this is a rip-off. $3.39 for 9.4oz of confectionary or powdered sugar, a little corn starch and vanilla flavor or cocoa powder. Just buy 1 pound of powdered sugar and add your own vanilla or cocoa. It will cost you less than a dollar.

Gluten-Free Cookies (all wheat and gluten-free, dairy-free)

For people with no food allergies: Still pay attention to the amount of sugar. Make sure they do not contain high fructose corn syrup or even fructose. Also, stay away from any cookies that use any form of hydrogenated fat. If you have time, you're better off making your own at home.

- Aunt Gussie's Gluten Free Kitchen (wheat and gluten-free, dairy-free, all natural): Chocolate Spritz; Chocolate Chip Almond; Sugar-free Vanilla Spritz.
- Cherrybrook Kitchen Gluten Free Dreams (peanut-free, dairy-free, egg-free, nut-free, wheat and gluten-free): Mini Chocolate Chip Cookies.
- Enjoy Life Soft Baked Cookies (gluten-free, no wheat, no dairy, no peanuts, no tree nuts, no eggs, no fish or shellfish): Chocolate Chip; Snickerdoodle.
- Enjoy Life Soft Baked Cookies (wheat and gluten-free, nut-free, dairy-free, peanut and tree nuts-free, egg-free, soy-free, fish and shellfish-free): Lively Lemon, Snickerdoodle, Gingerbread Spice, Double Chocolate Brownie.
- Gluten Free Cafe (gluten-free): Lemon Sesame Bar.
- Glutino Gluten Free Wafer Cookies (wheat and gluten-free): Vanilla; Strawberry; Chocolate; Lemon.
- Glutino Gluten Free Candy Bar (wheat and gluten-free): Chocolate Peanut Butter (contains dairy); Milk Chocolate (contains dairy); Dark Chocolate (no dairy).

- Ian's Cookie Buttons (wheat and gluten-free): Chocolate Chip; Crunchy Cinnamon.
- JK Gourmet Biscotti: Dried Peach Apricot; Lemon Poppyseed.
- Kinnikinnick Cookies (gluten-free, dairy-free, nut-free): Montana's Chocolate Chip.
- Kinnikinnick Kritters Animal Cookies (wheat and gluten-free, dairy-free, nut-free).
- Kinnikinnick S'moreables Graham Style Crackers (wheat and gluten-free, dairy-free, nut-free)
- KinniToos Sandwich Cremes Cookies (gluten-free, dairy-free, nut-free): Chocolate Sandwich; Vanilla Sandwich.
- Mary's Gone Crackers Love Cookies (organic, wheat and gluten-free): Ginger Snaps;
- Chocolate Chips; N'Oatmeal Raisin (without oats).
- Mi-Del Gluten Free Cookies: Cinnamon Snaps; Pecan Cookies; Arrowroot Cookies; Ginger Snaps.
  - Nana's Cookie Bars (no eggs, no dairy, no gluten, no refined sugar): Nana Banana; Berry Vanilla; Chocolate Munch.
- Nana's Cookies (no eggs, no dairy, no gluten, no refined sugar): Lemon; Chocolate Crunch; Ginger; Chocolate; Chocolate Chip; Oatmeal Raisin.
- Nana's Cookie Bites (wheat and gluten-free, no refined sugars, no transfats, no GMO, no cholesterol, no eggs, no casein, no cane or beet products): Ginger Spice; Fudge.
- Orgran Outback Animals (wheat and gluten-free, dairy-free, egg-free, yeast-free, GMO-free, soy-free, nut-free, vegan): Chocolate and Vanilla Cookies.
- Pamela's Old Fashion Cookies (wheat and gluten-free, dairy-free): Raisin Walnut; Spicy Ginger; Chocolate Chip.
- Pamela's Products Simplebites (all natural, wheat and gluten-free, no transfats): Mini Chocolate Chip; Mini Ginger Snapz; Mini Extreme Chocolate.
- Tree Huggin Treats (gluten-free, dairy-free, non GMO, all natural, no preservatives): Crispy Cat Toasted Almond; Mint Coconut.
- WOW Baking Company: Snickerdoodle; Oregon Oatmeal.- Jennies Coconut Macaroons (casein, gluten and peanut-free): Classic; Chocolate; Almond Flavored. Caution: These cookies are addictive. My current favorites.

GF Breads

- <u>EnerG</u> Tapioca Loaf; Light Tapioca Loaf; White Rice Yeast-Free Loaf; Brown Rice Yeast-Free Loaf; White Rice Loaf; Brown Rice Loaf; High Fiber Loaf; Corn Loaf.

SWEET SNACKS AND BARS

Gluten-Free/Casein-Free Healthy Snack Bars

<u>Please note</u>: I do not recommend you use bars as a substitute for real food. If you need sugar control, I recommend you pick the ones with low sugar and high protein (nuts) content. The protein content will help regulate the sugar levels in your blood.

GF Sweet Bars (all wheat and gluten-free, dairy-free)

- <u>Bobo's</u> Oat Bars (GF, non-GMO, 100% vegan, wheat-free): Cranberry, Coconut, Banana Chocolate, Strawberry, Apricot, Original.
- <u>Enjoy Life</u> Chewy Bars (gluten and dairy-free): Very Berry; Caramel Apple; Cocoa Loco; Sunbutter Crunch (no nuts).
- <u>Glutino</u> Organic Bars (gluten-free, cholesterol-free, low fat, low sodium): Chocolate and Peanuts; Wildberry; Chocolate and Banana; Apple; Chocolate, Blueberry.

GFCF, no grains, no rice, no sugar added

- <u>Baraka Bar</u>: Cocoa Almond; Spirulina Goji Berry; Goldenberry Pecan. My current Austin-made favorite. Raw, gluten-free, dairy-free and vegan.
- <u>Bio Genesis Ultra-Low Carb</u> (DF): Sweetened with Xylitol. Crispy; Chocolate Coconut; Peanut Butter Crunch. Total net carbs per bar: 4 g.
- <u>100% Organic Go Raw Bars</u>: Spirulina Energy Bar (total carbs 24 g); Live Pumpkin Bar (total carbs 22 g); Banana "Bread" Flax Bar (total carbs 15 g); Real Live Flax Bar (total carbs 31 g).
- <u>Kind Fruit and Nut Bars:</u> I love these for travel. Fruit and Nut Delight (total carbs 16 g); Macadamia and Apricot (total carbs 15 g); Almond and Coconut (total carbs 14 g); Nut Delight; Almond and Apricot; Macadamia and Apricot; Walnut and Date.
- <u>Kind Plus</u>: With additional nutritional elements added (antioxidants, calcium, protein, omega 3's): Cranberry and Almond; Almond and Cashew; Mango Macadamia; Almond, Walnut and Macadamia; Passion Fruit Macadamia; Strawberry Nut Delight.

- Larabar Organic Bars. Caution: Although these bars do not have added sugar, they are still pretty sweet. Be careful if your children tend to be affected by eating high amounts of sugar.
- Jocalat Organic Bars: Chocolate; Chocolate Hazelnut; German Chocolate Cake; Chocolate Coffee; Chocolate Mint; Chocolate Cherry.
- Larabar Bars sweetened with dates only: Peanut Butter Chocolate Chip; Chocolate Chip Cookie Dough; Chocolate Chip Brownie; Carrot Cake; Tropical Fruit Tart; Peanut Butter and Jelly; Peanut Butter Cookie; Cinnamon Roll; Cocoa Mole; Cherry Pie; Chocolate Coconut; Ginger Snap; Banana Bread; Cashew Cookie; Pecan Pie; Lemon Bar; Key Lime Pie; Coconut Cream Pie.
- Metagenics Ultra Meal Bars. Medical food bar sweetened with liquid fructose. Contains an average of 13 g sugar per bar: Chocolate Fudge; Chocolate Banana; Lemon Zinger; Chocolate Raspberry; Apple Cinnamon.
- Organic Food Bar sweetened with dates and agave nectar. Vegan Bar; Active Greens; Active Greens Chocolate; Cranberry; Belgium Chocolate Chip.
- Raw Organic Food Bars with fruit-based date sugar and agave nectar: Cinnamon Raisin; Chocolate Coconut.

Gluten-Free Breakfast Cereals

Honestly, I'm not a big fan of packaged breakfast cereals. They are mostly a refined product and contain a high amount of sugar which may be good for a quick burst of energy, but will spike your blood sugar and, if repeated daily, eventually will lead to hypoglycemia. But for a working mom, they are convenient. If you must, buy the ones with the least amount of sugar. Whether refined or not, sugar is sugar, no matter how it is labeled. If you have a little time, try to prepare a good hot cooked cereal that will provide more fiber and a low amount of sugar.

Instant Oatmeal and Hot Cereals

If you are highly sensitive to gluten, make sure to buy only certified GF oats.

- Arrowhead Organic: Yellow Corn Grits (gluten-free), Instant Oatmeal (wheat-free but not certified GF), Wheat Free 7 Grain Cereal (wheat-free but may contain gluten). Oat Bran (wheat-free but not certified GF). Rice & Shine (gluten-free), Steel Cut Oats (wheat-free but not certified GF). Rolled Oat Flakes (wheat-free but not certified GF).). Old Fashioned Oatmeal (wheat-free but not certified GF).).

- GlutenFreeda Instant Oatmeal (certified gluten-free oats, wheat-free): Apple Cinnamon with Flax; Maple Raisin with Flax; Banana Maple with Flax.
- Holly Au Natural (wheat and gluten-free): Hot Cereal; Porridge.
- Nature's Path Organic (wheat-free but not certified GF): Hot Oatmeal Maple Nut, Original, Apple Cinnamon.

GF Breakfast Cereals (all wheat, gluten-free and dairy-free)

- Arrowhead Mills: Organic Amaranth Flakes; Organic Maple Buckwheat Flakes; Puffed Corn; Puffed Rice; Puffed Millet.
- Barbara's Bakery Puffins: Original; Cinnamon; Honey Rice; Peanut Butter.
- Blue Roo: Gourmet Vita-Pro Cereal.
- CM Organics: Frosted Corn Flakes (gluten-free), Toasted Oats O's (may contain gluten).
- Enjoy Life Granola (wheat, dairy, peanuts, tree nuts, egg, soy, fish and shellfish-free): Very Berry Crunch; Cinnamon Crunch; Cranapple Crunch.
- Enjoy Life Perky's (wheat, dairy, peanuts, tree nuts, egg, soy, fish, shellfish-free): Crunchy Flax; Crunchy Rice.
- Erewon 100% organic Whole Grain Cereal (gluten-free): Cocoa Crispy Brown Rice; Crispy Brown Rice with Mixed Berries; Rice Twice' Crispy Brown Rice No Salt Added.
- EnviroKids Organic Cereal (gluten-free, low sodium, no preservatives, no additives): Koala Crisp; Organic Gorilla Munch; Organic Amazon Frosted Flakes. Organic Peanut Butter Panda Puffs;
- Glutino Cereal (wheat and gluten-free, no saturated fat, cholesterol-free): Honey Nut; Apple Cinnamon.
- Healthy Valley: Rice Crunch-Ems (gluten-free), Oat Bran O's, Oat Bran, Oat Bran with Raisins (may contain gluten).
- Kaia Foods Buckwheat Granola (gluten-free and raw): Cocoa Bliss; Raisin Cinnamon; Dates and Spices.
- Laughing Giraffe Organics (gluten-free, rice-free): Vanilla Almond Smakaroo; Walnut Pecan Cherry Ginger GF Granola; Cranberry Orange Cacao GF Granola.
- Nature's Path (gluten-free, rice-free): Mesa Sunrise Flax, Corn and Amaranth. My personal favorite; Organic Honey'd Corn Flakes; Organic Millet Rice Oat bran Cereal.
- Peace Cereal Organic: Mango Passion Corn and Oats (may contain gluten), Vanilla Almond Corn and Oats (may contain gluten).

- <u>Perky's</u> (gluten-free, rice-free): Nutty Flax; Nutty Rice.
- <u>Two Moms in the Raw</u> Gluten Free Granola (wheat and gluten-free, dairy-free, 100% raw, 100% organic): Blueberry Granola; Gojiberry Granola.

Chocolate Bars and Chips

Chocolate Bars

Dark chocolate has one of the highest amounts of helpful antioxidants around. Real chocolate should only contain cocoa butter, cocoa liquor, a little sugar, soy-based lecithin and vanilla. Choose the chocolate with the highest amount of pure cocoa in them. I would suggest no less than 70% cocoa content and higher, if you don't mind the bitterness. The higher the number, the bitterer it will be. If you are allergic to dairy products, do not eat milk chocolate or chocolate candies and snacks.

My personal favorite and reasonably-priced brand is Lindt from Switzerland. Other good brands are <u>Callebaut</u> (Belgium), <u>Cote d'Or</u> (Belgium), Dagoba Organic (US), <u>Scharffen Berger</u> (US), <u>Vosges</u> (US), <u>Vivani</u> (Germany), <u>Divine</u> (Germany), <u>Valor</u> (Spain), and <u>Valrhona</u> (France) and many more.

GF Chocolate Chips

Any good quality semisweet or bittersweet chocolate chip should be gluten-free. The only ingredients should be: cocoa liquor or paste, sugar, cocoa butter, vanilla and possibly an emulsifier like soy lecithin (if you're allergic to soy, take note.) If you would like to pay a little more:

- <u>Enjoy Life</u> Semi Sweet Chocolate Chips (wheat and gluten-free, contains no dairy, soy, peanuts, tree nuts, egg, fish or shellfish; contains no casein, potato, sesame or sulfites)
  - <u>Bob's Red Mill</u> Tropical Source Semi sweet Chocolate Chips (wheat, gluten, dairy-free)

ASSORTED SAVORY SNACKS

Wheat-free, Gluten-free Crackers, Chips, Nuts and Snacks

GF Beans Chips

A great new product made in Austin is <u>Beanitos,</u> a tortilla-like chip made with beans. They come in two flavors: Black Bean and Pinto Bean and Flax Seeds. Be careful, they are addictive. Corn-free, gluten-free, high fiber, low certified glycemic index, contain 4g of protein and 600mg of omega 3s per serving.

- Boulder Canyon: Gluten Free Rice and Adzuki Beans Snack Chips: Natural Salt.

GF Corn Chips

- Tortilla Chips: Ideally, all of these should be gluten-free but if you are cautious about them really being GF, make sure the bag says so. My favorite national brand is Garden of Eating. They taste great and are made with organic corn. Another good national brand is Kettle Brand.
- CM Organic Tortilla Chips (all fried): Assorted thin and thick types.
- Garden of Eden Organic Corn Chips (all fried): Blue Corn, Red Hot Blues, Yellow Chips, Sesame Blues, White Chips, Chili and Lime, Guacamole, Nacho Cheese.
- Guiltless Gourmet Corn Baked Chips: Baked Tortilla and Black Beans Chips (baked).

GF Crackers

- Blue Diamond Natural: Nuts and Rice Crackers: Pecan Nut-Thins. Hazelnut Nut-Thins. Almond Nut-Thins: Country Ranch and Original.
- Crunchmaster Multi-Seed Crackers (all natural, low sodium, cholesterol-free, wheat and gluten-free): Sweet Onion, Rosemary and Olive Oil.
- Two Mom's in the Raw Sea Crackers (dairy-free, wheat and gluten-free, 100% raw, 100% organic, no added oils, no added sugars): Tomato Basil, Pesto.
- EnerG (wheat and gluten-free): Sesame Pretzel Rings; Wylde Pretzel.
- EnerG Wheat-free Crackers (wheat and gluten-free, Milk-free, Lactose-free, egg-free): Original, Onion.
- Enjoy Life (no nuts, no soy, no dairy, no gluten) No Nuts Beach Bash and Mountain Mambo Nut-free Trail Mix.
- Explorer's Bounty Tribal Stone Crackers (gluten-free, fat-free): Original, Onion, Garlic.
- Glutino Crackers (wheat and gluten-free): Original, Vegetable, Multigrain Cheddar.
- Glutino Breadsticks (gluten-free, low fat, no preservatives, no additives, made with non-hydrogenated oils): Sesame, Pizza.
- Glutino Gluten-Free Pretzel Sticks and Twists (wheat and gluten-free, milk-free, casein-free, egg-free). Sesame Pretzel Rings; Unsalted Pretzel Twists.

- Mary's Gone Crackers Sticks and Twigs (organic wheat and gluten-free): Original; Onion; Black Pepper; Herb; Caraway; Curry; Chipotle Tomato; Sea Salt.
- Mrs. Crimble's Cheese Crackers (wheat and gluten-free): Sundried Tomato and Pesto, Original Cheese.
- San J Brown Rice Crackers (wheat and gluten-free) : Original; Sesame.

GF Dry-Roasted Veggie Snacks

Nothing can replace good fresh vegetables but in a hurry, I present you another form of healthy gluten-free snacks. Hot Wasabi Coated Peas; Lightly Salted Dry-Roasted Edamame (soybeans).

GF Raw Kale Chips

This is a new and very healthy snack. They are vegan, GF and CF. Because they are dried at a temperature no higher than 117F, it is a live and raw food full of green nutrients. Rhythm Superfoods produces them in Austin, TX.

- Raw Rhythm Kale Chips: Kool Ranch; Zesty Nacho.
- Kaia Foods Kale Chips (wheat and gluten-free, raw): Barbecue; Chili Lime; Sea Salt and Vinegar.

GF Lentils Chips

- The Mediterranean Snack Food Co. Baked Lentil Chips: Sea Salt; Sea Salt and Cracked Pepper; Cucumber Dill.

GF Packaged Nuts and Nut Butters

I prefer that you buy in the bulk section and save yourself some money; but if you need to buy packaged, the following are reliable:

GF Packaged Nuts (all are wheat and gluten-free)

- AustiNuts: Assorted Dry Roasted Nuts.
- Gensoy Roasted Soy Nuts: Unsalted; Zesty Barbeque; Deep Sea Salted; Hickory Smoked.
- Hawaiian Host Macadamia Nuts: Lightly Salted; Honey Glazed.
- MareBlu: Pecan Cinnamon Crunch; Pistachio Crunch; Almond Crunch; Cashew Crunch.
- Pepitas Organic Pumpkin Seeds: Sweet Cinnamon; Extra Hot; Barely Salted; Spicy Garlic; Dark Chocolate.

GF Packaged Nut Butters (all are wheat and gluten-free)

A very good source of plant-based protein. Great snack on a gluten-free cracker with a little all-fruits preserves.

- Arrowhead Organic: Crunchy Valencia Peanut Butter, Creamy Valencia Peanut Butter, Sesame Tahini.
- Artisana Raw Organic: Cashew Butter; Coconut Butter; Pecan Butter; Walnut Butter; Tahini (sesame seed butter).
- CM All Natural: Cashew Butter, Smooth Peanut Butter, Crunchy Peanut Butter.

GF Popcorn (all are wheat and gluten-free)

If you don't feel like making them at home, there are plenty of pre-made choices out there. Just remember, most of them are popped in dubious quality oil. Air-popped is always better. Organic is an even better idea.

- 479 degree Popcorn: Madras Coconut and Cashews; Chipotle Caramel and Almonds; Black Truffle and Cheddar (contains dairy); Ginger Sesame Caramel; Fleur de Sel (sea salt) Caramel; Vietnamese Cinnamon Sugar.
- Central Market Organics: Lightly Salted; White Cheddar Popcorn (has dairy).
- Newman's Own Organic Popcorn: Unsalted, Light Butter, Butter.
- Rocky Mountains Honest Popcorn (wheat and gluten-free, nut-free): Naked; White Cheddar (contains dairy); Caramel.
- Vic's: Yellow Cheddar (has dairy); White Cheddar (has dairy); White Popcorn, Half Salt, Caramel.

GF Potato Chips (all are wheat and gluten-free)

Stay with natural or organic if at all possible. This will avoid GMO potatoes. Another precaution: avoid any chips (potato, veggie, corn) that are fried in hydrogenated or partially hydrogenated oils. My own preference would go to baked, not fried corn chips. Here in Texas, we have a great brand called Guiltless Gourmet. They were designed to be fat-free, but they taste great and you're avoiding all that fried oil.

GF Potato Sticks (wheat and gluten-free)

- Stonewall Kitchen Potato Sticks: Salt and Pepper; Sour Cream and Chive; Chipotle Ranch.

GF Rice Cakes and Chips (all are wheat and gluten-free)

- <u>Lundberg Organic Rice Cakes</u>: Sesame Tamari, Wild Rice, Tamari Seaweed, Brown Rice, Mochi Sweet, Apple Cinnamon, Buttery Caramel, Honey Nut.
- <u>Lundberg Rice Chips</u>: Honey Dijon; Fiesta Lime; Sesame Seaweed; Pico de Gallo; Santa Fe Barbeque; Sea Salt.
- <u>Mr. Krispers</u> Baked Rice Krisps (wheat and gluten-free): Salt and Pepper; Barbecue; Nacho; Sour Cream and Onion (contains dairy).
- <u>Quaker Rice Snacks</u>: Apple Cinnamon, Sour Cream and Onion, Cheddar Cheese.

GF Japanese Rice Crackers (all are wheat and gluten-free)

- <u>Feng Shui</u> (wheat and gluten-free, no MSG, fat-free): Original Rice Crackers; Hot Wasabi Rice Cracker; Maki Rolls.
- <u>San-J</u> Sesame Brown Rice Crackers: Tamari; Black sesame; Sesame.

GF Soy Chips (all are wheat and gluten-free)

- <u>Glenny's Natural Soy Crisps</u>: White Cheddar, Creamy Ranch, Original BBQ.

GF Sprouted Seeds (all are wheat and gluten-free)

- <u>Kaia Foods</u> Sprouted Sunflower Seeds: Sweet Curry, Garlic and Sea Salt, Teriyaki.

GF Veggie Chips and Snacks (all are wheat and gluten-free)

- Use vegetable chips as much as possible and choose the oven-baked variety rather than the oil-fried variety.
- <u>Arrico</u> Vegetable Chips (fried).
- Baked <u>Latke Crisps</u>, made of potato (fried).
- <u>Central Market Organics</u>: Veggie Chips (potatoes, tomatoes, spinach), Bruschetta Veggie Chips (all fried).
- <u>Eden</u>: Vegetable Chips, Wasabi Chips (made with potato starch); Plantain chips (all fried).
- <u>Terra</u> Vegetable Chips (fried).
- <u>Tyrrells</u> Hand Fried Vegetable Chips (parsnip, beet and carrot)
- <u>Vege Chips</u>: Natural, BBQ, Lime Chili, Sweet and Sour, (cassava, tapioca flour and spices)

Meat Snacks (all are wheat and gluten-free)

- Tom Tom's Turkey Snack Sticks.
- The Buffalo Guys: Buffalo Jerky.

Gluten-Free Dry Pasta, Alternatives to Pasta, Prepared Pasta and Meals in a Box

Assorted GF Dry Pasta (all wheat and gluten-free, dairy-free)

- Ancient Quinoa Harvest GF Quinoa Pasta: Garden Pagodas; Veggie Curls; Rotelle; Elbows; Spaghetti.
- Deboles Rice Pasta: Corn Elbow Pasta.
- Eden Foods Buckwheat Pasta at Whole Foods and more online.
- Lundberg: Brown Rice Spaghetti Pasta.
- Mrs. Leeper's: All varieties Brown Rice Pasta.
- Orgran Gourmet Natural (gluten-free, wheat-free, dairy-free, egg-free, soy-free, yeast-free, GMO-free, vegan): Corn and Vegetable Pasta; Rice and Millet Pasta Spirals; Rice and Corn Pasta Macaroni; Rice and Corn Spaghetti; Vegetable Rice Pasta Spirals; Rice and Corn Pasta Penne; Rice and Corn Pasta Tortelli; Rice and Corn Lasagna Mini Sheets; Farm animals Rice and Corn Vegetable Pasta.
- Rustichella d'Abruzzo (organic gluten-free): Rice Spaghetti; Rice Penne Rigate; Rice Fusillotti; Rice Fusilli.

Canned Prepared Pasta Dishes

- Orgran (gluten-free, wheat-free, dairy-free, egg-free, yeast-free, soy-free, nut-free and vegan): Spaghetti in Tomato Sauce; Alternative Grain Spaghetti Tomato and Basil Sauce.

GF Boxed Meal Mixes (all wheat and gluten-free, dairy-free)

- Alter Eco Rice: Coral Red Jasmine; White Jasmine; Purple Jasmine; Ruby Red Jasmine; Black Quinoa; Pearl Quinoa.
- Annie's Homegrown (gluten-free, contains dairy): Rice Pasta and Cheddar.
- Edward and Sons: Roasted garlic organic mashed potatoes; Dairy-free Chreesy organic mashed potatoes; Home style organic mashed potatoes.
- Ian's Pizza and Pasta Kit (no wheat or gluten, no milk or casein, no soy or eggs, no nuts).

- Mrs. Leepers Gluten-free: Beef Lasagna; Beef Stroganoff; Cheeseburger Mac; Chicken Alfredo; Creamy Tuna (contains dairy).
- Namaste Foods: Gluten-free Taco Pasta: GF Pasta Pisavera: Non-dairy Say Cheez Pasta.
- Road's End Organics (wheat and gluten-free, dairy-free, casein-free): Delicious Golden Quick Gravy; Cheddar Style Chreese Sauce Mix; Alfredo Sauce Mix; Shiitake Mushroom Quick Gravy; Savory Herbs Gravy.
- Road's End's Organic (gluten-free, soy-free, lactose-free, cholesterol-free): Mac and Chreese Alfredo Style; Penne and Chreese Cheddar Style.

Gluten-Free Pasta Alternatives

GF Potato Gnocci

- Cucina Viva Potato Gnocchi.

GF Corn Polenta

Polenta is a traditional Italian side dish made out of corn grits.

- San Gennaro Polenta : Original, Sun Dried Tomato and Garlic, Basil and Garlic. This one is pre-cooked and ready to heat and serve. Slice, place in a baking pan, cover with tomato sauce, sprinkle with grated Swiss cheese or Parmesan, heat and serve. A quick and tasty side dish.

The others are dry mixes. Follow the instructions on the package.

- Alpina Savoie Polenta mix.
- Bellino Instant Polenta mix.
- Dal Raccolto From the Harvest Cornmeal.
- De La Estancia Organic Polenta Meal.
- Great River Organic Milling: Stone Ground Cornmeal (gluten-free).

Oils and Vinegars, Soy Sauces, Condiments

Olive Oils

Buy only organic first press extra virgin olive oil. It contains the highest amount of antioxidants, has not been overheated and oxidized and does not contains harmful chemicals.

- Centrum Assorted Extra Virgin Organic Olive Oils.
- CM Organics: Extra Virgin Olive Oils.
- Centrum: Organic Virgin Coconut Oil.

- MacNut: Organic Macadamia Nut Oil.

Wheat-free Vinegars and Soy Sauces

- Bragg Organic: Organic Apple Cider Vinegar.
- CM Organics: Balsamic Vinegar.
- Kame: Rice Vinegar.
- Nakano: Seasoned Rice Vinegar.
- Spectrum Organic: Balsamic Vinegar, White Wine Vinegar, Red Wine Vinegar, Apple Cider Vinegar.

GF Soy Sauces

- Bragg Liquid Aminos (soy-based organic liquid seasoning, like soy sauce but much better). Caution: some people claim that it contains traces of gluten through processing.
- San-J: Organic Whole Soybean Wheat-free Tamari Sauce (my favorite and the only one to be guaranteed GF).

GF Condiments

- CM Organic Mustard: Dijon: Yellow and Whole Grain.

CANNED PRODUCTS

Gluten-Free/Casein-Free Canned Beans and Chilies

- Amy's Organic Chili: Medium; Medium with Vegetables; Spicy; Medium Black Bean.
- Amy's Organic Refried Beans: Mild Green Chiles; Black Beans.
- Bearitos Organic Canned Refried Beans: Low Fat; Fat Free; Traditional Green Chili; Spicy.
- Central Market Organics: Pinto Beans; Black Beans; Kidney Beans; Garbanzo Beans.
- Eden Organic Canned Beans: Black Beans; Garbanzo and Black Soy; Aduki; Navy; Cannellini; Small Red Beans.
- Eden Organic Canned Rice and Beans: Pinto; Caribbean Black Beans; Cajun Small Red Beans; Green Lentils; Kidney Beans.
- SW Baked Beans: Pinquitos; Sweet Bacon; Maple Sugar; Black Beans; Kidney Beans; Red Beans; Butter Beans; Garbanzo Beans; White Beans.
- Westbrae Natural Organic: Black Beans; Pinto Beans; Kidney Beans; Vegetarian Chili Beans; White Beans; Soup Beans; Red Beans. Golden Corn; Sweet Peas.

- Westbrae Natural Organic Canned Beans: Garbanzo; Soy Beans; Lentils; Salad Beans; Pinto Beans; Kidney Beans; Chili Beans; Great Northern Beans; Soup Beans; Red Beans.

Gluten-Free and some Casein-Free Canned Soups

- Amy's Organic Soups: Potato Leek; Black Bean Vegetable; Butternut Squash; Lentils Vegetable; Chunky Tomato Bisque; Chunky Vegetable; Cream of Tomato (has dairy); Cream of Mushrooms (has dairy); Corn Chowder (has dairy).
- Blue Crab Bay: Clam Chowder (GFCF).
- Health Valley Organic Soups (all GFCF): Split pea; Lentil; Black Bean; Mushroom Barley; Tomato.
- Imagine Organic: Corn Chipotle Bisque; Cuban Black Bean Bisque; Creamy Portobello Soup; Creamy Broccoli Soup; Creamy Butternut Squash Soup; Creamy Tomato Soup; Creamy Potato Leek Soup; Creamy Sweet Corn Soup (all dairy-free); Lobster and Crab Bisque (contains dairy).
- Pacific Organic Soups: Creamy Roasted Carrot (contains soy milk); French Onion Soup (dairy-free); Roasted Red Pepper and Tomato (contains dairy); Creamy Butternut Squash (contains soy milk); Creamy Tomato (contains dairy).

Gluten-Free and Casein-Free Liquid Broths

- Central Market Organic Broths: Vegetarian Vegetable Broth (vegan); Free-Range Chicken Broth.
- Imagine Organic Broths: Free Range Chicken; No Chicken Broth; Vegetable Broth (vegan); Chicken Cooking Stock; Beef Flavored Cooking Stock; Vegetable Cooking Stock (vegan).
- Health Valley Broths: Beef Flavored Broth; Chicken Broth.
- Pacific Organic Broths: Free Range Chicken Broth; Beef Broth; Mushroom Broth (vegan); Vegetable Broth (vegan).

Canned Fish and Seafood

Sardines

These small wonders are very good for you in many ways. They are a good source of omega-3 fatty acids and natural calcium. Omega-3 fatty acids are very important for brain function. Squeeze a lemon or lime on top and add sea salt and freshly ground black pepper to make them even better to eat.

- Bela Olhao from Portugal: Hot Sauce; Lemon Sauce. My favorite brand.

- <u>Crown Prince</u>: Wild Caught Brisling Sardines in pure olive oil.

Other Canned Fish and Seafood

- <u>Canned Salmon</u>: Crown Prince, Taste, Sea Bear, Raincost, Rubinstein.
- <u>Canned Lobster Meat</u>: Looks Atlantic.
- <u>Canned Crab Meat</u>: Crown Prince, Taste, Chicken of the Sea.
- <u>Canned Tuna</u>: Be careful, Albacore is said to contain more mercury than the other type. Choose Tongol Tuna, Light Tuna in water, Yellow Fin.
- <u>Canned Central Market</u>: Ventresca (Tuna Belly Filet; a treat).

DRY MEALS AND SOUPS

Wheat-free, Gluten-Free and Dairy-Free Packaged Dried Meals

Beans Dried Meals

- <u>Fantastic</u>: Refried Beans Quick Mix.
- <u>Assorted Dry Beans Soup Mixes</u> from Cherchies, Cassoulets USA, Frontier Soups, Alessi.

Potato Dried Meals

- <u>Manischewitz</u>: Potato Latke Mix; Mashed Potato Mix; Yolk Free Noodle Pasta.
- <u>Panni</u>: Potato Shredded Dumplings, Pancake, Bavarian Dumpling, Spaetzle.

Rice Dried Meals

- <u>Thai Kitchen</u>: Rice Noodles.
- <u>Thai Kitchen</u>: Jasmine Rice; Spicy Thai Chili; Lemongrass and Ginger.
- <u>Thai Kitchen</u> Rice Noodle Bowls: Thai Ginger; Mushroom; Spring Onion; Roasted Garlic; Hot and Sour; Lemongrass and Chili.
- <u>Thai Pavilion</u> Stir-Fry Rice Noodles Mix: Authentic Pad Thai; Peanut Satay Simmer Noodles; Thai Red Curry; Green Curry Summer Noodles.
- <u>Thai Kitchen</u> <u>Coconut Milk</u>: Classic; Lite.
- <u>A Taste of Thai</u>: Thin Rice Noodles.
- <u>Lundberg Rice Sensations</u>: Moroccan Pilaf; Sesame Teriyaki.
- <u>Alessi</u>: Risotto a la Milanese; Arborio Rice with Tomatoes; Porcini Mushrooms.
- <u>Marrakesh Express Rice Mixes</u>: Wild Mushrooms; Parmesan Cheese (contains dairy); Wild Pecan Rice.

- <u>Casbah Rice Mixes</u>: Spanish Pilaf; Saffroned Jasmine Rice; Rice Pilaf; Lentil Pilaf; Nutted Pilaf.
- <u>Near East Rice Mixes</u>: Spanish Rice; Long Grain and Wild Rice; Sesame Ginger; Curry; Lentil; Wild Mushrooms and Herbs; Toasted Almonds; Original.
- <u>Tony Chachere's Creole Mixes</u>: Red Beans and Rice; Jambalaya; Gumbo (contains dairy); Dirty Rice.
- <u>Zatarian</u>: New Orleans Red Beans and Rice Mix.
- <u>Vigo Mixes</u>: Mexican Rice with Corn; Rice and Lentil Pilaf; Jambalaya Cajun Rice Mix (contains dairy).

Gluten-Free and Casein-Free Dried Soups

Dried Soup Mixes

- <u>Annie Chun's Rice Express Bowl</u>: Sprouted Brown Rice; Sticky White Rice; Sushi Wraps and Rice Bowl.
- <u>Dr. McDougall's Soup in a Cup</u>: Miso Noodle; Black Bean and Lime; Tamale; Split Pea; Tortilla Soup.
- <u>Fantastic World Foods Soup in a Cup</u>: Split Pea; Southwest Tortilla Bean; Buckaroo Bean Chili; Baja Black Bean; Summer Vegetable Rice; Classic French Onion (contains dairy); Creamy Potato Leek (contains dairy).
- <u>Health Valley Dried Soup Mix in a Cup</u>: Lentil; Creamy Potato (contains dairy); Zesty Black Bean.

Spices, Extracts and Flavorings

Salt

Natural sea salt a much healthier alternative to your "regular" table salts. Typically, table salt contains an anti-caking chemical like sodium aluminosilicate (which contains aluminum) which allows it to flow, but is not necessarily good for you. Natural salts, on the other hand, are a good source of sea minerals. I recommend the French sea salts most highly, and the Himalayan, Japanese, and Australian sea salts are also good choices.

Spices

If you can afford it, choose organic and non-irradiated spices. Buying them bulk will save you money and insure that the spices have not been sitting on the shelves for a long time. Some spice companies use wheat as a filler, so stick to **M & B (Morton & Bassett) Organic Spices**, **Frontier Organic Spices**, and **Central Market Organic Spices**.

Extracts and Flavorings

Caution for people allergic to wheat: Some brands of extracts contain wheat. Stick with certified organics and read the labels.

- Central Market Organic Extracts: Vanilla; Almond; Pure Lemon; Pure Orange; Pure Peppermint.

DF/CF Animal Milk Alternatives

Almond Milk

Blue Diamond is a good brand.

Coconut Milk

So Delicious Coconut Milk: Original, Unsweetened Original, Vanilla, and Unsweetened Vanilla.

Hazelnut Milk

An excellent source of plant-based protein, Calcium, Vitamin D and Riboflavin. Pacific Organic is the best source.

Hemp Milk

The new kid on the block and my new favorite, it is full of goodies. It has the highest amount of omega-3 fatty acids of all milk alternatives, 700 mg as well as 2,000 mg of omega-6 with GLA. It contains all 10 essential amino acids and contains a good amount of protein and digestible fiber. Provides essential vitamins A, B12, D, E, Riboflavin and Folic Acid. Essential minerals: Magnesium, Potassium, Phosphorus, Iron and Zinc. Living Harvest is the brand to get.

Rice Milk

Rice Dream Organic and Good Karma are good choices.

Soy Milk

Use only organic and non-GMO food source soy beans. Westsoy and Organic Valley are two reputable sources. Note: Do not purchase Silk. Their sources have not proven to be above GMO (Genetically Modified Organism) suspicions.

DRINKS

Bottled water, fruit juices, and fermented Kombucha tea are all GFCF and safe for you to drink. I prefer that you drink water; if you drink fruit juice, dilute it 50/50 with water. I also recommend bottled Kombucha tea, which is full of health-giving compounds.

GF Beers

- Greens': Dubbel Dark Ale; Triple Blond Ale; Amber Ale.
- Bard's Sorghum Malt Beer.
- Redbridge Sorghum Beer.
- And many more such as:
- Anheuser-Busch: Redbridge.
- Bard's Tale Beer: Bard's The Original Sorghum Malt Beer.
- Bi-Aglut: Birra 76 Bi-Aglut.
- Green's: Discovery Amber Ale, Pioneer Lager, Endeavour Double Dark Beer, Trailblazer Lager, Herald Ale, Pilgrim Cherry Beer, Mission Amber Beer, Pathfinder Dubbel Dark, Quest Triple Blonde.
- New France Beers: La Messagère.
- O'Brien Brewing: O'Brien Premium Lager, O'Brien Premium Light, O'Brien Brown Ale, O'Brien Pale Ale.
- Ramapo Valley Brewery: Honey Beer (formerly Honey Passover Beer).
- Sprecher Brewing: Shakparo Ale, Mbege.
- The Alchemist Pub & Brewery: Celia Framboise, Celia IPA, Celia Saison.

FROZEN GFCF PRODUCTS

Frozen Gluten-Free and Casein-Free Breakfast Products

Frozen GF Waffles (all GFCF unless specified otherwise)

- Lifestream Organic Waffles: Mesa Sunrise w Corn and Flax; Buckwheat; Buckwheat Wild Berry Gluten-free Waffles.
- Vans Wheat-free Waffles (gluten-free, eggless, vegan, dairy-free, no cholesterol, no transfats): Apple Cinnamon; Blueberry Buckwheat; Flax.

Frozen Breakfast Burritos (all GFCF unless specified otherwise)

- Amy's Organic: Burrito Especial w black beans, rice and tomato (wheat-free); Black Bean Burrito (dairy-free, wheat-free); Breakfast Burrito w black beans and tomatoes (dairy-free, wheat-free); Cheddar Cheese Burrito (wheat-free, contains dairy).

Frozen Enchiladas (all GFCF unless specified otherwise)

- Amy's Organic: Corn and Tomato Cheese (wheat-free, contains dairy); Black Bean and Vegetable; Enchiladas w black beans and Vegetables (dairy-free. wheat-free); Cheese Enchilada (non dairy cheese) w Beans, Corn and Tomato (wheat-free).

Frozen Organic Breakfast Potato Dishes (all GFCF unless specified otherwise)

- Cascadian Farms Organics (all gluten-free and dairy-free): Country Style Potatoes (potatoes, red peppers, onions); Crinkled French Fries; Shoe String Fries; Hash Browns; Spud Puppies; Straight Cut French Fries.
- Alexia Organics (all gluten-free and dairy-free): Hashed Browns; Oven Crinkles Classic and Salt and Pepper; Oven Reds w Olive Oil; Parmesan and Roasted Garlic; Yukon Gold Fries w Sea Salt; Oven Reds w Olive Oil; Sun-Dried Tomatoes and Pesto; Oven Fries w Olive Oil, Rosemary and Garlic ; Oven Fries w Olive Oil and Sea Salt.

Frozen Gluten-Free Baked Breads

- EnerG : Tapioca loaf; White rice loaf.
- Food for Life Gluten-free Breads: Brown Rice; White Rice; Rice Pecan; Rice Almond; Raisin Pecan; Millet.
- French Meadow Rice Bread (yeast-free): White Rice; Brown Rice.
- Gillian's: Cinnamon Raisin Rolls; French Rolls.
- Glutino Bagels.
- Kinnikinnick Foods: Italian White Tapioca Rice Bread; Candadi Yeast-Free Multigrain Rice Bread; Tapioca Rice Hot Dog Buns; Tapioca Rice Hamburger Buns; Tapioca Rice Cinnamon Buns.
- Rio's Brazilian Cheese Bread (gluten-free, contains dairy): Original; Pesto; Roasted Red Pepper.
- Udi's Gluten Free Foods: White Sandwich Bread; Whole Grain Bread (my current favorite, it tastes like the real thing).

GF Frozen Breakfast Products (all GFCF unless specified otherwise)

- Amy's Organic Hot Cereal Bowls: Cream of Rice; Steel Cut Oats.
- Glutino Cinnamon French Toast (wheat and gluten-free, milk-free, casein-free, cholesterol-free, egg-free, tree nut-free, peanut-free).
- Ian's Cinnamon French Toast Sticks (no eggs, no nuts, no soy).
- Kinnikinnick Foods Gluten Free Muffins: Chocolate Chips Muffins; Blueberry Muffins; Carrot Muffins.

- Kinnikinnick Foods Donuts (nut-free): Cinnamon Sugar; Maple Glazed; Chocolate Dipped.
- Kinnikinnick Foods Homestyle Waffles: Original; Cinnamon Brown Sugar.
- Udi's Gluten-Free Foods: Blueberry Muffins; Lemon Streusel Muffins.

GF Frozen Raw Pizza Crusts (all GFCF unless specified otherwise)

- Gluten Free Kneads Ancient Grains Pizza Crust.
- Udi's Gluten-Free Foods: Pizza Crusts.
- Gillian's Frozen Raw Pizza Dough.
- Chebe Raw Pizza Crust On The Go (yeast-free).

GF Frozen Raw Pie Crusts (all GFCF unless specified otherwise)

- Gillian's Quiche and Pie Crust (contains dairy)

Frozen Gluten-Free and Casein-Free Meals or Dishes

GF Frozen Tortillas (all GFCF unless specified otherwise)

- Food for Life Brown Rice Tortillas: Sprouted Corn Tortillas.

GF Frozen Pizzas (all GFCF unless specified otherwise)

- Amy's Rice Crust Cheese Pizza (gluten-free, contains dairy); Gluten-free, non-dairy Cheeze with Rice Crust (gluten and dairy-free).
- Glutino Gluten Free Pizzas: Spinach Soy Cheese Pizza; Spinach and Feta (contains dairy); 3 Cheese Pizza (contains dairy).

GF Frozen Potato Pancakes (all GFCF unless specified otherwise)

- Dr. Praeger's Sweet Potato Pancakes: Sweet Potato Littles; Broccoli Pancakes

Assorted Frozen Savory Pies (all GFCF unless specified otherwise)

- Amy's Organic: Mexican Tamale Pie (wheat-free with corn topping); Country Vegetable Pie (dairy-free, contains wheat); Broccoli Pot Pie (wheat-free, contains dairy).

Frozen Tofu Products (all GFCF unless specified otherwise)

- Amy's Organic: Vegetable Pot Pie with Tofu; Tofu Ranchero with roasted Potatoes and Black Beans; Tofu Scramble with Hash Brown and Veggies.

Frozen Bowls (all GFCF unless specified otherwise)

- Amy's Organic: Teriyaki w Tofu Brown Rice and Vegetables; Santa Fe Enchilada w Pinto Beans and Vegetables; Brown Rice and Vegetables; Low Sodium Brown Rice and Vegetables; Mexican Casserole Bowl (contains dairy).

Assorted GF and some CF Frozen Prepared Meals

GF Frozen Tamales (all GFCF unless specified otherwise)

- Ramiro's Tamale Company (Note: typically tamales are not made with wheat flour, only corn masa but it does not say gluten-free on the package): Pork Tamales - Hot; Pork Tamales - Mild; Beef Tamales; Chicken Tamales.
  - Texas Tamale Company (same comment as above): Black Bean Tamales; Beef Tamales; Pork Tamales; Chicken Tamales.

Frozen Pasta Dishes (all GFCF unless specified otherwise)

- Amy's Organic: Macaroni Soy Cheese (dairy-free, contains wheat); Tofu Vegetable Lasagna (dairy-free, contains wheat); Garden Vegetable Lasagna (rice pasta, gluten-free, dairy-free); Vegetable Lasagna (dairy-free, contains wheat).
- Caesar's Gluten-Free and Wheat-Free Pasta Dishes (GF, all contain dairy): Vegetable Lasagna; Cheese Lasagna; Stuffed Shells with Cheese in Marinara Sauce; Manicotti with Cheese in Marinara Sauce.
- Conte's Wheat and Gluten-Free Pasta: Potato Gnocchi; Potato and Cheese Pierogies (contains dairy); Spinach and Cheese Ravioli (contains dairy); Cheese Ravioli (contains dairy); Cheese Stuffed Shells (contains dairy).

Assorted Frozen Meals (all GFCF unless specified otherwise)

- Cedarlane Organic: Burrito Grande w black Beans and Basmati Rice; 3 Cheese Quesadillas (contains dairy).
- Gluten Free Cafe: Asian Noodles; Savory Chicken Pilaf; Lemon Basil Chicken (contains dairy); Fettuccini Alfredo (contains dairy).

- Glutino Gluten Free Dishes: Chicken Penne Alfredo (contains dairy); Chicken Pomodoro with Brown Rice and Vegetables (contains dairy); Chicken Pad Thai (contains dairy); Chicken Ranchero with Brown Rice (contains dairy). Macaroni and Cheese (contains dairy).
- Mimi's Organic Kitchen: Black Bean and Corn Chili; Spicy White Beans and Jalapeno Chili; Three Beans Chili w Rice.
- Organic Fairfield Farm Kitchens: Confetti Rice Pilaf and Chicken with Honey BBQ Sauce; Chicken Marsala with Mashed Potatoes (GF, contains dairy); Macaroni and Meat Sauce (dairy-free, contains wheat).
- S'Better: Chicken Fingers; Chicken Siciliano; Beef Corn Dog.

Frozen Indian and Asian Dishes (all GFCF unless specified otherwise)

- Amy's Organic: Rajmah Dal (gluten-free, dairy-free); Asian Noodle Stir Fry with Rice Noodles and Tofu (gluten-free, dairy-free); Thai Stir Fry with Vegetables and Rice (gluten-free, dairy-free); Indian Samosa Wrap with Potatoes, Peas and Tofu (dairy-free, contains wheat). Indian Palak Paneer with Creamed Spinach Cheese and Rice (gluten-free, contains dairy); Indian Mattar Paneer with Curried Peas, Cheese with Rice (gluten-free, contains dairy); Chana Masala (gluten-free, contains dairy).

Gluten-Free and Casein-Free Frozen Meats

Beef

- Meyer Natural Angus (no preservatives, additives or artificial flavors): Beef Patties and Burgers.
- Dakota Beef (no preservatives): Uncured All Beef Hot Dogs.

Bison or Buffalo

- Buffalo Organic (gluten-free, no transfats): Spicy Chicken Wings; BBQ; Honey and Garlic; Buffalo Hot Dogs.

Pork

- Organic Valley (no nitrates, no nitrites, no pesticides, not preserved, no antibiotics, no pesticides, no GMO): Pork Bratwurst; Organic Hardwood Uncured bacon).
- Beelers (gluten-free, no artificial ingredients, no preservatives, no antibiotics, no growth hormones, vegetarian fed): All Natural Mild Italian Sausage; Sausage Link; Breakfast Sausage; Hot Pork Sausage.

Turkey

- <u>Shelton's</u>: Uncured Turkey Bologna (no nitrates or nitrites added); Turkey Breakfast Strips (no preservatives, no artificial ingredients, gluten-free).

Assorted Frozen Meats

- <u>Garrett County</u>: Chicken Bites.
- <u>Organic Prairie</u> (all organic, gluten-free, dairy-free): Italian Chicken Sausage; Pork Bratwurst; Uncured Beef Hot Dogs; Hardwood Smoked Uncured Bacon (more choices available online).

Frozen Gluten-Free and Casein-Free Meat Substitutes

Frozen Chicken Substitute (GFCF)

Qorn Products are made out of mycoprotein (a type of mushroom - Fusarium venenatum). It's a very good vegetable protein source. Non Organic, but meat-free and soy-free.

- <u>Qorn Products</u>: Chick'n Patties; Chick'n Nuggets; Meat-free Grounds; Garlic and Herbs Cutlets; Tenders.

Veggie Burgers and Patties

- <u>Amy's Organic</u>: Bistro Burger (GFCF); California Veggie Burger (CF, contains wheat); Quarter Pound Veggie Burger (CF, contains wheat).
- <u>Boca Organic Soy Burgers</u> (all dairy-free, all contain wheat): All American; Classic Garden Vegetable; Vegan with Organic Soy.
- <u>Morningstar Organic</u> (all dairy-free, all contain wheat): Asian Veggie Patties; Garden Veggie Patties; ¼ Pounder; Soy Patties; Sausage Links; Bacon Strips.

Gluten-Free Frozen Cakes and Desserts

GF Frozen Cookies or Cookie Dough (all GFCF unless specified otherwise)

- <u>French Meadow Bakery</u> Cookie Dough (peanut-free): Chocolate Chip; Fudge Brownies.
- <u>Gluten Free Kneads</u> Cookie Dough: Snickerdoodle; Triple Chocolate Blast (my favorite).

Frozen GF Cakes

- Gillian's Foods Pumpkin Pie. (gluten-free, contains dairy).
- Julie's Organic Ice Cream with GlutenFreeda's Chocolate Cookies (GF, contains dairy).
- Pamela's New York Style Cheese Cake. (GF, contains dairy).
- Pamela's Coffee Cake. (GF, contains dairy).
- Peoples Pharmacy Flourless Chocolate Cake (GF, contains dairy but can be made dairy-free or soy-free with special advance order).
- Shabtai Gourmet Swiss: Chocolate Roll (GF, contains dairy); Florentine Lace Cookies (GF, dairy-free).
- Walker's: Meringue Nest (very sweet, contains eggs)

GFCF Frozen Desserts (all GFCF unless specified otherwise)

- Living Harvest Tempt (made with hemp milk): Coconut Lime; Mint Chip.
- NadaMoo Frozen Desserts: An Austin-grown product made with coconut milk and agave nectar. A very good product: Java Crunch; Creamy Coconut; Gotta Do Chocolate; Mmm... Maple Pecan; Vanilla...ahhh; Lotta Mint Chip.
- Organic Coconut Bliss. A frozen dessert made with coconut milk and agave nectar. Another great product. You'll never miss ice cream: Dark Chocolate; Pineapple Coconut; Chocolate Peanut Butter; Naked Coconut and many more. My current favorite: Chocolate Hazelnut Fudge. Yum!
- Soy Delicious (made with soy milk): Vanilla; Chocolate Velvet.
- Soy Dream (made with soy milk): Vanilla; Chocolate; Vanilla Fudge Swirl; Green Tea; Butter Pecan; Chocolate Fudge Brownies; French Vanilla.
- Rice Dream (made with rice milk, egg-free): Cocoa Marble Fudge; Vanilla; Neapolitan; Strawberry.
- Tofutti (made with soy milk): Vanilla; Almond Bark; Cuties Bars Choco and Vanilla.
- Temptation Non Dairy: Coffee; Chocolate; Peach Cobbler.

Frozen Sorbets or Sorbettos (all GFCF unless specified otherwise)

Unlike sherbet which contains dairy, sorbets (also known as sorbetto) are made only with fruit puree and a sweetener.

- Belizza: Acai; Acai Banana; Acai Mango.
- Haagen Dazs Sorbets: Raspberry; Strawberry; Lemon; Cranberry Blueberry; Mango.

- <u>Natural Choice Organic</u>: Banana; Strawberry; Kiwi; Lemon; Blueberry; Mango.
- <u>Pierre's Sorbets</u>: Lemon; Peach.
- <u>Savoy Sorbets</u>: Triple Lemon; Lavender; Chamomile Orange; Spiced Wine.
- <u>Sorbetto Classico</u>: Mango; Raspberry; Pomegranate; Blackberry Cabernet.
- <u>Talenti Italian Sorbetto</u>: Lisbon Lemon; Roman Raspberry.

Frozen Fruit Bars Great for dairy-free kids of all ages

- <u>Bluebell</u> Fruit Bars: Strawberry. - Dreyer's Fruit Bars: Strawberry; Lemonade; Tangerine; Grape; Lime. (Note: avoid the ones made with Splenda).
- <u>Dreyers Fruit Bars</u> (all dairy-free): Creamy Coconut; Tangerine; Lemonade; Strawberry; Grape; Limee; Kiwi and Mixed Flavors.
- <u>Natural Choice Organic Fruit Bars</u> (all dairy-free): Orange; Strawberry; Coconut; Raspberry.

REFRIGERATED GFCF PRODUCTS

- Refrigerated Milk and Yogurt Alternatives
- <u>Blue Diamond</u> Almond Milk: Original; Vanilla.
- <u>Central Market</u> Organics Soy Milk: Original; Vanilla; Chocolate
- <u>Silk</u> Pure Almond Milk: Original; Vanilla.- <u>So Delicious</u> Coconut Milk: Original; Vanilla. Unsweetened.- <u>Rice Dream</u> Milk: Original; Vanilla.- <u>Silk</u> Soy Milk: Plain: Vanilla; Chocolate:- <u>Silk</u> Soy Creamer: Original; Vanilla; French Vanilla; Hazelnut.
- <u>So Delicious </u>Coconut Milk Creamer: Original: French Vanilla; Hazelnut.

Coconut and Soy Milk Yogurts (all are dairy-free)

- <u>So Delicious</u> Coconut Milk Yogurt (vegan, dairy-free, soy-free): Strawberry Banana; Blueberry; Pina Colada; Plain; Vanilla.
- <u>WholeSoy</u> and Co (vegan, casein and dairy-free, gluten-free, no cholesterol): Cherry; Vanilla; Raspberry; Lemon; Blueberry; Peach; Strawberry; Plain. My current favorite brand.

Other Dairy-like but Dairy-free Products (all are dairy-free)

- <u>Tofutti</u>: Sour Supreme Soy Sour Cream (soy-based, dairy-free).
- <u>Tofutti</u>: Better than Cream Cheese Imitation Cream Cheese (soy-based, dairy-free): Plain, Herbs and Chives, French onion.

GF/Dairy-free Cheese Substitutes (all are dairy-free)

- Daiya Dairy-Free Cheese: Mozzarella Style and Cheddar Style. My friend Beth swears by them. She says it's the closest thing to the real thing she has ever tasted and I trust her.
- Follow Your Heart Vegan Gourmet: Cheddar; Mozzarella; Monterey Jack.
- Galaxy Nutritionals Rice Slices Cheese Substitute (dairy-free, soy-free, gluten-free, vegan): Swiss flavor; Mozzarella flavor; Pepper Jack flavor; American Cheese flavor.
- Galaxy Nutritionals Veggy (soy based cheese substitutes), (dairy-free, gluten-free, vegan): Pepper Jack flavor; American Cheese flavor; Swiss flavor; Mozzarella flavor.
- Soya Kaas (soy cheese substitute), (dairy-free, gluten-free, vegan): White Cheddar Style; Smoked Cheddar Style; Garlic and Herb Style; Jalapeno Mexi-Kaas; Monterey Jack Style; Mozzarella Style.
- Soy Natural Cheese Alternative: Monterey Jack Flavor; Jalapeno Flavor; Mozzarella Flavor; Mild Cheddar Flavor; White Cheddar Flavor.
- The Original Almond Cheese: Jalapeno Jack Style; Cheddar Style; Mozzarella Style.
- Tofu Rella Cheese Substitutes (dairy-free, soy-based tofu cheese, vegan): Cheddar Style; Garlic Herb; Monterey Jack Style; Mozzarella Style.

GF/Dairy-free Spreads

- Earth Balance: Non-GMO, non-hydrogenated, 100% expeller-pressed Natural Buttery Spread (dairy-free, soybean, palm, canola and olive oils): If you have soy allergies, there is a new one in a red-colored bucket that doesn't contain soy. Regular and Whipped.
- Promise Take Control Vegetable Oil Spread: Regular and Light. (dairy-free, non-hydrogenated, soybean, sunflower, canola, palm and palm kernel oils).
- Rice Butter Alternative (Lactose, dairy, gluten and corn-free, non-hydrogenated).
- Smart Balance: Organic Buttery Spread; Light and Whipped (dairy-free, non-hydrogenated, gluten-free. Palm fruit, soybean, canola, flax seed and olive oils).
- Spectrum Naturals: Non-hydrogenated Spread (dairy-free, canola oil). Tastes like butter.

PeoplesRx GF Desserts (gluten-free but contain dairy)

- Peoples Pharmacy: Exotic Carrot Cake (gluten-free, contains dairy); Almond Raspberry Tart (gluten-free, contains dairy): Pumpkin Cheese Cake (gluten-free, contains dairy).

Gluten-free Fresh Corn Products (all wheat and gluten-free)

- Tostadas Caseras: Corn Tostadas.
- El Milagro: Corn Tortillas and Blancas.
- Central Market: Fresh Tamales: Bean and Cheese; Pork-Beef-Ancho-Serrano; Chicken-Jalapeno-Tomatillo; Bean and Cheese.

Packaged Corn Products (all wheat and gluten-free)

- Bearitos Organic Tostadas Corn Shells
- Garden of Eatin': Organic Corn Taco Shells: Yellow Corn, Blue Corn.
- El Galindo: Corn Taco Shells and Chalupa Shells.
- Rio Rancho: Corn Tostada Shells.
- El Milagro: Corn Tostadas.

High quality Omega-3 Fatty Acids Sources

My favorite brand is **Barlean's** because they fresh-date their products so you always know it's fresh. Other good brands are **Spectrum** and **Udo's Oil**. You will find them in the refrigerated showcase.

- Barlean's: Fish Oil (orange-flavored), Cod Liver Oil (citrus-flavored), Assorted Flaxseed Oils with or without lignan (a beneficial prebiotic soluble fiber).
- Spectrum and other pharmaceutical grade fish oil or cod liver oil.

Recettes. *Recipes*

Recipes Introduction

Hello again, and welcome to my favorite GFCF recipes. This is where the fun begins, the hands get dirty and the rolling pin hits the dough.

Interestingly, I seem to get many more requests for breads, breakfast pastries, cookies, and desserts than I do for other foods. Of course, I will include all sorts of recipes (or it would be unbalanced), but I will offer you more baked products in this book than in my previous one.

Weighing Instead of Measuring Ingredients

Being a pastry chef by trade, I have always weighed the ingredients in every single recipe I have made during my entire professional life. As a pastry and baking teacher I have always insisted that my students do the same. Why? Because while pastry making is an art, it is also a science. Since a lot of pastry science has to do with chemical reactions, everything needs to be weighed precisely. I know some of you will groan at the idea of weighing everything, but, once you get used to it, you will thank me. Cup measuring is just too inconsistent. By weighing, you will get consistent results every time you bake. Therefore, in the baking and pastry section, all the recipes will be labeled in weight unless the measurements are too small, in which case I will use teaspoons and tablespoons. You'll see, it's really not that difficult, and once you get used to it, you will never want to go back.

Find a cheap electronic scale at your closest kitchen equipment store, Wal-Mart or Target. No need to spend a lot of money on some fancy expensive scale. In my classes I use a cheap scale that cost me about $30.00 at Bed, Bath and Beyond. A couple of suggestions: make sure they can weigh up to 6 or 7 pounds; check that they have a "tare" (zero out) button; also make sure they offer pounds and ounces as well as metric measurements (kilograms and grams). I will not torture you with metric recipes, but it could be helpful if you find French or foreign recipes online that you wish to try. I wonder why the U. S. hasn't shifted their measuring system to metric yet? I thought that was supposed to be done in the 1970s. Oh well. I'm used to it by now.

You will also find that using a scale will cut down on your dishwashing, as well as saving you time. To use, place your mixing bowl or container directly on the scale and push the start button; that will zero it out automatically; add your first dry ingredient; push the "tare" button, add the next ingredient and so on until you're done with the dry ingredients; switch containers for your wet or liquid ingredients, press the tare button and finish weighing all your wet ingredients. I use the mixing bowl as my measuring bowl so I don't have to wash an additional container.

To save space I used the contractions commonly used in the baking business. Please remember that 1 lb = 1 pound; 1 oz = 1 ounce; 1 qt = 1 quart; 1 pt = 1 pint; 1 cp = 1 cup; 1 Tbsp = 1 tablespoon; 1 tsp = 1 teaspoon.

Mixer

All my baking and pastry recipes are produced with a Kitchen Aid stand mixer. These are very similar to the larger professional Hobart 20-qt stand mixers I have used all my professional life. My favorite version is the least expensive one, the Artisan series with the tilt head feature that allows me easy access to the mixing bowl. You can find them almost anywhere for about $250.00. All my recipes are written with this type of mixer in mind.

Baking

As many of you already know, the oven temperatures I give you are only an indication. Every oven is different from gas to electric to convection. At work, I use a convection oven. If you do too, I suggest you lower the suggested temperature by 25 degrees Fahrenheit. Another suggestion is to turn you product halfway through the baking time so that your product bakes evenly. Most ovens do have hot spots, and this can cause uneven baking.

Dry Ingredients

Typically, gluten-free flours give better results when they are combined with one another. The base flour is always white or brown rice flour. Then a starch or two is added to give you a smooth mouth feel. Then you will need additional protein for hold, nutrients and flavor. This is where grains like millet, teff, sorghum and cassava come in handy. And finally, to hold it all together like gluten would, use a little xanthan gum. Be careful to not add too much, as it will make your dough too sticky and gummy. Beyond that, if you are a tinkerer, play around with different flours like quinoa or bean for additional flavor.

Here are some of the most used flours and their descriptions. Have fun!

Rice

Rice flour is the flour base you can't do without. You will use it as your main flour even if it's mixed with other flours for additional flavor or body. I prefer to use brown rice flour, as it contains more fiber, vitamins and minerals, but for cakes, white rice flour is better. My all time favorite is the very fine rice flour made by Authentic Flours. This is the brand I use for most of my cakes, cookies and desserts. It is more expensive and harder to find locally, but you can order it on the internet. Bob's Red Mill is another good choice and easier to find.

Corn, Potato and/or Tapioca Starches

Corn starch is a very good substitute for wheat flour when it is used in cake mixes, and to thicken sauces or soups. Usually all three of these starches are interchangeable. If you are allergic to corn, feel free to substitute potato starch. Another good starch is tapioca. I use it in my cake/pastry mix. If it's too difficult for you to find, stick to cornstarch, as long as you're not allergic to it.

Buckwheat

Unlike what its name might imply, buckwheat is not wheat. It is part of the sorrel and rhubarb family. Its texture is rustic and it has a strong flavor. My grandmother - Mamie - used it in her Crêpes de Sarrasin (buckwheat crêpes) recipe, which is a traditional form of savory crepe in the Brittany region of France. I haven't seen it in too many other recipes. It is very commonly used in Eastern Europe and Russia. You can use it to make a buckwheat bulgur. Buckwheat is a hardy plant providing phosphorus, magnesium, potassium, and calcium. It is also rich in vitamins A, B1, B2, PP and lysine.

Cassava Flour

This flour is usually used as a complement to rice flour to render cakes more moist and consistent in texture. It comes from a root widely used in South America. More than 500 million people in Africa and Asia use the cassava root as well. We still have a lot to learn about the many uses of this tuber. Don't be put off by its odor, as the odor cooks away and you will never be able to tell it was there. It is a good source of protein and minerals.

Chestnut Flour

188 | Living Gluten and Dairy-Free with French Gourmet Food

This flour is mostly used in Europe where chestnut trees are abundant. One of my favorite memories is eating finger-burning-hot roasted chestnuts from street vendors during winters in France. I remember being able to find them when I lived in New York, but they are nowhere to be found in Texas. Why would they be? We don't even have winters in Texas. Chestnut flour is typically found in desserts. It is sweeter and heavier than wheat flour. If used, mix it with rice flour to lighten it. Chestnuts are a good source of potassium, phosphorus, magnesium, iodine, iron, copper and sulphur. It also contains vitamins C, E, and B complex as well as lysine.

Coconut Flour

Coconut flour is made from coconut meat after most of the oil has been extracted to make coconut oil. Coconut flour is high in dietary fiber and protein, and is gluten-free. It has more fiber than gluten-based grains. Since coconut flour contains natural sugar from the coconut meat, baked goods need less added sugar. It has a mildly sweet coconut taste.

Quinoa

Although quinoa is a wonderful grain to cook with, it is rarely used as a flour due to its strong flavor. I will offer a couple of quinoa dishes; it's as easy to cook as rice. One thing to remember: make sure to rinse it in a fine mesh colander under running water, as these seeds protect themselves from birds with saponins. In other words, if it's not rinsed properly, it will taste like soap. Unless you said something naughty, you probably would not appreciate that taste in your mouth. Otherwise it is a wonderful ancient grain revered by the Incas centuries ago. It is very rich in protein, and was used as a travel food, mixed with lard and rolled in chia seeds into easy-to-transport, nutritious balls. Nowadays it is used to make wonderful salads and side dishes.

Millet

Another grain widely used on other continents. One of the oldest cereals, it was cultivated by Chinese peasants more than 5000 years ago. It is used throughout Asia and Africa. It can be grilled, crushed, germinated, roasted, and used as flour and flakes. In this country it is rarely used as flour. It is rich in potassium, magnesium, phosphorus and silica. It also contains vitamin A, B1, B2 as well as PP vitamins.

Gluten-Free Flour Mixes

In this book, I offer you different flour mix options. First, I give you the two gluten-free flour mixes I blend and use in my daily baking: the GF Pastry Flour Mix and the GF Bread Flour Mix, and they are the ones I will reference in my recipes. However, I do realize that you may not want to bother buying 6 different flours and blending them yourself. So I have found commercial flour blends that will be very good substitutes for the above mixes. My favorite brand is **Authentic Foods** gluten-free flour mixes: to replace my GF Pastry Flour blend, use GF Classical Blend. To replace my GF Bread Flour Mix, use Multi-Blend Flour or if you prefer more of a bean flavor, use Bette's Four Flours Blend. If this brand is difficult to find in your town, I also like **Bob's Red Mill** flour blends: for Pastry, use Bob's All Purpose GF baking Flour. For Baking, use GF Hearty Whole Grain Bread or GF Homemade Wonderful Bread. They are very good products and tend to cost a little less. Another very good brand is **King Arthur's** Gluten-free flour mixes: for Pastry, use their Gluten-Free Multi Purpose Flour. For Baking, use their Gluten-Free Bread Mix.

Please keep in mind that each flour blend is slightly different and you may have to adjust the recipe to achieve the proper consistency. If the mix is too wet, add a little flour mix; if the mix is too dry, add a little more water or alternative milk.

Arzu Grain Mix

This is something brand new. I am offering you two recipes created with this wonderful new gluten-free whole grain product called Arzu by World Wise Grains. It's a unique blend of buckwheat, quinoa, and legumes (garbanzo and white Northern bean flakes). It gives you 8 grams of protein and 6 grams of fiber. It takes only minutes to prepare and can be served in an endless variety of ways, from breakfast cereal to dinner side dishes. It comes in the following flavors: Original, Chai and Southwest. For more recipes and healthy advice, check www.worldwisegrains.com.

Wet Ingredients

Soy Milk

This is the easiest alternative "milk" available. If you can find it, I suggest you use organic soy milk, only so you know it's not made from GMO soy. Its texture is the closest to cow's milk and, for the most part, it reacts the same way. Please note: because some brands contain a lot of sugar, buy unsweetened only and add the sweetener of your choice in the recipe. This way you have control over the amount and quality of sweetness you wish. Taste many different brands to find the one whose flavor you like the best. Use the same amount as cow's milk. You can also find soy "creamer" that can be used instead of half & half.

Rice Milk

Being French, this is not my favorite milk substitute. It's too thin for my taste; I prefer something creamier. On the other hand, if you want a lighter recipe with less fat content, by all means, use rice milk. Even when unsweetened, rice milk tends to be a little sweeter than soy milk, so take that into account in your recipes.

Almond Milk

This is one of my two current favorite milk substitutes. The other one is coconut milk. I love its flavor, slightly almond-y, but not overwhelmingly so. It's a perfect replacement for cow's milk as it has the same cooking and baking qualities. It's a good alternative to soy milk if you are allergic to soy, and it's also a little creamier than rice milk. Buy plain and unsweetened.

Coconut Milk

My other current favorite milk substitute. I love its flavor, and it contains the good kinds of fats. Being very creamy, it's very good for custards. It is a little more expensive than soy milk. If you don't care for the coconut flavor, or if it would interfere with the overall recipe flavor, stay with soy or almond milk. Please be sure to use the coconut milk available in milk cartons, not the canned coconut milk, which is a very different product that will give you completely different results.

Other Alternative Milks

We do have a lot more choices these days. We can also choose hazelnut, walnut, pecan and even hemp milk (yes, you can drink it. It's not against the law!) Unfortunately, they are harder to find and certainly more expensive to buy. Check my shopping list for more details.

Other Assorted Ingredients

Fats

To replace butter, my two favorite healthy fats are extra virgin olive oil and virgin coconut oil. I know that's a lot of virgins, but they're worth it. For the olive oil try to find a brand that does not have too strong a flavor. Italian and American olive oils should do well for you. Spanish oils tend to have a stronger flavor. If you can afford it, avoid other vegetable oils as they tend to be highly processed. Another fat I use when I need to "cream" a fat with sugar is non-hydrogenated, non-GMO oil spreads or margarines. If you are allergic to soy, there is even one brand that does not use soy. Check the shopping list.

Crème Chantilly - Whipped Cream

Again, nowadays it's somewhat easy to find soy-based "whipped cream". By all means, use them for your strawberry shortcake or "vacherin". It gives pretty good results, but be aware that it does not stay "whipped" for very long. Add it to your dessert at the last minute. And for your own sake, do NOT use that gross "whipped topping" out there. You know the name. That stuff will kill you faster than if you ate a pound of fresh butter every day. It's loaded with hydrogenated fat.

Sugar

I know, picky-picky. If you can, avoid refined white sugar. Use organic turbinado sugar instead. It's healthier for you. It still contains beneficial vitamins and minerals.

Gelatin or Kanten?

Although I'm not vegetarian or vegan, I'm not crazy about using gelatin. It believed to contain MSG. How it's made makes me cringe, and lots of funky chemicals are used to "purify" it. Avoid! Instead use agar-agar, also known as kanten. It is derived from red algae, so it is plant-based and the process is a lot more straightforward. The only problem is that it takes a little longer to prepare. Use 1 tsp of agar-agar powder per cup of liquid. Let sit for a few minutes, bring to boil gently and stir well until it's fully dissolved. Cool down to gel. When using agar-agar with acidic fruits or juices, use 25% more agar powder per cup of juice. To substitute with gelatin, 1 teaspoon of agar powder equals 1 tablespoon of gelatin.

Leavening

To help bread rise there is no substitute for yeast. I use dry instant yeast. It is easy to measure and use. Mix it with some warm liquid and little sugar to activate it. Let it foam up and add to your recipe. This is the best way to use it for gluten-free recipes, as you do not have the elasticity offered by the gluten in regular wheat flour. Make sure to buy gluten-free yeast. If you are avoiding yeast, use baking powder instead.

Another good way to help your bread, muffins, cookies, scones and cakes to rise is to use baking soda and baking powder. They are both chemical leavening agents acting on the acidity present in the recipe. Most likely, you will use baking powder, but sometimes the recipe will call for baking soda as well.

Another forgotten leavening agent is eggs. They will help your product rise, and their protein will provide structure. For some light desserts, egg whites are mixed with a pinch of sea salt or cream of tartar, some sugar and whipped to soft peaks. Make sure not to over-whip them, or they will lose all their leavening power.

For all of these above ingredients please check the **Master Shopping List** (Appendix C)

A Few Baking Notes from Chef Alain

Although a lot of you miss your favorite croissants, Danish pastries and puff pastry, there is no way to make a gluten-free version of these wonderful products. What makes them work is gluten's ability to stretch and expand. Some breads and brioche are possible to make, but please don't expect the same texture and flavor. The magic of gluten makes a world of difference in these products.

A few of my GF friends asked me to provide basic baking recipes. Although I understand their needs, I felt that there are plenty of good basic recipe sources in other American books and web sites. Since this book's title contains "…with French Gourmet Food", I will offer mostly French recipes. To make these GF friends happy, I will provide you a few of the recipes I used during my GF baking classes. Thank you for your understanding.

Now let's get rolling, baking or cooking. Don't forget to wash your hands, and see you in the kitchen. A bientôt!

Chef Alain Braux

Pains. *Breads*

Mélange de Farine a Pain Sans Gluten. *Gluten-Free Bread Flour Mix*

This nutritious blend works best in baked goods that require elasticity, such as breads, wraps and pie crusts. This recipe is good for a 2 pound Provencal Boule bread recipe.

Yield: 2 lbs 8 oz

This recipe is **GFCF**

INGREDIENTS

- **6 oz Soy flour**
- **6 oz Chickpea flour (garbanzo bean flour)**
- **8 oz Cornstarch or Potato starch**
- **8 oz Tapioca flour**
- **12 oz White rice flour**

PROCEDURE

1. Weigh all ingredients in a large bowl placed on a scale. Don't forget to zero out between weights. Thoroughly combine all ingredients.

2. Store in a container with a tight lid in your refrigerator until needed.

3. You can double or triple these recipes to make as much flour mix as you need.

Boule de Pain à la Provençale. *French Provencal Boule*

This bread is best if eaten within two days. To crisp and freshen, place the bread in a preheated oven (350F) for 5 minutes. It will keep up to two months sliced in your freezer, wrapped in plastic wrap (or a Ziploc bag) and again in foil. Take out as many slices as you need and toast back to freshness. Modified slightly, this recipe also makes French baguettes and Crusty dinner rolls.

Yield: 8 servings (One 2 lb, 12-oz loaf or four 11-oz baguettes)

Oven Temp: 400F

This recipe is **GFCF**

INGREDIENTS

- **1 lb 8 oz Gluten-free bread flour mix (see separate recipe)**
- **4 tsp Xanthan gum**
- **2 tsp Sea salt**
- **2 Tbsp Turbinado sugar**
- **2 Tbsp Active dry yeast**
- **2 Tbsp Dried herb of choice**
- **or Herbes de Provence mix with lavender**
- **2 Garlic cloves (optional)**
- **1 lb 4 oz Warm water (10 oz)**
- **2 Tbsp Extra virgin olive oil**
- **Rice flour or cornmeal for dusting**

PROCEDURE

1. Grease or lightly spray a 9 x 5 x 5" 2-pound loaf pan. Dust with white rice flour or cornmeal. If you choose to do a boule, prepare a baking pan with a sheet of baking parchment.

2. In a large measuring cup, weigh the warm water (~110F) and olive oil. Mix together.

3. Weigh all the dry ingredients in your mixing bowl.

4. With the paddle attachment, start the mixer at slow speed; add the warm water/olive oil into the dry ingredients until the dough is the consistency of your "ear lobe" (squeeze to feel how soft it is).

5. When the dough has the right consistency, mix for an additional 4 minutes at high speed.

6. With a large spatula or dough scraper, transfer the dough into the baking pan. Spread evenly. Spray with olive oil spray to prevent the dough from crusting. Sprinkle with Herbes de Provence. Cover with a clean towel. Place in a warm place to rise about 50 percent (about 45 min - 1 hour).

7. For a boule, place the dough on a table dusted with gluten-free flour. Flour your hands and round the dough. Place on sheet pan with baking paper. Spray with olive oil to prevent the dough from crusting. Sprinkle with Herbes de Provence. Place in a warm place to rise

about 50 percent (about 45 min - 1 hour).
8. Preheat your oven at 400F.
9. When the dough springs back when pressed in lightly, place in oven and bake for 25-30 minutes.
10. When baked, the bread will sound hollow when tapped and register between 200 and 220F internal temperature on an instant read thermometer.
11. Let the bread cool for 10 minutes before removing from the pan.

Variation 1: French Baguettes

Yield: 4 baguettes

1. Grease and lightly spray two double French bread pans and dust with white rice flour or cornmeal. Prepare the recipe as above.
2. Weigh the dough. Divide the dough into four equal parts. Roll each part into the shape of a French baguette and place each in a French bread pan. They should be about 10-12 inch long.
3. Place a clean kitchen towel over the dough and place the pans in a warm area to rise for approximately 35-40 minutes. The middle of each baguette should rise to the top of the pan and be double its original size.
4. Preheat oven at 400F.
5. Bake bread in the lower tier of the preheated oven for 15-20 minutes. After the first 15 minutes, check your bread for browning. If it's well browned, cover it loosely with a piece of aluminum foil. When baked, your bread should sound hollow when tapped and register 200-220F internal temperature on an instant read thermometer.

Variation 2: Crusty Dinner Rolls

Yield: Makes 24 rolls

1. Line a large cookie sheet with parchment paper and lightly spray with oil.
2. Prepare the French Baguette recipe.
3. Using a large ice cream scoop (about 1/4 cup capacity), scoop dough balls, well spaced, onto your cookie sheet.
4. Cover lightly and let rise in a warm place for 35-40 minutes.
5. Bake in a preheated 400F oven for 15-20 minutes.

6. When baked, the rolls will sound hollow when tapped and register 200-220F internal temperature on an instant read thermometer.

Chef's Tips:

✓ Crunchy crust: For a traditional baguette crust, place a small ovenproof bowl with approximately ½ to 1 cup warm water on the lowest rack of your preheated oven. Bake bread in the lower third of the oven. After the bread has been baking for 15 minutes, carefully remove the water bowl. Finish baking to dry off.

✓ Shiny top: For a shinier crust, 5 minutes before the end of baking, brush the top of your loaves with a little olive oil. Return to the oven and finish baking.

✓ Crusty bottom: For a crustier bottom, remove your loaves from the pan after baking and place it directly on the oven rack to bake for an additional 3 to 5 minutes.

✓ Herbal alternatives: Vary the flavor of your bread by adding different dried or freshly chopped herbs or freshly minced garlic to your dough.

Pain Sans Gluten a la Farine de Sarasin. *Gluten-Free Buckwheat Bread*

This is a heavy but tasty bread. It will last a long time.

Yield: One 2 lb, 4-oz loaf

Oven Temp: 425F

This recipe is **GFCF**

INGREDIENTS

- 8 oz Water, warm
- 7 oz Soy or Almond milk, warm
- 1 Tbsp Agave nectar
- 2 tsp Instant dry yeast
- 3 oz Eggs (about one and a half)
- 8 oz Buckwheat flour
- 6 oz Brown rice flour
- 1 tsp Sea salt
- 1.5 tsp Xanthan gum

PROCEDURE

1. Place a measuring cup on top of the scale. Zero it out. Weigh and mix together water, soy milk, agave nectar, and yeast. Cover and let sit in a warm place for about 15 minutes until the mix foams. Add the beaten eggs. Mix in.

2. Place your mixer's bow on the scale. Zero it out. Weigh the buckwheat, rice flour, salt and xanthan gum.

3. Fit the mixer with the whisk attachment. Start the mixer at low speed.

4. While running, pour the liquids into the flours. The batter should be soft. Pour into a paper or aluminum-lined 9 x 4 x 4 loaf pan. It should be halfway full.

5. Cover with a clean towel. Place in a warm place. Let the dough rise for about an hour until it rises 50 percent more.

6. Meanwhile preheat your oven at 425F.

7. Bake the bread for about 35 to 40 minutes until it sounds hollow. Let cool for a few minutes. Take out of the pan and place on a grid to dry.

Pain au Quinoa. *Quinoa Bread*

This wonderfully scented bread will also offer you a good amount of plant-based protein. Enjoy this nutty-flavored GF bread.

Yield: One 2 lb loaf

Oven Temp: 350F

This recipe is **GFCF**

INGREDIENTS

- **2 oz Water, warm**
- **2 tsp Turbinado sugar**
- **3 tsp Instant baker's yeast**
- **12 oz Brown rice flour**
- **4 oz Amaranth flour**
- **6 oz Quinoa flour**
- **½ tsp Sea salt**
- **¼ tsp Xanthan gum**
- **4 oz Quinoa seeds**
- **10 oz Water, warm**

PROCEDURE

1. Measure the water, sugar and yeast in a small ceramic or glass bowl. Mix well. Cover. Place in a warm place. Let sit for about 15 minutes until the yeast becomes active and starts foaming.
2. Weigh the flours and seeds (brown rice, amaranth, quinoa, salt, and quinoa seeds) in your mixer's bowl. With the paddle attachment, start your mixer at low speed. Add your yeast mix and enough warm water to reach "ear lobe" consistency. Scrape the sides of the bowl. Switch to medium speed and mix the dough well for another minute, but do not overmix.
3. Spray your loaf pan with olive oil. Empty the dough into the pan. Cover with a clean towel and let rise in a warm space for about 45 minutes until it is 50 percent higher.
4. Preheat your oven to 350F.
5. Brush the top of your loaf lightly with water and sprinkle quinoa seeds on top. Bake on the middle rack for about 45 minutes or until a small knife blade comes out clean.

✓ Chef's Tip: If you do not have access to amaranth flour, feel free to use sorghum or garbanzo bean flour.

Brioche au Chocolat et a l'Orange en Casserole. *Chocolate and Orange Brioche in French Oven Pot*

This is a variation on an old brioche recipe I used to make for the Hotel du Pilon in the Alps in my youth.

Yield: One 2 lb loaf in a French oven pot (also known as a Dutch oven) or bread pan

Oven Temp: 350F

This recipe is **GFCF**

INGREDIENTS

- **2 oz Water, warm**
- **2 tsp Turbinado sugar**
- **2 tsp Instant baker's yeast**
- **2 oz Rice milk, warm**
- **2 oz Olive oil**
- **8 oz Eggs (around 4)**
- **1 lb 2 oz Brown rice flour**
- **4 oz Turbinado sugar**
- **½ tsp Sea salt**
- **¼ tsp Xanthan gum**
- **The zest of 2 oranges**
- **4 oz Bittersweet chocolate chips**

PROCEDURE

1. Weigh the warm water, sugar and yeast in a small ceramic or glass bowl. Mix well. Cover. Place in a warm place. Let sit for about 15 minutes until your yeast becomes active and starts foaming.

2. Weigh the wet ingredients in a large measuring cup: warm rice milk (or water), oil, and eggs. Mix together.

3. Weigh the dry ingredients in your mixer's bowl: brown rice flour, sugar, gum, orange zest and chocolate chips. Start mixing with the paddle attachment at low speed. Pour in your wet ingredients and mix until your dough reaches the "ear lobe" consistency. Scrape the sides of your bowl. Switch to medium speed and blend well for another minute. Do not overmix.

4. Line a 2 quart French oven pot with aluminum foil, folding the excess foil over the edges. Cut off the foil at a one inch overhang. Spray with olive oil. If you do not have such a pot, use your regular 2 pound bread pan. Cover with the pot's lid or a clean towel and let rise in a warm area for about 45 minutes, or until it has risen about 50 percent.

5. Preheat your oven to 350F.

6. Bake on the middle rack for about 45-50 minutes (depending on whether you used the pot or the pan) or blade comes out clean. Cool for a few minutes. Take out of the pot or pan. Let cool on a grid.

Pain de Mais aux Herbes de Provence. *Corn Bread with Herbes de Provence*

This is a GFCF version of Bob's Red Mill corn bread I improved for my Peoples Pharmacy customers. I offer them with our daily GF fresh soups.

Yield: One 9x9x2 cake pan or 9" round pan or about 12 medium muffins

Oven Temp: 350F

This recipe is **GFCF**

INGREDIENTS

- **6 oz Eggs (about 3)**
- **1 tsp Sea salt**
- **14 oz Unsweetened almond milk**
- **4 oz Olive oil**
- **1-20 oz package of Bob's Red Mill Cornbread Mix**
- **1 Tbsp Provencal herbs**

PROCEDURE

1. Preheat your oven at 350F.

2. Weight the eggs, salt, almond milk and olive oil in your mixer's bowl.

3. With the paddle attachment, start mixing at low speed and add the content of the corn bread mix and the Herbes de Provence (optional). Mix for a few seconds to gather the ingredients. Scrape the bowl. Switch to medium speed and mix well for another 2 minutes until the batter is smooth.

4. Spray your cake pan with olive oil spray. Pour your mix into the pan. Spread evenly.

5. Bake on the middle rack at 350F for about 30 minutes. Turn the pan around half way. It is ready when the blade of a small knife comes out clean.

6. Let cool. De-pan. To serve with soup, I cut it into 2"x2" squares.

Pain Brioché aux Amandes. *Brioche-Style Almond Bread*

I love almonds, everything almond. Here is one of my favorite almond breads. It's even better when toasted and spread with your favorite fruit spread or preserves.

Yield: One 2 quart French oven pot or one 2 lb bread pan

Oven Temp: 350F

This recipe is **GFCF**

INGREDIENTS

- **2 oz Water, warm**
- **2 tsp Turbinado sugar**
- **2 tsp Instant baker's yeast**
- **14 oz Brown rice flour**
- **2 oz Corn starch**
- **1.5 oz Turbinado sugar**
- **4 oz Almond flour**
- **6 oz Raw whole almonds**
- **½ tsp Xanthan gum**
- **½ tsp Sea salt**
- **10 oz Almond milk, warm**
- **4 oz Eggs (about 2)**
- **½ tsp Almond extract**

PROCEDURE

1. Weigh the warm water, sugar and yeast in a small ceramic bowl. Mix well. Cover and let foam for about 15 minutes to activate the yeast.
2. Weigh the liquid ingredients in a large measuring cup: warm almond milk, eggs, and almond extract.
3. In your mixer's bowl, weigh your dry ingredients: rice flour, corn starch, sugar, almond flour, gum, and sea salt.
4. Start your mixer at low speed with the paddle attachment. Pour the yeast mix and the other liquid until the consistency is soft, but not liquid. Switch to medium speed and mix another 2 minutes until your mix is smooth.
5. Prepare your pot or pan. Line it with aluminum foil. Cut the overhang at one inch. Spray with olive oil.
6. Pour the batter into the pot or pan. Cover with the lid or a clean towel. Let rise in a warm space for about 45 minutes or until your bread is risen about 50 percent. Place a few raw almonds delicately on top of your bread to decorate it.
7. Preheat your oven at 350F.
8. Bake on the middle rack with or without lid for about 45 minutes or until the blade of a small knife comes out clean. Cool down. De-pan carefully. Eat as is with butter or margarine or my favorite, raspberry preserves.

Pain d'Epices de Mamie. *Mamie's Spiced Bread*

When I was little, for special occasions my grandmother, Mamie, would prepare this very special tea bread for us. It was savored mostly over the Holidays, drizzled with a little honey. It was so tempting to eat the whole loaf in one sitting, but she knew better. We were allowed only one slice per afternoon "goûter" (snack).

Yield: One 2 lb bread pan

Oven Temp: 350F

This recipe is **GFCF**

INGREDIENTS

- **10 oz Soy milk, warm**
- **12 oz Locally harvested honey**
- **6 oz Light brown sugar**
- **10 oz Brown rice flour**
- **8 oz White rice flour**
- **2 oz Chestnut flour (or use 20 oz of GF Bread Flour Mix)**
- **½ tsp Xanthan gum**
- **2 tsp Baking soda**
- **1 tsp Ground cinnamon**
- **1 tsp Ground ginger**
- **½ tsp Ground cardamom**
- **½ tsp Ground clove (or use 1 Tbsp Spice blend)**

PROCEDURE

1. Preheat your oven to 350F.
2. Weigh the milk, honey and sugar in a saucepan. Place on low heat and stir until the sugar is completely dissolved.
3. Weigh the dry ingredients in your mixer's bowl: brown rice flour, white rice flour, chestnut flour (or GF bread flour mix), xanthan gum, baking soda, and the spices.
4. Start your mixer at low speed with the paddle attachment and pour the liquids into the dry ingredients. Once the ingredients come together, stop the mixer and scrape the sides of the bowl. Switch to medium speed and mix another 2 minutes until it is smooth.
5. Prepare your pan. Line it with aluminum foil. Cut the overhang at one inch. Spray with olive oil.
6. Pour the batter into the pan. Bake for 45 minutes to one hour, or until the blade of a small knife comes out clean. Allow to cool. De-pan carefully. Let cool fully before your slice and enjoy it.

✓ Chef's Tips: if you don't care for the spice, make it without. It still tastes great. This bread holds very well wrapped in aluminum foil in a dry place. Do not refrigerate, but keep in an airtight box. The older, the better.

Petit Déjeuner. *Breakfast*

Mélange de Farine de Pâtisserie Sans Gluten. *Gluten-free Pastry Flour Mix*

Yield: 2 lbs 3 oz

INGREDIENTS

- 11 oz Brown rice flour
- 11 oz White rice flour
- 7 oz Potato starch
- 6 oz Tapioca starch
- 2 tsp Xanthan gum

PROCEDURE

1. Weigh all ingredients together in a bowl on top of your scale.

2. Mix and sift together.

3. Store in an airtight container in the refrigerator.

Petit Déjeuner A Votre Santé. *A Votre Santé Healthy Home-made Breakfast Cereal*

This recipe is one I created for myself, based on the work of Dr. Budwig of Germany. It is low in sugar, full of soluble fiber and beneficial omega-3 fatty acids. The soy or coconut yogurt will provide live probiotics as well.

Servings: about 30

Prep Time: 10 min.

Finishing Time:

20 min.

INGREDIENTS

To Start:

- **1 bag of GF Rolled Oats (Bob's Red Mill for example)**

Or

- **Maple Glazed Buckwheat Flakes (Nature's Path)**

Add:

- **1 cup sliced raw Almonds**
- **1 cup raw Walnut or Pecan pieces**
- **1 cup raw Sunflower seeds**
- **1 cup raw Pumpkin seeds**
- **2 cups Raisins or Currants or dried Blueberries**

PROCEDURE

1. In a large bowl, mix the cereals with the fruits and nuts.

2. Place in a glass or metal storage container with a tight lid.

3. When ready to use, measure ½ cup into a bowl.

4. Add the ground flax seeds or whole chia seeds (good for omega-3 fatty acids and good fiber for digestion).

5. Pour 1 to 2 ounces of alternative milk of your choice.

6. Add 1 heaping Tbsp of alternative yogurt.

7. Top it off with 1 Tbsp of fruit-flavored Fish or Cod Liver oil, or Flaxseed oil.

8. Mix well. Let it sit for 10 minutes to let the cereal absorb the liquids.

✓ Chef's tip: In Winter, I let my breakfast warm up at 200F in my toaster oven for another 10 minutes while I get ready for work. Another way to do it hot is to boil your milk and add to your cereal mix, stir, and then add the additional ingredients.

- 1 cup candied Ginger

Just before eating, add:

- 2 tsp Flax seeds (ground) or Chia seeds (whole)
- 2 oz Soy, Almond, Coconut, Hazelnut, or Rice milk (your choice)
- 1 Tbsp unsweetened Soy or Coconut Yogurt
- 1 Tbsp Fish or Cod Liver oil (preferably fruit flavored) or Flaxseed oil

Crêpes Petit Déjeuner au Quinoa. *Quinoa Pancakes*

This is a tasty alternative to your regular pancakes and so much healthier for you. Enjoy them with your favorite topping.

Servings: About 12 pancakes depending on size.

This recipe is **GFCF**

INGREDIENTS

- **4 oz White rice flour**
- **2 oz Quinoa flour**
- **1 tsp Baking powder**
- **1 Tbsp Turbinado sugar**
- **8 oz Eggs (around 4)**
- **10-12 oz Soy milk**
- **Coconut oil for cooking**

PROCEDURE

1. Weigh the flours, baking powder and sugar in your mixer's bowl. With the whisk attachment, start mixing at low speed.

2. Add the eggs and the soy milk progressively until there are no lumps. Switch to medium speed and whisk for another minute until the batter is smooth. Let rest for at least 30 minutes.

3. Heat your frying pan. When hot, pour about 2 oz of batter into the pan. Cook until colored on one side. Flip over and finish cooking.

✓ <u>Chef's Tips</u>: This will make fluffy and nutty pancakes filled with fiber and protein. Top them with your favorite topping. I personally like to make a cake with them, alternating butter (or margarine) and fruit preserves in between.

Gaufres de Bruxelles. *Brussels Waffles*

I know this is not really French, but it is made in the French section of Brussels (just kidding!) When we lived there, Brigitte and I loved to get one of these covered with whipped cream and fresh strawberries as a special treat. In Belgium they use beer instead of baker's yeast. Feel free to substitute part of your milk with a good GF beer (do not heat the beer). Cheers!

Servings: 6

This recipe is **GF.** Can be made **GFCF.**

INGREDIENTS

- **12 oz Soy or Almond milk, warm**
- **1 tsp Turbinado sugar**
- **1 tsp Instant baker's yeast**
- **10 oz GF Bread Flour mix**
- **¼ tsp Sea salt**
- **3 oz Butter or non-hydrogenated margarine, melted**
- **3 Egg yolks**
- **3 Egg whites**
- **¼ tsp Sea salt**
- **1 tip of a knife of Cream of tartar**
- **2 Tbsp Turbinado sugar**

PROCEDURE

1. Warm the alternative milk to body temperature. Mix in the yeast and sugar. Let sit covered until it starts to foam, about 15 minutes.
2. Warm your waffle iron.
3. Meanwhile, weigh the flour and salt in your mixer's bowl. When the yeasted milk is ready, start mixing the batter at low speed with the whisk attachment. Add the egg yolks and the milk progressively, then switch to medium speed. The batter should be soft, but not as liquid as a crepe batter. Adjust with additional milk if necessary. Pour into a large bowl.
4. In a separate mixer bowl, weigh the egg whites, salt, cream of tartar and sugar. Whisk at medium speed until they foam up nicely then switch to high and whip until the meringue forms soft peaks.
5. With a rubber spatula, fold half of the egg whites carefully to lighten the mix. Add the other half and fold carefully to keep the batter light. Voila, ready to cook.
6. Cook according to the manufacturer's instructions

✓ Chef's Tips: Sprinkle your waffles with GF powdered sugar or top them with drizzled honey, melted chocolate or any fruit of your liking.

Biscuits aux Canneberges et Noix. *Cranberry Walnut Scones*

One of my favorites breakfast indulgence. While not really French in creation we have adopted this melt-in-your-mouth pastry as ours.

Yield: 8 scones
Oven Temp: 400F
This recipe is **GF**.
Can be made **GFCF**

INGREDIENTS

- 3 oz Brown rice flour
- 3 oz White rice flour
- 2.5 oz Tapioca, corn or potato starch
- 3 oz Almond flour
- 2 ½ tsp Baking powder
- ½ tsp Xanthan gum
- ½ tsp Sea salt
- 2 oz Butter or margarine, cold, cut in small pieces
- 3 oz Cranberries, dried *
- 3 oz Walnut pieces **
- 4 oz Heavy whipping cream or Soy creamer (4 oz)
- 4 oz Eggs (2)
- 1 Tbsp Honey or Agave nectar
- 2 tsp Vanilla extract

PROCEDURE

1. Preheat your oven at 400F.
2. Line a baking pan with baking paper, or spray your pan with olive oil spray and dust with rice flour.
3. In your mixing bowl, weigh together brown rice flour, white rice flour, almond flour, tapioca starch, xanthan gum, baking powder and sea salt. Blend together at slow speed with the paddle.
4. In a separate bowl, weigh cranberries and walnut pieces. Add to dry mix and give it a few turns.
5. Cut the cold butter or margarine into small pieces. Add to the dry mix.
6. In a third bowl, weigh the heavy cream (soy creamer), eggs, agave nectar and vanilla.
7. Starting your mixer at the slowest speed, mix in the butter until it reaches pea size. Add the liquid ingredients and mix only until the dough comes together. Stop the mixer. If needed, finish mixing with a spatula.
8. Using an ice cream scoop #12 (you can find them at baking or restaurant supply store such as Ace Mart or Williams Sonoma, and sometimes at your grocery store baking department). Scoop an even scoopful of the dough and drop onto the baking pan. Make sure to separate them by at least 2 inches. If you don't mind uneven-looking scones, you can form the dough into 8 scones by hand.
9. Press each dough piece gently with your

fingers to flatten it a little. Brush with a
little beaten egg and sprinkle with
cinnamon sugar if desired.

10. Bake on the middle rack for 12-15
minutes. The bottom should be golden
colored when done.

✓ Chef's Tip: For an eggless version, you can replace the eggs with 2 Tbsp
of EnerG egg replacer. You can also replace the first 3 ingredients with
the GF Pastry Flour Mix.

* You can replace dried cranberries with any dried unsulphured fruit of your
choice: raisins, blueberries, strawberries, ginger, etc...

** You can replace the walnut pieces with other nuts of your choice: pecan,
hazelnut or macadamia, or seeds such as sunflower and pumpkin.

Petits Gâteaux aux Bluets et Citron. *Blueberry Lemon Muffins*

Yield: 12 medium muffins

Oven Temp: 350F

This recipe is **GFCF**

INGREDIENTS

- 6 oz Brown Rice flour
- 3 oz Stone-ground Cornmeal
- 3 oz Tapioca starch, Corn starch or Potato starch
- 2 Eggs
- ½ tsp Xanthan gum
- 2 tsp GF Baking powder
- ½ tsp Baking soda
- ½ tsp Sea salt
- 4 oz Unsweetened soy or other alternative milk, warm
- 6 oz Creamy honey or agave nectar
- 4 oz Olive oil
- 2 oz Egg (one)
- The zest of a lemon
- The juice of a lemon
- 8 oz Blueberries, fresh or frozen
- 1 Tbsp Brown rice flour

PROCEDURE

1. Preheat your oven at 350F.
2. Spray your muffin pans with olive oil spray. Dust with brown rice flour or use paper inserts.
3. In your mixer's bowl, weigh all the dry ingredients. Using the whisk attachment, mix together at slow speed until well blended.
4. In small pan, weigh the milk and then warm it up to body temperature over low heat. Add the additional wet ingredients and whisk together.
5. While your mixer is going at low speed, add the wet ingredients into dry ingredients. Mix well but gently.
6. In a separate bowl, toss the fresh or frozen blueberries with brown rice flour, add to mix and mix gently by hand with a rubber spatula.
7. Scoop into paper cups.
8. Bake on middle rack for 18-20 minutes until done.

✓ Chef's Tip: You can substitute the first 3 ingredients with 12 oz GF Pastry Flour Mix.

Petits Gâteaux d'Automne aux Fruits Rouges. *Autumnal Red Fruit Muffins*

This colorful and tasty cake can be made either as a pound cake or as muffins. I like it as a muffin in the morning.

Yield: One 2 lb loaf or 12 medium muffins

Oven Temp: 350F

This recipe is **GFCF**

INGREDIENTS

- 8 oz plain Soy or coconut yogurt
- 4 oz Olive oil
- 4 oz Eggs (2)
- 6 oz Cassava flour
- 2 oz Chestnut flour
- 4 oz Turbinado sugar
- ½ tsp Xanthan gum
- 1 tsp Baking soda
- ¼ tsp Sea salt
- 8 oz Raspberries
- 4 oz Blueberries

PROCEDURE

1. Preheat your oven at 350F.
2. Prepare your muffin pans. Spray with olive oil and sprinkle with rice flour, or use paper inserts.
3. Weigh your wet ingredients in a large measuring cup: yogurt, olive oil and eggs. Mix them together. Set aside.
4. Weigh the dry ingredients in a large mixing bowl: cassava and chestnut flours, sugar, gum, baking soda and salt. Mix well with a whisk.
5. For this recipe, the mixing will be done by hand. Make a well at the center of your dry ingredients, pour the wet ingredients and, using a strong hand whisk, mix well until there are no more lumps. Sprinkle the berries on top of the batter and fold gently with a rubber spatula.
6. Using an ice cream scoop, drop the batter into the paper cups, about ¾ full. Sprinkle with coarse sugar for decoration.
7. Bake 12-15 minutes on the middle rack until the blade of a small knife comes out clean. Cool. Take them out of the muffin pan carefully and enjoy.

✓ Chef's Tip: If you have a hard time finding chestnut and cassava flour, replace them with 8 oz GF Bread Flour Mix.
✓ Off season, you can replace the red fruits with frozen mixed red berries. Toss them still frozen with a little rice flour before mixing into the batter so they don't sink to the bottom.

Petits Gâteaux a la Noix de Coco et Graines de Pavot. *Coconut Lemon Poppy Seed Muffins*

Yield: 6 muffins.

Oven Temp: 350F

This recipe is **GFCF**

INGREDIENTS

- **2 oz Coconut flour**
- **1 ½ tsp Poppy seeds**
- **¼ tsp Baking powder**
- **2 Tbsp Coconut oil, melted to slightly warm**
- **2 Tbsp Coconut or Soy or Almond milk**
- **3 Eggs**
- **3 Tbsp Honey**
- **2 tsp Lemon extract**
- **¼ tsp Sea salt**

PROCEDURE

1. Preheat your oven at 350F.
2. Weigh and combine the coconut flour, poppy seeds and baking powder in your mixer's bowl.
3. In a large measuring cup, weigh and blend together coconut oil, coconut milk, eggs, honey, lemon extract, and salt.
4. Start your mixer at low speed with the paddle attachment. Add the wet ingredients into the dry ingredients. Mix thoroughly then increase the mixer's speed until there are no lumps.
5. Scoop the batter into muffin cups. Sprinkle with shredded coconut.
6. Bake at 350F for about 15 minutes or until the blade of a small knife comes out clean.

Gâteaux pour le Goûter. *Tea Time Poundcakes*

Gâteau Moelleux aux Bananes et Noisettes. *Moist Banana and Hazelnut Pound Cake or Muffins*

Unlike some people, I love ripe, almost dark bananas. That's when their flavor is at its peak. The subtle flavor of hazelnuts adds another layer to this moist pound cake or muffin.

Yield: One 2 lb loaf or 12 medium muffins

Oven Temp: 350F

This recipe is **GFCF**

INGREDIENTS

- **4 oz Hazelnuts, toasted and chopped**
- **12 oz Bananas, very ripe (about three)**
- **4 oz Turbinado sugar**
- **½ tsp Sea salt**
- **1 pinch Black pepper, ground**
- **6 oz Eggs (about 3)**
- **4.5 oz Hazelnut flour**
- **2.5 oz Potato starch**
- **1 tsp Baking soda**

PROCEDURE

1. Preheat your oven at 350F.
2. Toast the hazelnuts for about 10 minutes until fragrant and light brown. Let cool. Chop coarsely.
3. If using a loaf pan, spray with olive oil and coat with rice flour. Do the same for muffin pans, or use paper inserts.
4. Peel the bananas. Place them in your mixer's bowl. Add the sugar, salt and pepper. Mix them well with the paddle.
5. Add the eggs one by one and cream well between additions.
6. In a separate bowl, weigh the flour, starch and baking soda. Whisk together. Stop the mixer. Add the dry mix into the wet mix all at once. Add the chopped hazelnuts. Start mixing at low speed until it gathers. Switch to medium speed and mix well for another minute until smooth.
7. Pour the batter into the pan or scoop into the paper cups. Decorate with whole hazelnuts and bake. Loaf: bake on the middle rack for 35-40 minutes or until the blade of a small knife comes out clean. Muffins: bake for 12-15minutes.

Quatre-Quarts au Citron. *Lemon Pound Cake or Muffins*

This is a traditional French pound cake recipe. "Quatre-quarts" means four quarts. The traditional recipe calls for 4 equal amounts of butter, sugar, eggs and flour. These proportions are slightly different, but the name stayed. The lemon adds a special flavor to it. Enjoy!

Yield: One 2 lb loaf or 12 medium muffins

Oven Temp: 350F

This recipe is **GFCF**

INGREDIENTS

- **6 oz Eggs (3)**
- **6 oz Turbinado sugar**
- **½ tsp Sea salt**
- **6 oz non-hydrogenated Margarine**
- **4 oz White rice flour**
- **2 oz Potato starch**
- **½ tsp Baking soda**
- **½ tsp Xanthan gum**
- **The zest of 2 Lemons**

✓ Chef's Tips: Feel free to substitute orange zest for lemon zest.

PROCEDURE

1. Preheat your oven at 350F.
2. If using a loaf pan, spray with olive oil and coat with rice flour. Do the same for muffin pans or use paper inserts.
3. Weigh your dry ingredients in a separate bowl: rice flour, starch and lemon zest. Set aside until needed.
4. Weigh the eggs, sugar and salt in your mixer's bowl. Start mixing at medium speed with the whisk until light.
5. Gently melt the margarine in a small pan over low heat. Don't let it get too hot or it will cook the eggs when they are combined. Switch the mixer speed to low. Pour the melted margarine slowly into the egg mix while mixing. Stop the mixer.
6. Add all the dry ingredients. Mix slowly until it comes together. Switch to medium speed and whisk another minute until the batter is smooth.
7. Pour the batter into the pan or scoop into the paper cups. Decorate with whole hazelnuts and bake. Loaf: bake on the middle rack for 35-40 minutes or until the blade of a small knife comes out clean. Muffins: bake for 12-15minutes.

Gâteau a la Noix de Coco and aux Canneberges. *Coconut Cranberry Walnut Bread*

Yield: One (9x5x5″) loaf

Oven Temp: 350F

This recipe is **GFCF**

INGREDIENTS

- **1 lb Eggs (about 8)**
- **4 oz Coconut oil, melted**
- **4 oz Coconut or Soy or Almond milk**
- **4 oz Turbinado sugar**
- **1 tsp Vanilla extract**
- **½ tsp Sea salt**
- **3 oz Coconut flour**
- **1 tsp Baking powder**
- **4 oz Dried cranberries**
- **2 oz Walnut pieces**

PROCEDURE

1. Preheat oven at 350F.
2. In a large measuring cup, weigh and blend together eggs, oil, coconut milk, sugar, vanilla and salt.
3. In your mixer's bowl, weigh and combine coconut flour with baking powder.
4. Start your mixer at low speed with the whisk attachment. Mix liquids into dry ingredients to form a soft batter. Increased the speed to medium and whip until there are no lumps.
5. Fold in cranberries and nuts with a rubber spatula.
6. Grease your loaf pan with coconut butter or line with aluminum foil. Pour the batter into the loaf pan.
7. Bake at 350F for about 50-60 minutes until a small knife's blade comes out clean. Remove from pan and cool on rack.

Petits Gateaux Secs. *Cookies*

Cookies au Chocolat et Pecans. Chocolate Chip and Pecan Cookies

Chocolate chip cookies are an American favorite. This recipe gives you a chance to experience the childhood memories of these simple cookies. They are recommended as a special treat to feed the soul of the GF child within that wants to come out and be a kid again.

Yield: About 20 pieces when using scoop #24.

Oven Temp: 350F

This recipe is **GF**. Can be made **CF**

INGREDIENTS

- **4 oz Butter** *
- **4 oz Almond butter** **
- **4 oz Agave nectar**
- **1 Tbsp Vanilla extract**
- **2 oz Egg (1)**
- **10 oz Gluten-free Pastry Flour Mix**
- **1 tsp Xanthan gum**
- **2 tsp Baking soda**
- **1 tsp Baking powder**
- **¼ tsp Sea salt**
- **6 oz Dark chocolate chips**
- **6 oz Pecan or walnut pieces**

PROCEDURE

1. Preheat your oven to 350F.
2. Weigh butter, almond butter, agave, and vanilla in the mixer's bowl. Cream together at medium speed.
3. When the above mix is creamed, add eggs one by one and mix well.
4. Sift together GF flour mix, baking soda, baking powder and salt. Add chocolate chips and pecan pieces. Mix together.
5. Add all dry ingredients into wet ingredients. Mix until dry ingredients are incorporated, but do not overmix.
6. With an ice cream scoop #24, scoop the dough on baking pans covered with baking paper. (If you do not have a scoop, you can use a tablespoon.)
7. Flatten the dough to the desired thickness with your fingers.
8. Bake at 350F for about 12 minutes or until the bottom is golden color. Cool and Serve.

* If you're dairy-free, feel free to substitute Earth Balance or other non hydrogenated vegetable shortening for the butter.

** You're welcome to substitute peanut, cashew, or hazelnut butter to almond butter for fun or according to your specific allergies.

Brownies à la Farine de Coco. *Coconut Flour Brownies*

In this recipe, I like to combine the flavors of the dark chocolate and coconut flour. Use a chocolate with at least 70% cocoa content. These are very moist brownies that your kids will ask for again and again.

Servings: 24 bars

Oven Temp: 350F

Prep Time: 20 min.

Cooking Time: 30 min.

This recipe is **GFCF**

INGREDIENTS

- 8 oz Coconut oil
- 8 oz Brown sugar
- 8 oz. Bittersweet chocolate
- 4 tbsp Agave nectar
- 2 tsp Vanilla extract
- 4 tbsp unsweetened Cocoa powder
- 4 whole Eggs
- 4 oz Turbinado sugar
- 1 pinch of sea Salt
- 6 oz Coconut flour
- 1 tsp Baking powder
- 2 oz Coconut "half & half" creamer

PROCEDURE

1. Preheat oven to 350 degrees.
2. Grease and dust an 11x8 pan with coconut oil and cocoa powder.
3. Place coconut oil, brown sugar, chocolate, agave nectar, and vanilla extract in a medium sized pot and melt on low heat, stirring until everything is well blended and smooth.
4. Sift in the cocoa powder. Mix well.
5. Remove from heat and cool down.
6. Beat the eggs, turbinado sugar and vanilla extract together in your stand mixer at high speed until frothy.
7. Meanwhile, weigh and mix together the coconut flour and baking powder.
8. Switch your mixer to low speed. Mix in the cooled chocolate mixture and sugar. Alternatively add in the flour with baking powder and coconut creamer, gently mixing after each addition.
9. Pour mixture into the prepared pan. Bake the brownies for 30 minutes or until the top of the brownies is crisp and the edges begin to pull away from the pan. (The center of the brownies will be dense and soft to the touch.)
10. Cool the brownies in the pan on a wire rack until cool.
11. Gently flip the brownie over a cutting board, cut into bars and serve.

Petits Gâteaux Secs à la Noix de Coco et au Citron et Citron Vert. *Lemon-Lime Coconut Flour Cookies*

The sourness of the lemon and lime flavors enhances the coconut sweetness. Merveilleux!

Yield: About 2 dozen cookies

Oven Temp: 350F

This recipe is: **GFCF**

INGREDIENTS

- **6 oz Butter or non-hydrogenated margarine**
- **6 oz Turbinado sugar**
- **1 Tbsp Lemon peel, grated**
- **2 tsp Lime peel, grated**
- **4 oz Coconut flour**
- **2 oz GF Pastry Flour Mix**
- **1 tsp Baking soda**
- **1 tsp GF Baking powder**
- **½ tsp Sea salt**
- **4 oz Eggs (2)**
- **2 Tbsp Lemon juice**
- **1 Tbsp Lime juice**

PROCEDURE

1. Pre-heat your oven to 350F.

2. With the paddle attachment, beat the butter/margarine, sugar, lemon peel and lime peel in your mixer's bowl.

3. When light and creamy, add the eggs one at a time until incorporated. Add the lemon and lime juices a little at a time until absorbed.

4. Weigh the coconut flour, GF Pastry flour mix, baking soda, baking powder, and salt in another bowl.

5. Stir into the wet mixture and continue mixing at medium speed.

6. Shape the dough into 1-inch balls. Place 2 inches apart on baking sheets covered with parchment (baking) paper.

7. Bake 10-12 minutes or until set. Immediately remove from the pans and cool in a wire rack.

Sablés Diamants. *Shortbread Cookies with Raspberry Dots*

I used to make these cookies the traditional way during my apprenticeship at Auer in Nice. I created this GF version for you.

Yield: About 2 dozen cookies

Oven Temp: 350F

This recipe is: **GF**

Can be made **CF**

INGREDIENTS

- **4 oz Turbinado sugar**
- **8 oz Unsalted butter or Earth Balance margarine**
- **¼ tsp Sea salt**
- **4 oz Eggs (2)**
- **1 tsp Lemon Juice**
- **1 Lemon zest**
- **1 tsp Vanilla extract**
- **12 oz GF Pastry Flour Mix**
- **3 oz White rice flour**
- **1 cup Crystallized sugar for rolling**

PROCEDURE

1. Weigh the sugar in your mixing bowl. Cut the butter/margarine into small pieces and add. Add salt.
2. Using the paddle attachment, start the mixer at low speed until it comes together, then switch to medium speed and cream well until light and fluffy.
3. Weigh the eggs, lemon juice, zest and vanilla extract. Beat together with a fork. Add to mix a little at a time. Cream well between additions.
4. Weigh the dry ingredients separately. Add them all at once. Give a short mix until the dough comes together.
5. Divide into two 1 lb pieces. Roll each into a log about 2 inches in diameter. Roll the log in crystallized sugar. Wrap tightly in plastic film. Refrigerate at least 2 hours or overnight.
6. The next day, preheat your oven to 350F.
7. Slice each roll into ½ inch slices. Place them on a baking pan covered with wax or baking paper. Space them one inch apart. With a small spoon, drop a small dollop of raspberry preserves at the center of each cookie.
8. Bake for 8 to 10 minutes or until the bottom of the cookies are golden brown. Let cool. Enjoy with dairy-free frozen dessert.

Macarons Meringues à la Noix de Coco. *Coconut Macaroon Meringues*

These wonderfully chewy coconut macaroons taste ever better when dipped in melted chocolate.

Yield: About 2 dozen 1 oz cookies

Oven Temp: 300F

This recipe is: **GFCF**

INGREDIENTS

- **4 oz Egg whites, room temperature**
- **1 pinch Sea salt**
- **½ tsp Cream of tartar**
- **4 oz Granulated sugar**
- **8 oz Shredded coconut**
- **4 oz Powdered sugar**

PROCEDURE

1. Preheat your oven to 300F.

2. Weigh the egg whites with the cream of tartar and salt in your mixer's bowl. Start whipping at medium speed with the whisk attachment until half-whipped.

3. When the meringue slides off the edge of the bowl, increase speed to high and add the sugar in a rainfall manner until it is all absorbed. Whip to firm peaks (when you take a little bit of meringue off the bowl, it stands up).

4. Stop the mixer. Take the whisk away. Weigh the coconut and powdered sugar in a separate bowl, then fold in with a rubber spatula.

5. Drop 1 oz cookies with a teaspoon onto pans lined with baking paper.

6. Bake for about 30 minutes at 300F. When you squeeze one with your fingers, it should still be moist at the center. Let cool.

7. Melt some dark chocolate and dip halfway. Place on a sheet pan covered with wax paper. Refrigerate. Eat whenever you need a GFCF treat.

Biscuits Croquants au Chocolat et Amandes. *Almond Butter Chocolate Chip Crisps*

This is a recipe I adapted from my friends at Arzu, Kim and Kristen. Arzu is a wonderful GF grain and legumes mix that can be used in many recipes. I chose to make cookies with their Chai mix.

Yield: About 20 cookies

Prep Time: 10 min.

Baking Time: 8-10 min.

Oven Temp: 350F

This recipe is **GFCF**

INGREDIENTS

- **8 oz Raw almond butter**
- **8 oz Agave nectar**
- **2 tsp GF Vanilla extract**
- **4 oz Eggs (2)**
- **8 oz Chai Arzu mix**
- **2 Tbsp Raw cocoa powder**
- **2 tsp Baking soda**
- **4 oz Dark chocolate chips**

PROCEDURE

1. Preheat your oven to 350F.

2. Weigh the almond butter and agave nectar together in your mixer's bowl on top of your scale. Cream together. Add vanilla. Add eggs one at a time and continue to cream.

3. Weigh and mix together Chai Arzu, cocoa powder, baking soda, and chocolate chips. Add to the creamed mix and mix well.

4. Using a small ice cream scoop (#24), scoop out cookies on sheet pans covered with baking paper. In a pinch, a tablespoon will also work.

5. Bake at 350F for 8-10 minutes until the edges are firm. If you prefer this cookie chewy, bake it less.

6. Store in an airtight container at room temperature.

Biscuits Quinoa aux Chocolat, Pecans et Orange. *Chocolate-Pecan-Orange Quinoa Cookies*

I love these tasty and chewy cookies. They're easy to make and easy to eat. Enjoy!

Yield: About 12 cookies

Oven Temp: 350F

This recipe is: **GFCF**

INGREDIENTS

- 2 oz non-hydrogenated margarine
- 2 oz Turbinado sugar
- ¼ tsp Sea salt
- 6 oz Soy or coconut yogurt
- 2 oz Raisins
- 2 oz Pecan pieces
- 2 oz Semisweet chocolate chips
- ¼ tsp Orange extract
- 2 oz Quinoa flour
- 1.5 oz White rice flour
- 1 tsp Baking powder

PROCEDURE

1. Preheat your oven at 350F.

2. Weigh the margarine, sugar and salt together in your mixer's bowl. With the paddle attachment, cream together at medium speed until light and fluffy. Add the yogurt and orange extract. Mix well.

3. In a separate bowl, weigh the flours and baking powder. Whisk together. Add the raisins, pecans, and chocolate chips. Toss with the flour mix.

4. Add to the mixer and mix well. Do not overmix.

5. Drop onto baking pans covered with wax or baking paper. Dipping your fingers in cold water, flatten the cookies.

6. Bake at 350F for 6-8 minutes until they start to color at the edges.

7. Cool down. Store in an airtight container at room temperature.

Langues de Chat. *Cat's Tongue Cookies*

In France, this crispy cookie is usually served with ice cream or sorbet. It is sometimes filled with ganache and dipped in chocolate. Typically, it is squeezed from a pastry bag into a long shape. In this recipe, we'll just drop the batter with a spoon to make it easier for you.

Yield: About 30-40 cookies

Oven Temp: 350F

This recipe is: **GFCF**

INGREDIENTS

- **2 oz Non-hydrogenated margarine or 2 oz olive oil**
- **2 oz Turbinado sugar**
- **1 Pinch of salt**
- **4 oz Eggs, beaten (2)**
- **2.5 oz White rice flour**
- **3 oz GF Pastry Flour Mix**
- **The zest of 1 lemon**

PROCEDURE

1. Preheat your oven at 350F.

2. Whisk the margarine until creamy.

3. Add the sugar and salt. Mix well.

4. Add the beaten eggs a little at a time. Whisk well until absorbed in the mix.

5. Add the flours and lemon zest. Whisk well until all the lumps are gone.

6. Using a teaspoon, drop little mounds of batter on a pan covered with baking paper. Make sure to give them at least one inch space between each other as they spread a lot.

7. Bake for 8-10 minutes until the edges are lightly brown. Cool down. Store in an airtight container.

✓ <u>Chef's Tips</u>: If you wish, you can place a dab of ganache on the inside of one cookie and press another one over it. Dip them halfway in melted chocolate. Refrigerate for a while. Enjoy with frozen dessert like coconut ice cream, soy ice cream or fruit sorbet.

Escargots à la Pate d'Amandes. *Almond Paste Snails*

I learned to make these cookies during my apprenticeship at Auer in Nice, right across the street from the Opera House... in case you're going there for your next vacation. They really are very simple to make, but you need a little expertise in using a pastry bag... and fast fingers to catch them.

Yield: about 20 - 1 ounce cookies

Oven Temp: 400F

This recipe is **GFCF**

INGREDIENTS

- **1 lb Pure almond paste (make sure to buy the 50% almond, 50% sugar type)**
- **2 to 3 Egg whites**
- **2 tsp Apricot jam**
- **Candied red cherries for decoration**
- **40 Pine nuts for decoration**
- **2 oz Apricot glaze**

✓ <u>Chef's Tips</u>: Now start a race between your fingers and the escargots and see who wins.

PROCEDURE

1. In your mixer's bowl, weigh all the ingredients but reserve one egg white to adjust consistency.

2. Starting on low speed with the paddle, mix all the ingredients. When they get together, increase the speed to medium. Adjust the consistency to a thick paste but not too soft, or it will run in the oven.

3. Fill a pastry bag fitted with a large star tip with the batter. Stick the baking paper on the baking sheet with a little batter at all four corners. With your pastry bag "draw" a 2 inch long stick and finish with a scroll, making the shape of a snail. When all done, place one half of a candied cherry on top of the scroll and 2 pine nut at the tip of the stick to look like the escargot's "horns". Let dry at room temperature for at least 30 minutes to allow for crusting.

4. Preheat your oven at 400F.

5. Place your baking pan(s) on the middle rack and bake for 8-10 minutes, or until the cookies have a light brown color. Do not overcook or they will be dry. If you wish, you can glaze your cookies with apricot glaze using a pastry brush.

Hors D'Œuvres. *Appetizers*

Tapenade. *Tapenade*

This is a wonderful appetizer loaded with black olives and a touch of capers. Its original name comes from a loose translation of the Provencal word "tapeno" which means "capers". In my modest opinion, they should have called it "olivado" since there are many more olives. Go figure!

Servings: 4

Prep Time: 30 min.

INGREDIENTS

- **1 garlic clove, chopped fine**
- **2 Tbsp capers, drained and chopped fine**
- **8 oz pitted black olives Niçoises**
- **¼ tsp freshly ground black pepper**
- **8 anchovies filets in oil, drained**
- **8 to 10 Tbsp extra virgin olive oil**
- **Any GF toasts, crackers or rice crackers you prefer**

PROCEDURE

1. Chop the capers and garlic finely with a chef's knife.

2. Place the olives in the bowl of a food processor fitted with the metal blade. Chop by pulsing until coarse.

3. Add the chopped garlic and capers, pepper and anchovies. Pulse until finely chopped.

4. Add the olive oil and incorporate with a few additional pulses.

5. To enjoy, top each cracker with tapenade and munch with delight.

✓ Chef's Tips: Please do not over-process. This should not be a cream or a paste. It tastes a lot better if you leave it kind of chunky.

Crêpes aux Courgettes. *Zucchini Appetizer Crepes*

This recipe comes from my sister Isabelle in Nice, France. I hope you enjoy them as much as I did when I was last in Nice.

Servings : 4-6

Yield : about 12 crepes depending on the size

Prep Time: 20 min.

Cooking Time: 20 min.

This recipe is **GFCF**

INGREDIENTS

- **10 oz Soy or Rice milk**
- **1 Tbsp Pastis (optional)**
- **6 oz Eggs (3)**
- **½ tsp Sea salt**
- **4 oz Brown rice flour**
- **1 oz Garbanzo bean flour**
- **4 medium Zucchinis**
- **2 Tbsp Olive oil**
- **4 Parsley sprigs, chopped**
- **1 pinch Sea salt**
- **1 pinch Black pepper, ground**

✓ <u>Chef's Tips</u>: Feel free to drink a nice "aperitif" of Pastis with this appetizer. Tastes just like Nice because Nice is nice.

PROCEDURE

1. Prepare the crepe batter: in a blender bowl, weigh the soy or rice milk, Pastis (Anis-flavored liquor served before lunch in the Provence-Cote d'Azur region. Optional), eggs, and salt. Whirl a little at low speed to break up the eggs. Add the rice and garbanzo flour, and blend first at low speed then high until all ingredients are well blended. Pour into a large ceramic bowl. Cover and let rest for at least 30 minutes.

2. Meanwhile, prepare your zucchinis. Wash them. Cut both ends off. Cut in quarters lengthwise, and then slice thinly.

3. Heat the olive oil in a frying pan. Add the sliced zucchini; add salt and pepper and sauté until tender. Take off the heat. Sprinkle with the chopped parsley and toss together. Let cool.

4. When everything has had a good "sieste" (nap), adjust the batter consistency if needed. Add more milk if you need to thin it down; it should be similar to a very thin pancake batter. Add the cooked zucchinis and mix carefully.

5. Heat more olive oil in a clean frying pan at medium heat. Pour about 2 ounces of batter into the pan, swirl to cover the bottom of the pan, and cook until golden at the bottom. Flip over and finish cooking. Place on a heated plate. Sprinkle with a little more chopped parsley and eat with a little crème fraiche or dip into plain soy or coconut yogurt.

Socca de Nice. *Socca from Nice*

Socca is a snack made from chickpea cooked like a large, thin crepes in Nice. It's another memory from my youth. When I was an apprentice at Auer near the Cours Saleia (the flower market in Nice), I was sent once in a while on Sundays to buy socca for all of us. It is a very simple dish, but as with most of us, remembrance makes everything taste better. Every time I go back home to visit my family, I make sure to make a special trip to the flower market and savor a piece of hot and still crunchy socca. You should too. Tell them I sent you.

Servings : 4-6

Servings: 4 -6

Oven set on **Broiler**

Prep Time: 10 min.

Baking Time: 4-5 min.

This recipe is **GFCF**

INGREDIENTS

- **8 oz Garbanzo bean flour**
- **1 tsp Sea salt**
- **Tbsp Extra virgin olive oil**
- **2 lbs (1 qt) Water**

PROCEDURE

1. Preheat your broiler.
2. Weigh garbanzo bean flour and salt in a large mixing bowl.
3. Add the olive oil and water progressively while mixing vigorously with a hand whisk. Mix until without lumps. Let rest for an hour.
4. Oil a baking pan with high edges with olive oil. Pour the batter into the pan. The batter should only be about 1/8th of an inch thick. If needed, prepare more pans.
5. Broil carefully. It will cook very quickly, so keep an eye on it. Cook it until it is a golden color. If it is slightly burned in spots, that's okay. We all like it like that.
6. Cut it in pieces with a pizza cutter. Eat it while it's still hot with cracked black pepper on it. That's the way we eat it in Nice.
6. . Place on a heated plate. Sprinkle with a little more chopped parsley and eat with a little crème fraiche or dip into plain soy or coconut yogurt.

✓ Chef's Tips: If you happen to have a wood fired oven or grill, so much the better. That is the traditional way to cook socca. Follow the same instructions.

Trempette Arzu aux Epinards et Artichauts. *Arzu Spinach and Artichoke Dip*

Looking for a great TV snack? This yummy, gluten-free, dairy-free ARZU Spinach and Artichoke Dip is for you!

Servings : 4-6

Servings: Ten 3 oz servings

Prep Time: 20 min.

Baking Time: 10 min.

Oven Temp: 400F

This recipe is **GF**. Can be made **CF**

INGREDIENTS

- ¼ cup Olive oil
- ½ White onion, finely chopped
- 1 Carrot, finely minced
- 1 Leek, finely minced or additional ½ chopped onion
- 4 Garlic cloves, minced
- ½ Jalapeno, minced
- 1 tsp Dry mustard
- ¼ tsp Nutmeg, ground
- 1 tsp Savory or thyme
- 1-14 ounce Can Artichoke hearts, rinsed, drained and chopped
- 8 oz Fresh baby

PROCEDURE

1. Preheat your oven at 400F.
2. Heat olive oil in a 6-quart sauce pan over medium heat. Add chopped onion, carrot and leek. Sauté until onions are transparent.
3. Add minced garlic and jalapenos and cook until soft.
4. Add rinsed artichoke heart pieces and fresh spinach or entire package of frozen spinach (including liquid). Cook until all ingredients are heated and the liquid is mostly evaporated.
5. Add spices: dry mustard, nutmeg, savory, sea salt, and black pepper.
6. Add the dry Arzu to the spinach mixture. Slowly add stock to mixture and blend all ingredients together until creamy. Add additional stock if needed.
7. Turn heat down to low and cover pot for 5-10 minutes, stirring occasionally.
8. Take off the heat. Add sour cream or sour cream substitute and blend well.
9. Pour into a ceramic or glass baking dish. Top with grated cheese or non-dairy parmesan cheese if desired. Place in the oven and gratin until the cheese bubbles and gets a nice golden color.
10. Serve with fresh sliced vegetables such as zucchini, bell peppers, carrots, etc or gluten free/dairy free chips or crackers.

spinach or frozen
- 1 cup Original Arzu
- 1 cup GF Chicken or
  Vegetable stock
- ¾ cup Sour cream or
  dairy-free sour cream
- ½ tsp Sea salt
- Black pepper to taste
- 2 Tbsp Parmesan or
  Romano cheese,
  grated, or non-dairy
  parmesan cheese

✓ Chef's Tips: You can choose to bypass the whole oven procedure and pour this dip in a crock pot on low to keep it warm while you dip your chips and veggies into it.

Soupes. *Soups*

Soupe de Santé Verte d'Alain. *Alain's Healthy Green Soup*

When I feel "barbouillé" or "pas dans mon assiette", like when I feel a cold or flu coming on, I take a large bowl of this soup, go to bed, sweat it out and I usually feel a lot better the next day. Since I always have these ingredients at hand, this soup is very easy to put together in a few minutes.

Servings: 1

Yield: 2 soup bowls

Prep Time: 5 min.

INGREDIENTS

- **2 cups filtered or spring water**
- **4 cups of mixed field greens, or any greens you happen to have**
- **8 broccoli or cauliflower florets**
- **1 carrot, sliced**
- **2 garlic cloves**
- **1 tsp fresh ginger**
- **1 Tbsp fish oil**
- **1 Tbsp miso paste**
- **1 tsp sea salt**
- **½ tsp cayenne pepper**
- **1 tsp turmeric spice**

PROCEDURE

1. Bring water to boil.

2. Meanwhile, put all the ingredients listed in your blender's jar. Be creative and add any fresh vegetables you have in your fridge. What you put in is probably what you need.

3. If you want it to be thicker, you can add 1 cup of cooked rice, a small cooked sweet potato, or even a raw egg for additional protein.

4. Pour hot water over the ingredients and start blending slowly, then at high speed until finely pureed.

5. Enjoy hot and go to bed to detox your body with a good sweating.

✓ Chef's Tips: This is a hot but raw soup. The water is boiled, but the vegetables are not cooked. All the vitamins, minerals and chlorophyll are fully active and ready to help you feel better. Enjoy!

Soupe Gaspacho. Gazpacho *Soup*

As most of you probably know, this is a classic Spanish soup, but it is appreciated during the hot summer all over the Mediterranean basin. This is a simple recipe, but the results will depend largely on the quality of your fresh vegetables.

Servings: 4

Prep Time: 20 min.

Cooking Time: 20 min.

INGREDIENTS

- 4 genuinely ripe medium tomatoes (local and in season is best)
- 2 medium cucumbers, sliced
- 2 celery branches, sliced
- 4 Tbsp extra virgin olive oil
- 2 Tbsp parley, chopped
- 2 Tbsp fresh basil, chopped
- 2 large garlic cloves, chopped
- 1 Tbsp sea salt
- 1 tsp black pepper, freshly ground
- Tabasco to taste
- 1 slice of dried GF bread, cubed (optional)

PROCEDURE

1. If you wish, you can peel your tomatoes by plunging them in boiling water for a minute or until the skin detach from the fruit; pick up with a slotted spoon and drop in a container filled with iced water; let cool and peel.

2. You can also decide to take the seeds out. In that case, quarter your tomatoes and squeeze the seeds out.

3. Place the quartered tomatoes, sliced cucumber and celery in a food processor and process fine.

4. Add olive oil, parsley, basil, cloves, salt and pepper and Tabasco to taste and finish blending.

5. One trick I learned from a friend is to add cubes of dried GF bread and blend with the soup at the end to thicken this wonderful soup. Adjust seasoning to taste.

6. For best flavor, serve this soup at room temperature and sprinkle with chopped parsley.

Soupe de Légumes au Bœuf. *Beef Vegetable Soup*

This is a very flavorful recipe I put together for Peoples Pharmacy. It is very earthy and healthy. If you don't have the time to prepare it tonight, why don't you stop by our store and get a bowl? That was easy, wasn't it?

Servings: 4-6

Prep Time: 15 min.

Cooking Time: 45-50 min.

This recipe is **GFCF**

INGREDIENTS

- 1 Tbsp Olive oil

- ½ **White onion,** **chopped**
- 2 **Garlic cloves,** **chopped fine**
- ½ **Celery branch,** **chopped**
- 1 tsp Sea Salt
- 8 oz Grass-fed Beef (stew 1" cubed or ground)
- 1 can (15 oz) tomatoes, diced
- 1.5 oz Tomato paste
- 1 Medium Yukon Gold potato, cubed
- 1 Carrot, sliced thin
- 1 Zucchini, sliced
- 8 oz Fresh Green beans, quartered (or frozen)
- 1.5 qt organic Beef broth
- ½ tsp Black pepper, ground

PROCEDURE

1. In a large soup pot, sauté chopped onions, garlic and celery in olive oil until translucent.

2. Add the beef and cook for a few minutes, stirring once in a while until the beef begins to brown.

3. Add cubed potato, tomatoes with juice, sliced carrot, zucchini, green beans, tomato paste, and spices. Sauté all together to get all the flavors blended.

4. Add the beef broth. Bring to boil, simmer for 45-50 minutes or until the meat is tender.

5. When soup is ready, add chopped parsley and GF Worcestershire sauce. Stir in and serve.

- 1 Bay leaf
- ½ tsp Dried marjoram
- ½ tsp Dried thyme leaves
- ½ Tbsp GF Worcestershire sauce
- ½ Tbsp Parsley, chopped

Soupe de Courgettes. *Zucchini Soup*

I love this soup in summer while the zucchini are fresh and flavorful. This can be eaten cold with a little soy or coconut creamer added to it.

Servings: 4-6

Prep Time: 10 min.

Cooking Time: 1 hour

This recipe is **GFCF**

INGREDIENTS

- **1 Tbsp Olive oil**
- **2 medium onions, chopped**
- **1 Garlic clove, chopped finely**
- **1 tsp Sea salt**
- **6 medium Zucchinis, sliced**
- **1 Bay leaf**
- **½ tsp Black pepper, ground**
- **½ tsp dried Oregano**
- **½ tsp dried Sage**
- **½ tsp dried Thyme**
- **½ tsp dried Rosemary**
- **2 qt organic Vegetable broth**
- **4 oz Brown rice, rinsed**

PROCEDURE

1. In a large soup pot, heat the oil and sauté onions, garlic and salt until the onions are transparent.
2. Add the zucchinis and spices and stir into the other ingredients for a few minutes.
3. Add the vegetable broth. Bring to boil and simmer for about 40 minutes. At this point, you have two choices: you can puree the whole soup in a blender or leave it as is. I like to blend half, and leave half with zucchini slices for a better mouth feel.
4. Add the rice; cook another 20 minutes until the rice is done. Enjoy!

✓ Chef's Tips: If you wish you can sprinkle parmesan or cheese substitute over the soup just before eating.

Soupe de Tomates à la Niçoise. *Niçoise-style Tomato Soup*

Like most people from Southern Europe - France, Italy and Spain, we love tomatoes. Here's a simple but flavorful tomato soup the way we do it in Nice.

Servings: 4-6

Prep Time: 15 min.

Cooking Time: 30 min.

This recipe is **GFCF**

INGREDIENTS

- **2 Tbsp Olive oil**
- **2 medium White onions, chopped**
- **2 Garlic cloves, sliced**
- **1 tsp Sea salt**
- **3 lbs (about 12) ripe Tomatoes**
- **2 tsp Sugar**
- **5-6 Basil leaves**
- **2 tsp dried Thyme**
- **1 Bay leaf**
- **1 Clove**
- **1 tsp Black pepper, ground**
- **1 qt Vegetable broth, as needed**
- **5-6 Parsley sprigs**
- **1 Garlic clove, chopped finely**
- **1 Tbsp Olive oil**
- **1 cup Rice or tapioca (optional)**

PROCEDURE

1. In a large soup pot, sauté the onions, garlic and salt in olive oil until golden.
2. Clean and quarter your tomatoes. Add to the onion mix. Add sugar, basil, thyme, laurel, clove and black pepper. Bring to boil and cook at medium-low heat for about 20 minutes until the tomatoes are tender.
3. Process the whole soup in a food processor with the metal blade until coarse, but not pureed. Put back into the pot and dilute with the vegetable broth to your taste. Bring to boil.
4. At this point, you could leave this soup as is. It can be enjoyed hot or cold.
5. Or, you could add the thickener of your choice: rice, tapioca or even some leftover mashed potatoes. I'll let you decide. Me, I like the rice. Cook another 20 minutes to cook the rice or tapioca.
6. Just before serving, mix the finely chopped parsley and garlic with the olive oil. Stir into the soup and serve.

Soupe aux Lentilles et à la Tomate. *Lentil Tomato Soup*

Another Peoples Pharmacy soup created by Nancy at the North Lamar store. Thank you, Nancy!

Servings: 4-6

Prep Time: 10 min.

Cooking Time: 1 hour

This recipe is **GFCF**

INGREDIENTS

- **1 Tbsp Olive oil**
- **½ White onion, chopped**
- **2 Carrots, diced**
- **1 Celery branch, diced**
- **1 tsp Sea Salt**
- **2 Garlic cloves, minced**
- **1 tsp dried Oregano**
- **1 tsp dried Basil**
- **1 Bay leaf**
- **½ tsp Black pepper, ground**
- **2 cups dry Lentils, rinsed**
- **1 can (15 ounce) crushed tomatoes**
- **1 qt organic Vegetable broth**
- **½ cup Baby spinach, rinsed and thinly sliced**
- **1 Tbsp Apple cider vinegar**

PROCEDURE

1. In a large soup pot, heat oil over medium heat.
2. Add chopped onions, carrots, and celery; cook and stir until onion is tender.
3. Stir in garlic, bay leaf, oregano, and basil; cook for another 2 minutes.
4. Add in vegetable broth, lentils, and tomatoes. Bring to a boil.
5. Reduce heat, and simmer for at least 1 hour.
6. When ready to serve stir in spinach and vinegar, and cook until it wilts. Serve.

✓ Chef's Tips: This is a very warming winter soup. To add a little flavor to it, I like to add a spoon of plain soy or coconut yogurt to it and stir.

Soupe de Poix Chiches à la Sauge. *Garbanzo Bean Soup with Sage*

It is not common for sage to be used in a soup. Here it goes very well with the sturdiness and earthiness of the garbanzo beans . Give it a try; It will surprise you!

Servings: 4-6

Prep Time: 10 min.

Cooking Time: 1 1/2 hours

This recipe is **GFCF**

INGREDIENTS

- 2 qt Water
- 1 lb organic dry Garbanzo beans, soaked overnight
- 2 medium Onions, sliced
- 2 large Carrots, sliced
- Heart of lettuce leaves, sliced
- 1 Garlic clove
- 10 fresh Sage leaves
- 1 sprig fresh Thyme
- Salt and Pepper to taste
- 2 Tbsp Olive oil

PROCEDURE

1. In a large pot, put together the water, beans, onions, carrots, lettuce, garlic, sage and thyme. Caution: Do not add the salt at this time or the beans will be tough.
2. Bring to boil. Simmer for about one and a half hours until the beans are tender.
3. Adjust the seasoning with salt and pepper. When serving, drizzle olive oil over the plate.

Salades. *Salads*

Vinaigrette de Santé d'Alain. *Alain's Healthy Salad Dressing*

This is not a magic potion - like the one of Asterix and Obelix comic book fame (the fans will know what I'm talking about) - but pretty darn close. It is loaded with ingredients known to help keep your heart healthy.

Servings: about 30

Prep Time: 15 min.

This recipe is **GFCF**

INGREDIENTS

- **1 cup apple cider vinegar or fresh lemon or lime juice**
- **4 cloves of fresh garlic, peeled and sliced**
- **1-2" piece of Ginger, peeled and sliced**
- **3 Tbsp Dijon-style Mustard**
- **1 tsp Sea Salt**
- **½ tsp Cayenne Pepper**
- **1 cup extra-virgin olive oil (or 2 cups olive oil, no flax seed oil)**
- **1 cup of flax seed oil for an extra boost of omega 3 fatty acids**
- **2 Tbsp GF Tamari Sauce**

PROCEDURE

1. Place the first set of ingredients in the blender. Blend at high speed until garlic and ginger are well processed.
2. Meanwhile, measure olive oil and flax seed oil into a measuring cup.
3. Through the hole in the blender's lid, pour the oil slowly into the above mix until it's fully absorbed.
4. If you want an additional burst of flavor, add the GF Tamari Sauce.

5. Note: If you find this dressing a little too acid (I love it that way) you can change the acid to oil proportions from 1:2 to 1:3. That is 1 cup of acid (vinegar or lemon juice) to 3 cups of oil blend (for example, 2 cups Olive oil and 1 cup Flax Seed oil).

✓ Chef's Tips: I prepare this amount and store it in the refrigerator in a squeeze bottle. That way, when I want to put together a quick salad, I just place some salad on a plate, shake the bottle of dressing and squeeze some of it on top of your salad. Voila!

Taboulé de Quinoa. *Quinoa Tabouleh*

This is a nice and refreshing alternative version to the traditional tabouleh made with cracked wheat. Enjoy!

Servings: 4

Oven Temp: 350F

Prep Time: 15 min.

Cooking Time: 45 min.

This recipe is **GFCF**

INGREDIENTS

- **2 cups Quinoa grains**
- **4 cups water**
- **4 Tomatoes, diced**
- **1 small Cucumber, diced**
- **1 small Onion, diced**
- **1 bunch Parsley**
- **Tbsp Olive oil**
- **1 cup Mint, chopped finely**
- **½ tsp Sea salt**
- **Black pepper to taste**
- **½ cup Pine nuts**

PROCEDURE

1. Bring the water to boil. Add the quinoa; bring back to boil while stirring. Take off the flame. Cover and let sit for about 10 minutes. When popped open, fluff with a fork and let cool until needed.
2. Meanwhile, in a separate bowl place the olive oil, diced tomatoes, onion, and cucumber. Add salt and pepper. Toss all together. Let sit.
3. Chop the parsley and mint finely. Add to the vegetable mix. Stir together. Add your cooked quinoa and toss gently together. Refrigerate until needed.
4. Toast the pine nuts in a frying pan or in your toaster oven until blond.
5. Serve the quinoa tabouleh on colorful plates and sprinkle the toasted pine nuts over.

Salade Niçoise. *Niçoise Salad*

Here's another classic from my hometown, Nice. Also called "la salade du soleil" (salad of the sun) in our region. It is loaded with fresh produce bought from the daily neighborhood open market or picked fresh from the garden. This salad will evolve with the seasons. It will be slightly different in Spring than in Summer. I will give you a modern version. Have fun and be proud of your own version. Needless to say, this is a whole meal to be enjoyed with family and friends.

Servings: 4

Prep Time: 40 min.

This recipe is **GFCF**

INGREDIENTS

- **1 head of fresh lettuce or your favorite garden salad**
- **8 heirloom tomatoes, firm and not too ripe**
- **½ lb of new small potatoes or small red potatoes**
- **4 oz haricots verts or green beans (about ¾ cup)**
- **2 small artichokes, peeled and sliced or 1 can artichoke hearts (optional)**
- **1 colorful pepper (green, red, yellow)**
- **8 oz canned tuna pieces in water**
- **1 celery branch with leaves**
- **2 green onions or 2**

PROCEDURE

1. Cut the salad leaves from the core, wash and drain properly.
2. Wash the tomatoes; cut them in 8 parts, do not slice them (it looks prettier and you won't have tomato seeds all over the salad). Sprinkle them with sea salt and let sit in your refrigerator.
3. Hard-boil the eggs; cool and peel them and cut them in quarters.
4. Cook the potatoes until tender but not too soft. Drain, cool and set aside. Cut in halves.
5. Steam your haricots verts for 5 minutes or until al dente. Drain, cool, set aside. Cut in 2 inch pieces.
6. Peel and mince the green onions or shallots.
7. Place the anchovy fillets between two paper towels to pat them dry.
8. Wash the pepper; cut the top off; take the seeds out and slice thin.
9. Wash the celery and cut into small dice.
10. If you wish to use fresh artichokes, pull the outer leaves out and with a small knife, cut out the outer part to expose the heart. Rub with a half fresh lemon all over to keep it from darkening. Slice thin and

shallots

To decorate your salad:

- 6 eggs, hard-boiled
- 2 oz small black olives Niçoises (about 1/3 cup)
- 8 anchovies filets in olive oil, patted dry

Red Wine Vinaigrette:

- 8 Tbsp extra virgin olive oil
- 2 Tbsp red wine vinegar
- ½ tsp sea salt
- ¼ tsp freshly ground black pepper

reserve. Or drain canned artichoke hearts.

11. Using a large deep platter or salad bowl, place the salad leaves at the bottom; add a layer of tomatoes, a few potato halves, a few cut haricots verts, a few slices of artichoke (optional), a couple of slices of colorful pepper, tuna pieces, a couple of pinches of diced celery and green onion slices.

12. Repeat this operation until you run out of ingredients.

13. Prepare your vinaigrette. Dress and toss the composed salad gently.

14. Decorate the top of your salad with hard-boiled egg quarters, small black olives and anchovy fillets.

15. Bon Appétit!

✓ Chef's Tips: If you want to prepare a luxury version of this salad, you can replace the canned tuna with fresh grilled tuna.

✓ Other options are fresh shelled green peas or beans, add a few leaves of parsley or basil; add finely minced garlic. You can use any salad greens you like or even mixed field greens (my favorite). Have fun and be creative. Just don't go too far out there or you will not be able to call it "Salade Niçoise" any more.

Salade aux Petits Poix et Poivrons. *Peas-full Egg Salad*

This is a fun and happy salad. It is a colorful twist to the traditional egg salad. Have fun and don't throw peas at each other. It's supposed to be peas-full.

Servings: 4-6

Prep Time: 20 min.

This recipe is **GFCF**

INGREDIENTS

- **12 hard boiled large Farm Eggs**
- **1 cup frozen organic Peas, thawed and drained**
- **1 Celery branch, diced**
- **1 Yellow bell pepper, diced**
- **1 Red bell pepper, diced**
- **4 Green onions, minced**
- **½ cup Organic mayonnaise**
- **¾ tsp Curry powder**
- **½ tsp Paprika**
- **Lemon juice to taste**
- **Sea salt and black pepper to taste**

PROCEDURE

1. In a large mixing bowl, combine mayo, peas, diced celery and bell peppers, green onions, and spices.

2. Peel your hard boiled eggs. Rinse and chop them (I use a tomato slicer). Add to the mayo-veggie mixture.

3. Add lemon juice, salt and pepper to taste.

4. Mix well and serve with baby greens or as a super spring sandwich. Enjoy!

Salade de Pâtes au Thon. *Garden Pasta Tuna Salad*

Here is a nice change for a pasta salad. It uses my special dressing, but feel free to substitute with your own choice. Serve it over a nice mix of field greens.

Servings: 4-6

Prep Time: 20 min.

This recipe is **GFCF**

INGREDIENTS

- **12 oz water-packed Tuna, drained and flaked**
- **2 large tomatoes, diced**
- **2 medium Cucumbers**
- **2 small Red bell peppers, seeded and diced**
- **1/2 cup Green onions, chopped**
- **½ tsp Sea salt**
- **1/4 tsp Black pepper, ground**
- **2 celery branches, chopped**
- **2 cups Small shell GF pasta, freshly cooked**
- **½ cup Alain's Healthy dressing**
- **1 Tbsp dried dill weed**

PROCEDURE

1. Cook your GF pasta as usual. Drain and run under cold water to cool it down. Set aside.

2. Meanwhile, slice the cucumbers in half lengthwise, scrape out the seeds with a spoon, salt them lightly and set them cut side down on paper towels to dry for about 10 minutes, then dice.

3. Combine first 6 ingredients in large bowl. Mix in the pasta.

4. Add the salad dressing and dill and blend well.

Viandes et Œufs. *Meats and Eggs*

La Daube a la Niçoise. *Niçoise-style Daube*

This is a slightly different version of the Daube Provencale above. It contains mushrooms and brandy. It brings a whole new dimension to this dish. If you have the time, try it as well and let me know which one you like best.

Servings: 4-6

Prep Time: 20 min.

Cooking Time: 4 hours

This recipe is **GFCF**

INGREDIENTS

- **2 oz dried Cèpes mushrooms**
- **2 Onions, sliced**
- **2 Garlic cloves, whole**
- **4 Carrots, sliced**
- **1 Celery branch, sliced**
- **2 sprigs fresh Thyme**
- **2 sprigs fresh Rosemary**
- **2 Bay leaves**
- **2 lbs beef stew meat: shank or chuck, cut into 3 inches pieces (ask your friendly butcher)**
- **Salt and Pepper to taste**
- **6 large ripe Tomatoes, peeled and seeded or 2**

PROCEDURE

1. Soak your dried cèpes in water.

2. In a frying pan with 1 Tbsp of lard, sauté the onions, garlic, celery and herbs until very soft.

3. Salt and pepper the cut meat to your taste. Heat the other Tbsp of lard in your soup pot and sauté the meat at high heat. It will seal the juices in and prevent the meat from falling apart. Continue to cook for another 10 minutes while stirring once in a while.

4. Add the sautéed onion mixture, crushed tomatoes, red wine, brandy and the cayenne pepper. Fill up with enough water to just cover the meat. Bring to boil, reduce the heat and simmer covered for 3 hours, or until the meat is tender.

5. After 3 hours, add the soaked mushrooms and adjust seasoning to your taste. Cook for an additional hour at a simmer.

6. If you wish, spoon out the fat from the top and serve. Another way to de-fat this meal is to let it cool in your refrigerator over night. Scoop out the congealed fat and warm up to serving temperature. The flavors will have aged overnight and your daube will taste even better. For Pete's

small cans crushed tomatoes

- 1 cup Red wine (Bordeaux)
- 1 cup Brandy of choice: Grappa, Cognac or Armagnac
- ½ tsp Cayenne pepper
- 2 Tbsp Lard to sauté meat and veggies
- Parsley, chopped for decoration

sake, do not heat it up in a microwave oven. Sacrilege!

✓ Chef's Tips: Serve this daube over cooked gnocchi and sprinkle with parmesan or your favorite cheese alternative.

Le Ragout de Porc aux Câpres. *Pork Stew with Capers*

This winter dish is full of southern French flavors. Enjoy it over a wide GF pasta.

Servings: 4-6

Prep Time: 15 min.

Cooking Time: 1 ½ hours

This recipe is **GFCF**

INGREDIENTS

- **2 lbs Pork shoulder (see procedure)**
- **1 Tbsp Lard**
- **1 onion, chopped**
- **1 Celery branch, chopped**
- **6 fresh Sage leaves**
- **1 sprig Thyme**
- **1 Bay leaf**
- **10 sprigs Parsley**
- **2 Tbsp White rice flour**
- **2 Egg yolks**
- **2 cups Dry white wine**
- **2 Tbsp Capers, drained**
- **1 Tbsp Cornichons (French pickles), chopped**
- **Sea salt and Pepper to taste**
- **Parsley, chopped for decoration.**

PROCEDURE

1. Ask your butcher to debone and cut the meat into 2 inches cubes. Sprinkle your meat with salt and pepper to taste.

2. In a large heavy pot over high heat, sauté the meat with the lard until the meat is colored. Lower the heat. Add onion, celery and herbs and cook until the onion is soft. Lower the heat still more, and cook, covered, for about an hour until it is tender.

3. When done, take the meat out of the pot and reserve on a platter in a warm place.

4. Going back to your pot, add the white wine (deglaze it); add the chopped capers and cornichons; add the yolks and keep on stirring until the sauce thickens. Do not allow to boil. Put the meat back and toss all the ingredients together.

✓ Chef's Tips: This meat is wonderful served over wide GF pasta. Sprinkle with chopped parsley for decoration.

Cotes d'Agneau au Romarin. *Rosemary Lamb Chops*

Nothing complements the flavor of lamb better than rosemary. My quick-broil method makes this dish very fast and easy to prepare. With this dish you not only enjoy great taste, but also add an excellent source of protein, vitamin B12, selenium, zinc, and vitamin B3.

Servings: 4

Prep and Cooking Time: 15 min.

This recipe is **GFCF**

INGREDIENTS

- **8 Lamb chops**
- **4 Tbsp Fresh lemon juice**
- **2 Tbsp Fresh rosemary, chopped**
- **2 Garlic cloves, chopped or pressed**
- **¼ tsp Sea salt**
- **¼ tsp Black pepper, ground**

PROCEDURE

1. Start your broiler. Place a heavy duty glazed cast iron or stainless steel pan on the top rack, about 5 inches from the broiler. Make sure it's large enough to hold all the chops at once. Preheat your pan for at least 10 minutes. (Make sure the handle is made of metal too!)

2. Chop your garlic and let sit for at least 5 minutes.

3. Mix together lemon juice, rosemary, garlic, sea salt, and pepper. Rub lamb chops with this mixture. Set aside on a plate.

4. Once your pan is hot, place lamb chops in the pan and return to broiler for about 4-5 minutes, depending on the thickness of the lamb. The lamb is cooked quickly as it is cooking on both sides at the same time. The internal meat temperature should be 165-170F.

✓ Chef's Tips: To make sure the meat juices are sealed in and the meat is moist, make sure your pan is very hot. Please handle with caution. If you can plan in advance, allow the lamb chops to marinate for a few hours to allow the marinade to develop even more wonderful flavor.

Poulet Farci aux Riz et Figues. *Roasted Chicken Stuffed with Rice and Figs*

A wonderful and sweet way to cook a chicken. I'll bet you never tasted such a treat!

Servings: 4-6

Oven Temp: 400F

Prep Time: 20 min.

Cooking Time: 45 min.

This recipe is **GFCF**

INGREDIENTS

- **1 large free range Chicken and its giblets**
- **2 Tbsp Olive oil**
- **2 medium Onions, sliced**
- **Salt and Pepper to taste**
- **10 Black figs in season**
- **8 oz White rice**
- **1 pint Water**
- **Cayenne pepper to taste**
- **Sea salt to taste**

PROCEDURE

1. Ask your friendly butcher or famer to empty the chicken but reserve the giblets. They will add a whole lot of flavor to this dish.

2. Place your rice in a colander; rinse with warm water until the draining water is clear, taking the starch out of the rice.

3. In a large pot, heat the oil at medium heat. Saute the onions until they become transparent.

4. Chop the giblets coarsely. Cut the tail and bottom off each fig. Cut each into eight sections.

5. Add the figs and giblets to the onions and cook until the giblets turn from pink to brown. Add the water, salt and pepper. Add the rice and mix well. Bring to boil and simmer for 20 minutes, or until the rice is cooked. Let cool a little.

6. Preheat your oven at 400F.

7. Dry the inside of your chicken carefully. Stuff ¾ of the way with the rice stuffing. Reserve the rest for later. Sew up with white thread.

8. Place the chicken in an oiled oven dish. Sprinkle with cayenne and sea salt. Bake on the middle rack for about 45 minutes. To make sure the chicken is cooked, poke it with a sharp object. If the juice coming out is yellow, it's ready. If it comes out

pink, not ready yet. Add more time.

9. When the chicken is cooked, take it out and let rest for 5 minutes. It will be easier to cut that way. Meanwhile, warm up the reserved rice stuffing and serve them together.

La Polenta de Ménage au Poulet. *Family-Style Polenta with Chicken*

I like this easy dish. It uses premade polenta that you can find at your nearest health food store and the chicken is easy to cook. Dinner is ready in 30 minutes.

Servings: 4-6

Oven Temp: 400F

Prep Time: 20 min.

Cooking Time: 10 min.

This recipe is **GFCF**

INGREDIENTS

- **2 premade Polenta logs**
- **2 Tbsp Olive oil**
- **1 whole Chicken breast cut in 2 inches chunks**
- **Sea salt and Pepper to taste**
- **1 Onion, chopped**
- **1 Garlic clove, chopped**
- **2 ripe tomatoes, peeled and seeded or 1 (15 oz) can crushed tomatoes**
- **½ tsp dried Thyme**
- **½ tsp Sea salt**
- **¼ tsp Cayenne**
- **Grated Swiss cheese or Swiss-style alternative cheese**

PROCEDURE

1. In a large pot, heat the oil over medium heat. Sauté the chicken pieces with salt and pepper until golden.
2. Add the onion, garlic and herbs. Keep on cooking until the onion is melted and the chicken fully cooked.
3. Add the tomatoes and bring back to a boil. Let simmer for another 10 minutes to allow the flavors to blend.
4. Meanwhile, oil an oven dish large enough to hold everything. Slice your polenta into half inch slices. Line the bottom of the dish with them. Pour the tomato/chicken sauce over them. Sprinkle with grated Swiss cheese or alternative cheese.
5. Bake on the middle rack for about 10 minutes or until the cheese is turning golden. Bon Appétit!

Tian de Courgettes au Riz. *Zucchini and Rice Egg Dish*

In the South of France, this egg dish is usually prepared a day ahead and eaten cold the next day as a picnic dish. It is also very good hot. Try both ways and see which way you like best.

Servings: 4-6

Oven Temp: 325F

Prep Time: 30 min.

Baking Time: 45 min.

This recipe is **GF**. Can be made **CF**

INGREDIENTS

- ½ cup White rice
- 1 cup water
- 2 Tbsp Olive oil
- 1 oz thick Bacon, cubed
- 1 Onion, slices
- 1 Garlic clove
- 2 lbs Zucchini, halved and sliced
- 10 Basil leaves, chopped
- 3 Eggs
- 2 oz Parmesan or alternative cheese
- Sea salt and Pepper to taste

PROCEDURE

1. Preheat your oven at 325F.
2. Rinse the rice well in cold water to eliminate the starch. Cook it as you usually would, al dente.
3. Heat olive oil in a frying pan, then add the bacon. Sauté for a while to melt the fat. Add the onions and garlic. Sauté until the onion is soft. Add the sliced zucchinis and cook some more until they are tender. Let cool.
4. In a separate bowl, beat the eggs with the chopped basil, salt, pepper and parmesan or alternative cheese. Mix into the zucchini mixture. Finally, add the cooked rice and fold together gently.
5. Oil a heavy cast iron or gratin dish. Place the whole preparation into it. Press it tight.
6. Bake on the middle rack for about 40-45 minutes or until set. Cool down to room temperature. Eat immediately, or refrigerate overnight. If you do decide to take it on a picnic, cut it up into individual servings.

Galettes de Sarasin Complete. *Brittany-Style Savory Crêpes*

Although my grandmother, Mamie, was from Normandy, she used to make us these dinner crepes once in a while. When I worked in Brittany for a summer season, I used to love to go to "une crêperie" (a crepes restaurant) and indulge in my Mamie's memory... and my pleasure "bien sur". I adapted her recipe for your enjoyment.

Servings: 4 to 6

Prep Time: 20 min.

Cooking Time: 30 min.

This recipe is **GFCF**

INGREDIENTS

- **8 oz Buckwheat flour**
- **2 oz Garbanzo bean flour**
- **½ tsp Xanthan gum**
- **½ tsp Sea salt**
- **¼ tsp Black Pepper, ground**
- **1 lb (1 pint) Soy or almond milk**
- **4 oz Eggs (2)**
- **1 Tbsp Olive oil**
- **1 lb (1 pint) Water**

PROCEDURE

1. Weigh your wet ingredients in a large measuring cup or bowl: soy or almond milk, eggs, oil, and mix well together. Weigh your water separately.
2. Weigh the two flours with salt and pepper in your mixer's bowl. With the whisk attachment, start mixing at low speed.
3. Add the liquid progressively as the machine runs. Adjust the consistency to fairly liquid with the water. Pour into a large ceramic bowl. Let rest covered for at least 1 hour.
4. When ready, heat some olive oil or coconut oil in your frying pan. Depending on the size of your pan, pour enough batter to cover the whole pan while whirling the batter around the pan. Cook until the sides turn light brown and start to detach from the sides of the pan. Flip over and finish cooking. Reserve on a hot plate kept warm. Cook all the crepes until your batter is used up.
5. All over France, you can order your "galettes" with a multitudes of fillings. "La complete" is usually a slice of baked ham, an egg (sunny side up), grated Swiss cheese over it and folded like an envelope. In my region, we like it filled with ratatouille (see recipe in Side Dishes), folded and sprinkled with grated cheese and gratine under a broiler.
6. For Casein-free, replace the cheese with

Swiss-style cheese alternative (see shopping list) and voila! To serve, place a crepe back into the pan on medium heat, place the ham slice at the bottom, then the egg, then the cheese or you can do ham and cheese only, or use ratatouille as a filling and so on. Your culinary imagination is the limit. For sugared crepes, see the desserts section for Crepes Suzettes.

✓ Chef's Tips: To keep the crepes from sticking, my grand-mere used to dip a baguette "crouton" (butt end of the baguette) in oil and rub the bottom of the pan with it. I use a strong paper towel folded in four.

Poissons et Fruits De Mer. *Fish and Seafood*

Ma Façon Rapide de Préparer des crevettes ou Coquilles de St. Jacques. *Alain's Quick Way to Prepare Poached Shrimp or Scallops*

When I come back home tired from working all day in my professional kitchen, I don't want to spend a lot of time in my home kitchen. I came up with this quick and tasty way to poach shrimp and scallops. I'm not sure it's a "new" way but it works. Give it a try, it's really easy. Serve them on top of GF pasta or with a composed salad and Voila! Dinner is served in no time at all.

Servings: 2

Prep Time: 3 min.

Cooking Time: 3-4 min.

This recipe is **GFCF**

INGREDIENTS

- **8-12 oz Peeled shrimp or scallops**
- **1 Tbsp Extra virgin olive oil**
- **1 Tbsp Coconut oil**
- **½ tsp of your favorite spice blend: Herbes de Provence, Cajun, or Chili**
- **1-2 pinches of Sea salt depending on your spice blend choice**
- **Mixed green salad with your favorite salad dressing, or GF pasta dish**

PROCEDURE

1. Heat an enameled cast iron pan like Le Creuset, a cast iron pan or heavy stainless steel frying pan on your stove over medium heat.

2. Add the oils to the pan. Allow them to warm up, but not to smoke. Add the spice blend of your choice and salt, and allow it all to warm up to develop the flavors.

3. When the spices sizzle, add your peeled shrimp or scallops and poach gently (do not fry) over medium-low heat. They will render their juices and create a wonderful sauce. Flip shrimp or scallops over; finish cooking.

4. You can either toss the cooked seafood with cooked pasta and top with your choice of alternative cheese, or, in the summer, top a mixed salad with them and drizzle the sauce over it. Wonderful!

✓ Chef's tip: A "healthier" way to prepare them is to poach them in fish stock using the same spices and principle. Enjoy!

Le Rouget a la Niçoise. *Red Mullet a la Niçoise*

Here is a nice and fairly easy way to prepare fish. You may have to ask your fish monger to special order the red mullet for you.

Servings: 4-6

Oven Temp: 325F

Prep Time: 20 min.

Cooking Time: 15 min.

This recipe is **GFCF**

INGREDIENTS

- **4 whole Red mullets**
- **1 can (28 oz) crushed Tomatoes**
- **4 Anchovies filets**
- **Lemon slices**
- **½ cup Black olives (Niçoises), pitted and sliced**
- **½ cup Capers, drained**
- **Parsley sprigs**
- **1 Lemon juice**
- **Olive oil to drizzle**
- **Salt and Pepper to taste**

PROCEDURE

1. Preheat your oven at 325F.
2. Ask your friendly fish monger to scale and gut the fish, but leave them whole.
3. Heat a large frying pan filled with about half an inch of olive oil. Bring the oil temperature to 350F and fry the fish, about 3 minutes on each side.
4. Oil an oven dish with olive oil. With a slotted spatula, place each fish carefully in the dish. Cover with the crushed tomatoes. Place two lemon slices and one anchovy filet on each fish. Sprinkle with sliced olives, capers and 2 parsley sprigs. Squeeze a lemon juice over all.
5. Bake at 325F for 15 minutes until all is heated. Serve over rice.

Thon Façon Côte d'Azur. *Tuna Côte d'Azur-style*

Tuna is a very meaty fish, the closest to red meat. It works well with bold flavors. This recipe provides you all the aromas of Provence.

Servings: 4

Prep Time: 20 min.

Cooking Time: 30 min.

This recipe is **GFCF**

INGREDIENTS

- **1-2 pounds tuna filet, about 1 ½ inches thick, cut into 4 filets by your fishmonger**
- **1 Tbsp olive oil**
- **A few sprigs of savory**
- **A few sprigs of thyme**
- **A few rosemary leaves**
- **Sea salt and freshly ground pepper to taste**

Sauce:

- **3 Tbsp olive oil**
- **1 medium onion, sliced thin**
- **4 garlic cloves, minced**
- **1-28 oz can of Glen Muir crushed tomatoes with basil**

PROCEDURE

1. Ask your friendly fishmonger to cut you a nice thick slice of tuna steak, cut into 4 filets.

Prepare the fish:

2. Brush the tuna steaks with olive oil, and then sprinkle the herbs all over them on both sides. Press them in. Let sit at room temperature for 3 to 4 hours.

Prepare the sauce:

3. Heat the oil in a saucepan on medium heat, sauté the onion and garlic until soft but not caramelized. Add the canned tomatoes with the juice. Add the herbs, salt and pepper. Simmer for a while until the liquid has mostly evaporated.
4. Lower the heat; add the chopped capers and black olives. Stir in gently. Adjust seasoning if necessary. Set aside.

Cook the tuna:

5. Remove the herbs from the tuna. Sprinkle with salt and pepper.
6. In a large frying pan on high heat, warm up the oil. Add your tuna filets and sear no more than 4 minutes per side. Remove the skin and serve.

- ½ tsp sea salt
- ½ tsp dried savory
- ½ tsp dried rosemary leaves
- ½ tsp dried thyme
- ½ tsp sea salt
- ½ tsp freshly ground black pepper
- 2 Tbsp capers, drained and chopped
- ½ cup black small olives Niçoises, drained and chopped fine

- 2 Tbsp olive oil
- Sea salt and freshly ground pepper to taste
- Chopped parsley

Serve the tuna

7. Place on heated plates, spoon the sauce over each filet and sprinkle with chopped parsley.

✓ Chef's tip: I serve this fish with oven-roasted Rosemary new potatoes. Délicieux!

Risotto aux Crevettes. *Shrimp Risotto*

Even though this is a dish originating in northern Italy, the ladies in the Comte de Nice came up with their own version. It can also be served with mussels, scallops or even sautéed Poutine.

Servings: 4-6

Prep Time: 20 min.

Cooking Time: 15 min.

This recipe is **GFCF**

INGREDIENTS

- 1 Tbsp Olive oil
- 1 medium Onion, sliced
- 2 pinches Sea salt
- 12 oz Arborio rice, rinsed
- 1 can (15 oz) crushed tomatoes
- 1 tsp Provencal herbs
- 1 pinch Saffron
- 1 qt Vegetable broth
- 2 oz Raisins
- 2 oz Pine nuts
- 2 Green onions, sliced
- Sea salt and Pepper to taste
- 1 lb Small shrimps, peeled
- ½ cup Vegetable broth
- 1 tsp Provencal herbs

PROCEDURE

1. In a large cast iron pot, heat the olive oil and sauté the onions with the salt until transparent. Add the rice. Stir well to coat the rice with the flavored oil. When the rice takes on a light golden color, add the tomatoes, broth, herbs, saffron, scallions, raisins and nuts. Salt and pepper to taste.

2. Bring to boil gently and cook about 20-25 minutes until the rice has absorbed the broth. Check for consistency. The rice should be creamy but slightly crunchy at the center.

3. Meanwhile, poach your shrimps in some vegetable broth perfumed with Herbes de Provence. When cooked, add to the rice with its cooking sauce and mix carefully. Cook another 10 minutes at low heat. Stir once in while to make sure the rice does not burn at the bottom of the pot.

4. Serve hot. Sprinkle with chopped parsley.

Accompagnements. *Side Dishes*

Les Macaronis à La Provençale. *Provencal-Style Macaroni*

This is a nice change from macaroni and cheese, and a lot healthier.

Servings: 4

Prep Time: 10 min.

Cooking Time: 15 min.

This recipe is **GF**. Can be made **CF**

This recipe is **GFCF**

INGREDIENTS

- 12 oz GF Macaroni
- 3 qt water
- 2 Tbsp Olive oil
- 2 medium Onions, chopped
- 2 Garlic cloves, chopped
- ½ tsp Sea salt
- 1 lb ripe Tomatoes, peeled and seeded or 1 can (28 oz) organic crushed tomatoes with basil
- 1 Tbsp Herbes de Provence blend
- Sea salt and Pepper to taste
- Parmesan or alternative cheese to sprinkle

PROCEDURE

1. In a large pot, cook your pasta al dente as you usually would. Drain and rinse.

2. Meanwhile, heat the olive oil in a pot. Sauté the onions and garlic with the salt until light brown. Add the crushed tomatoes with basil and the Herbes de Provence. Cook for 15 minutes until the flavors are well blended.

3. Add to pasta. Toss gently. Serve. Sprinkle with parmesan or alternative cheese.

Ratatouille. *Ratatouille*

This wonderful dish is the essence of Provence. The best time to prepare it is in the Summer when the tomatoes are full of flavor. If you want to prepare it at other times, I recommend using Muir Glen organic crushed tomatoes with basil. I know, it's a sacrilege, but it helps you savor this dish in all seasons. You can savor ratatatouille as a main dish, soup, side dish, or as a great pizza topping. Here's the version Helene taught me. Enjoy!

Servings: 4

Prep Time: 20 min.

Cooking Time: 1 hour

This recipe is **GFCF**

INGREDIENTS

- ½ cup vegetable broth
- 3 Tbsp extra virgin olive oil
- 1 medium white onion, peeled and cut in half moons
- 2 garlic cloves, minced
- 1 small green bell pepper, cut in thin slices
- 1 small red bell pepper, cut in thin slices
- 3 small eggplant, cut into 1 inch pieces
- 3 medium zucchini, cut into 1 inch pieces
- 3 large perfectly ripe tomatoes, or 1-28 oz

PROCEDURE

1. Peel and chop onions and garlic. Toss together in a bowl and let sit for 5 min.

2. Cut green and red bell peppers, take the seeds out, cut in four sections and slice thin.

3. In a large skillet or pot, heat the vegetable broth and olive oil over medium-high heat; add the onions, garlic and bell peppers and sauté for 5 minutes, or until tender.

4. Add the eggplant, zucchini and tomatoes (or canned tomatoes); mix well and cook for 10 more minutes until they start to soften.

5. In a separate bowl, mix the tomato paste and red wine together. Stir in the parsley, basil, Provence herbs and spices.

6. Add this flavorful mix to the vegetables and stir well. Lower the heat to simmer and continue to cook, covered, one more hour until all the vegetables are melted, like a stew or thick soup.

- **Muir Glen Organics crushed tomatoes with basil**
- **3 oz tomato paste (skip if you use ripe fresh tomatoes)**
- **½ cup red wine (the secret ingredient)**
- **1 Tbsp fresh parsley, chopped fine**
- **1 Tbsp fresh basil, chopped fine**
- **1 Tbsp Herbs de Provence blend**
- **1 tsp sea salt**
- **½ tsp freshly ground black pepper**

7. Serve in white porcelain bowls to show off the ratatouille's bright colors (remember, we eat as much with our eyes as with our mouth) and sprinkle with a few fresh parsley leaves.

- ✓ <u>Chef's Tips</u>: This dish can be a satisfying dish by itself, eaten warm or at room temperature. The flavors seem to bloom better at these temperatures than when hot.
- ✓ It also is a wonderful side dish with a sautéed filet of white fish.
- ✓ Another trick I learned from Helene is to prepare or buy a par-baked GF pizza crust and top it off with ratatouille mixed with one beaten egg and bake. The ratatouille tends to be runny so the egg holds it together. Sprinkle your favorite grated alternative cheese on top: Swiss-style or others. Enjoy!

Epinards aux Raisins et aux Pignons. *Spinach with Raisins and Pine Nuts*

I like this recipe. Simple, healthy and tasty. What more could we want?

Servings: 4

Prep Time: 15 min.

Cooking Time: 5 min.

This recipe is **GFCF**

INGREDIENTS

- **2 lbs (2 bags) Spinach**
- **4 Tbsp olive oil**
- **4 oz Pine nuts**
- **2 oz Raisins, soaked and drained**
- **Salt and Pepper to taste**

PROCEDURE

1. Prepare a bowl with iced water and ice cubes to cold-shock the spinach.

2. Bring a large pot of salted water to boil. Drop 1 lb of spinach at a time. Bring water to boil. With a slotted spoon, pick up the spinach and drop them into the cold water to stop them from cooking too much. Drain while you're cooking the next batch. Press as much water out of them as you can.

3. When your spinach is dry, heat olive oil and toast the pine nuts at low heat. When they reach a golden color, add the raisins, spinach, salt and pepper. Voila!

Les Tomates au Four a la Provençale. *Oven-Baked Tomatoes Provençale*

There's nothing much to say about this classic of Provencal cuisine dish. Made with in-season, beautiful, juicy tomatoes, some people say it's better than... I'll let you fill in the gap.

Servings: 4

Oven Temp: 400F

Prep Time: 15 min.

Cooking Time: 15-20 min.

This recipe is **GFCF**

INGREDIENTS

- **4 large Tomatoes**
- **1 Garlic clove, chopped**
- **1 Anchovy filet**
- **1 bunch Parsley, chopped**
- **Sea salt and Pepper to taste**
- **4 oz GF Bread crumbs**
- **Olive oil to drizzle**

PROCEDURE

1. Preheat your oven at 400F.
2. Cut your tomatoes into halves. Squeeze them to get most of the juice and seeds out. Flip them over a grid and let them drain further.
3. Meanwhile, crush the garlic with the anchovy in a mortar or small food processor. Add the chopped parsley. Mix well or pulse a few times in the food processor. Salt and pepper to taste.
4. Oil an oven dish. Place your 8 half tomatoes in the dish side by side. Fill them with the garlic mix. Cover with a generous amount of GF bread crumbs. Drizzle with olive oil.
5. Bake on the middle rack at 400F for about 15-20 minutes until the tomatoes are cooked.
6. Enjoy with a fish dish.

Risotto de Quinoa aux Poivrons Rouges. *Quinoa Risotto with Red Bell Peppers*

This is another simple but healthy recipe. Easy to prepare and tasty. Enjoy!

Servings: 4

Prep Time: 15 min.

Cooking Time: 10 min.

This recipe is **GFCF**

INGREDIENTS

- **2 Red bell peppers, seeded and sliced**
- **1 carrot, sliced thin**
- **½ cup Vegetable broth**
- **1 Tbsp Olive oil**
- **2 Parsley sprigs**
- **½ tsp Sea salt**
- **¼ tsp Paprika**
- **½ tsp Cayenne pepper**
- **2 cups Quinoa grains, rinsed**
- **4 cups Vegetable broth**

PROCEDURE

1. Wash, seed and slice the red bell peppers. Slice the carrot. Place in a pot with the vegetable broth and olive oil. Cook covered at low temperature until the carrots are tender, about 10 minutes. Cool down.

2. Meanwhile, bring the 4 cups of vegetable broth to a boil. Add the quinoa. Bring back to a boil. Take off the heat. Let sit, covered, for another 10 minutes until the quinoa absorbs all the liquid.

3. Pour the cooked vegetables with the liquid in a blender. Add the spices and herbs. Process until pureed into a sauce.

4. When the quinoa is ready, fluff up with a fork. Add the vegetable sauce and mix carefully.

Tomates Farcies à la Viande de Bœuf. *Beef-Stuffed Tomatoes*

This is another classic of the Southern France region. Feel free to substitute the ground beef with ground turkey if you prefer.

Servings: 4

Oven Temp: 350F

Prep Time: 20 min.

Cooking Time: 30 min.

This recipe is **GF**. Can be made **CF**

INGREDIENTS

- **4 large ripe Tomatoes**
- **2 Tbsp Olive oil**
- **1 Onion, sliced**
- **1 Garlic clove, chopped**
- **½ tsp Sea salt**
- **1 oz bacon, cubed**
- **4 large Chard leaves, chopped finely**
- **2 large ripe Tomatoes**
- **1 lb Grass-fed ground Beef, Bison or Turkey**
- **2 Tbsp Parsley, chopped**
- **Sea salt and Pepper to taste**
- **2 Eggs**
- **4 oz Parmesan or alternative CF cheese**

PROCEDURE

1. Preheat your oven at 350F.
2. Cut all the tomatoes in half. Squeeze out as much juice and seeds as possible. Place 8 halves upside down on a grid to drain. Chop the remaining two.
3. In a large heavy pot, heat the olive oil, sauté the bacon, onions and garlic with the salt until the onions are transparent. Add the chopped chard leaves, chopped tomatoes, ground beef or bison, chopped parsley and salt and pepper to taste. Cook on medium heat for 15 minutes. Allow to cool.
4. Add the eggs and parmesan or alternative cheese to the filling. Stuff each tomato half with the filling in a mounded shape.
5. Place them in an oiled baking dish. Drizzle with olive oil and cook at 350F for 30 minutes. This is a complete meal in itself. Enjoy it with a mixed salad.

Purée de Pommes de Terre a l'Ail. *Mashed Potatoes with Garlic*

You know how we love to add garlic to anything in the South of France? Well, I have done it to a classic: mashed potatoes. They are very creamy and flavorful.

Servings: 4

Prep Time: 15 min.

Cooking Time: 12-15 min.

This recipe is **GFCF**

INGREDIENTS

- **4 medium Yukon Gold potatoes, cubed**
- **3 oz Olive oil**
- **3 oz Soy or Almond milk, unsweetened**
- **4 Garlic cloves, pressed**
- **2 Scallions, chopped**
- **½ tsp Sea salt**
- **½ tsp Black Pepper, ground**

PROCEDURE

1. Fill the bottom of the steamer with 2 inches of water.
2. While steam is building up in the steamer, press the garlic and let it sit for at least 5 minutes.
3. Cut potatoes into 1/2-inch cubes with the skin on.
4. Steam for 12-14 minutes until done.
5. Place them in your mixer's bowl. Using the paddle attachment, mash the cooked potatoes with olive oil, garlic, and unsweetened soy or almond milk. Mix in chopped scallions, salt and pepper to taste. Depending on the potatoes, you may need to add a little more milk.

✓ Chef's Tips: I like to spread it into a baking dish, cover it with parmesan or alternative cheese and bake "au gratin" for about 10 minutes at 400F.

Haricots Verts avec sa Vinaigrette et Amandes. *Haricots Verts in Almond-Garlic Vinaigrette*

This green and healthy dish features the slim and crunchy haricots verts. I like to toss them in a light vinaigrette and add toasted almonds for additional texture.

Servings: 4

Prep Time: 15 min.

Cooking Time: 4-5 min.

This recipe is **GFCF**

INGREDIENTS

- **1 oz Slivered Almonds**
- **3 oz Vegetable broth**
- **12 oz Haricots Verts (green beans), trimmed and cut in quarters**
- **3 Tbsp Olive oil**
- **1 Tbsp Apple cider vinegar**
- **1 tsp French spicy mustard**
- **1 Garlic clove, crushed**
- **½ tsp Sea salt**
- **¼ tsp Black pepper, ground**

PROCEDURE

1. Toast slivered almonds in a frying pan until golden. Set aside.
2. Clean and cut ends of haricots verts. Cut in two or four sections.
3. Place the vegetable broth in a sauté pan. Bring to a boil.
4. When broth is steaming, add haricots verts. Stir.
5. Cover with lid. Cook for 4 minutes until al dente.
6. Meanwhile, in a large bowl, prepare the vinaigrette with olive oil, vinegar, mustard, garlic and spices.
7. When the haricots verts are ready, toss them with the vinaigrette and toasted almonds. Sprinkle with chopped parsley.

Riz Sauvage au Romarin et Baies de Goji et Noix. *Rosemary Wild Rice with Goji Berries and Walnuts*

I like this side dish for its lightness, assorted flavors and colors.

Servings: 4

Oven Temp: 350F

Prep Time: 15 min.

Cooking Time: 60 min.

This recipe is **GFCF**

INGREDIENTS

- 4 oz **Walnut Pieces, toasted**
- 3 oz **Goji berries, soaked**
- 3 oz **Vegetable broth**
- 3 oz **Crimini mushrooms, sliced**
- ½ **White onion, chopped**
- 1 **Garlic clove, chopped**
- 1.5 tsp **Fresh Rosemary, chopped**
- 1 tsp **Sea Salt**
- ½ tsp **Black pepper, ground**
- 8 oz **Wild Rice**
- 1 pt **Vegetable broth**

PROCEDURE

1. Preheat your oven at 350F.
2. Soak the Goji berries in very hot water for twenty minutes, or until ready to use.
3. Prepare all the vegetables, spices and herbs.
4. In a sauté pan, weigh the vegetable broth. Heat over high heat until it starts to steam. Add all the vegetables, the drained goji berries, and the herbs and sauté in broth for 5 min or until tender.
5. Rinse rice in cold water and drain. Add to veggies and cook together for a couple of minutes.
6. Pour this mix into an oven dish. Add the pint of vegetable broth. Cover with aluminum foil and bake for 45 minutes or until the rice is cooked.
7. As the baking time draws to a finish, toast the walnuts pieces over medium heat in a skillet for about 10 minutes, stirring often to prevent burning.
8. When ready to serve, top with the toasted walnuts.

Desserts. *Desserts*

Classique Mousse au Chocolat. *Classic French Chocolate Mousse*

This is a lighter version of the classical, rich chocolate mousse, made the way I learned to prepare it at my first 4-star hotel job in the South of France.

Servings: 4

Prep Time: 20 min.

This recipe is **GF**. Can be made **CF**

INGREDIENTS

Step 1:

- **8 oz Bittersweet chocolate (70% cocoa content)**
- **2 oz Butter or non-hydrogenated margarine, cut in small pieces**
- **2.5 oz Egg yolks (8)**

Step 2:

- **4 oz Egg whites (8)**
- **1 pinch Sea salt**
- **2 oz Turbinado sugar, finely ground**

Step 3:

- **4 oz Heavy whipping cream**
- **1 Tbsp Turbinado sugar**
- **2 drops of vanilla extract**

PROCEDURE

1. Weigh the chocolate in a dry bowl. Set over a simmering water bath. Melt to warm (110F) or until all the lumps are melted. You can also melt your chocolate carefully in a microwave oven at low power until melted, about 2 minutes.
2. Remove from the heat. Add the butter or margarine and stir until melted.
3. Add the egg yolks, mixing well with a whisk.
4. Weigh your egg whites, sea salt and sugar in your mixer's bowl. With the whisk attachment, whip at medium speed until it forms a soft meringue (soft peaks). Fold gently into the chocolate mixture in two batches.
5. In a cold bowl, whip the cream, sugar and vanilla with a hand whisk until soft peaks form (or use the Soy Whip or whipped topping).
6. Fold gently into chocolate mousse. Transfer the mousse to your prettiest large serving bowl or individual cups or ramekins. Chill for several hours before serving.
7. You may choose to decorate them with additional whipped topping rosettes and chocolate shavings or colorful sprinkles.

✓ Chef's Tips: Feel free to substitute the whipped cream with Soy whipped cream.

Soufflé aux Framboises Léger comme un Nuage. *Light as a Cloud Raspberry Souffle*

This is a very healthy, very light, melt-in-the-mouth version of the traditional soufflé recipe. Unlike the traditional recipe, it does not contain any flour, just a touch of corn starch. I learned this recipe at a famous French health spa.

Servings: 4

Prep Time: 20 min.

Cooking Time: 12 min.

This recipe is **GF.**

Can be made **GFCF**

INGREDIENTS

- 4 - 3 3/4 " (7 3/4 fl oz) Ceramic ramekins
- 4 oz Raspberries fresh or frozen (about 1 cup)
- ¼ tsp Fresh lemon juice
- ¼ cup Powdered sugar
- ½ tsp Corn starch

- 2 Egg yolks
- 4 Egg whites
- 1 pinch Sea salt
- 2 Tbsp Granulated sugar
- 2 Tbsp Butter or Earth Balance margarine, at room temperature
- 2 Tbsp Granulated sugar

PROCEDURE

1. Preheat your oven at 400°F standard or 350°F convection.

2. With a pastry brush, brush the inside of the ramekins with the softened butter or margarine. Sprinkle with granulated sugar. Turn the ramekins around to allow the sugar to stick evenly. Tap out the excess sugar gently.

3. In a food processor or blender, blend the raspberries, sugar, corn starch and lemon juice together. If you don't mind the seeds, leave this mix alone. Otherwise, strain the seeds out.

4. Add the egg yolks to the fruit mixture. Blend well. Pour into a large mixing bowl.

5. In a grease-free stand mixer bowl, start whisking the egg whites with the salt and sugar at medium speed, allowing them to fluff up gently. When all your ingredients are ready, increase the speed until they form soft peaks. (Do NOT over whip, or they will form lumps while mixing.)

6. Add 1/3rd of the whipped egg whites into the fruit mixture. Mix in gently with a hand whisk to lighten the mix. Add the rest of the egg whites and fold gently with a rubber spatula. With a spoon, carefully fill your prepared ramekins with the

Raspberry Sauce

- ½ cup Raspberries, fresh or frozen
- ¼ cup Powdered sugar
- ¼ tsp Fresh lemon juice

soufflé mixture. Level the tops carefully with a spatula or the back of a knife. With your right thumb, clean the inside edge of each ramekin to allow your soufflé to rise straight up.

7. Bake at 400°F (350°F convection) for about 12 minutes or until the sides are light brown and firm to the touch.

8. Sprinkle the top with powdered sugar and serve with the raspberry coulis (optional).

9. **Raspberry Coulis**: process all ingredients in a food processor or blender. Strain through a fine mesh strainer or chinois. Refrigerate. Serve in a sauceboat with your hot soufflés. Pour sauce over soufflés just before eating. Bon Appétit!

✓ Chef's Tips: You can replace the granulated sugar with finely processed turbinado sugar.
✓ The thin layer of butter/margarine spread inside the ramekins will allow the soufflé mixture to rise without sticking to the edge. The sprinkled sugar will bring an additional slight crunchiness to your soufflés. Be very careful not to allow your fingers to touch the inside of your ramekins once they have been prepared or your soufflé will stick and rise sideways.

Crème Brulée à la Lavande. *Lavender Crème Brulée*

I created this recipe for my first Classical French Desserts class. All my students loved it. It's not that difficult; give it a try!

Yield: 4 ramekins

Oven Temp: 350F

Prep Time: 15 min.

Cooking Time: 40 min.

This recipe is **GFCF**

INGREDIENTS

- **1 lb (pint) Soy or Coconut creamer**
- **1 tsp Lavender flowers, dried**
- **¼ tsp Vanilla extract**
- **¼ tsp Agar powder**
- **3 oz Egg yolks (6)**
- **1.5 oz Turbinado sugar**
- **1 pinch Sea salt**
- **GF Powdered sugar**

PROCEDURE

1. Preheat your oven at 350F.
2. Whisk the soy creamer, agar powder and lavender together in a 1 quart stainless steel pan. Bring to boil on low heat and cook while stirring for about one minute. Set aside to allow the lavender to steep and to cool down the liquid. Meanwhile, bring some water to boil in a 2-qt pot.
3. Whisk the egg yolks, sugar, and salt until the sugar is incorporated. Do not over whip, as it will create too much foam.
4. Temper the egg/sugar mix with the soy creamer mix. That is, add a little of the warm lavender soy creamer to the egg yolk mix a little at a time while whisking gently. Repeat until all the soy creamer is mixed with the sugared egg yolks. Strain the mixture to get any lumps and lavender out. Skim the foam off.
5. Set shallow individual ramekins or gratin dishes on a towel in a deep oven pan (a doubled-up paper towel will do the trick as well). The purpose of the towel is to insulate the bottom of the ramekins from the strong oven heat. <u>Note</u>: If you bake your crème brulées in a convection oven, you will not need the paper towel at the bottom of the pan.
6. Divide the custard mixture equally among the dishes. Pour boiling water into the deep pan halfway up the sides of the ramekins.
7. Bake at 350F until the custard is just set, about 35-45 minutes depending on ramekin size and oven type. Cool down to

room temperature, then refrigerate.

8. To finish, start your broiler. Dab any moisture from the top of the baked custards. Sprinkle with an even layer of powdered sugar. Caramelize the sugar under the broiler; place the custards very close to the heat so the sugar caramelizes quickly before the custard warms up too much. When it cools, the caramelized sugar will form a thin, hard crust.

9. Serve within an hour or two. If the custards are held for too long, the moisture in the custards will soften the caramel.

✓ Chef's Tips: For a deluxe version (like in fancy restaurants), flavor with a vanilla bean instead of extract. Split 1 vanilla bean in half lengthwise and scrape out the tiny seeds. Simmer the pods and seeds with the creamer. Remove the pods and continue with the basic recipe.

Ma Marquise Préférée au Chocolat. *My Favorite Chocolate Marquise*

Why is this marquise my favorite? Is she pretty? Is she rich? Nope! She's a very simple yet yummy chocolate lady. What's not to love? I hope you like her too.

Servings: 4-6

This recipe is **GF**.

Can be made **CF**

INGREDIENTS

- **8 oz Dark chocolate (70% cocoa)**
- **2 Tbsp Butter or Coconut oil**
- **12 oz Vanilla Soy or Coconut yogurt (2 pots)**
- **1-2 pinches Black pepper, ground**
- **2 Egg yolks**

PROCEDURE

1. Heat a 2 quart pot filled halfway full of hot water. Let the water simmer but not boil.
2. Weigh your chocolate and butter/oil in a metal bowl slightly larger than the pot you will be using for the bain-marie (double boiler). Place the bowl over the bain-marie and melt the chocolate gently while stirring.
3. Meanwhile, weigh the yogurt and the black pepper into a cold mixing bowl. Whisk together.
4. Pour the melted chocolate mix over it and whisk well. Add the egg yolks and finish whisking until smooth.
5. Pour in small ramekins or a large bowl. Refrigerate for a few hours or overnight. If you feel like it, decorate with whipped cream, soy whipped cream, or a few chocolate shavings.

✓ Chef's Tips: If you want to add additional flavor, add mint, coffee or any flavor you like. Play with your food. It's OK, I promise.

Pots de Cocos. *Coconut Pots*

Here is another simple yet tasty dessert. Don't you love coconut? I do.

Servings: 4-6

Oven Temp: 350F

Prep Time: 15 min.

Cooking time: 30 min.

This recipe is **GFCF**

INGREDIENTS

- 1 lb (pint) Coconut milk (from a carton, not from a can)
- 2 oz Shredded coconut
- 1-2 pinches Sea salt
- 1 tsp Vanilla extract
- 6 oz Turbinado sugar
- 6 oz Eggs (3), beaten

PROCEDURE

1. Preheat your oven at 350F.
2. Weigh all the ingredients except the eggs in a large bowl. Whisk well.
3. Add the beaten eggs and whisk together until smooth.
4. Pour this batter into ramekins placed in a baking dish. Place the dish on the middle rack of your oven. Pour hot water halfway up the ramekins' sides.
5. Bake for about 20-30 minutes until they feel firm to the touch and not wiggly at the centers. Let cool. Refrigerate until needed.

✓ Chef's Tips: I enjoy this dessert with a raspberry coulis (sauce) like the one for the raspberry soufflés. The tartness brings out the coconut sweetness and flavor.

GF Beignets aux Pommes. *Apple Fritters*

When I was a kid, I loved these apple fritters. My mom would make them only during Mardis Gras. She taught me how to prepare them, and later I learned a different recipe during my apprenticeship. I love them sprinkled with turbinado sugar. You can also cover them with powdered sugar "snow".

Yield: About 16 beignets

Oil Temp: 350F

Prep Time: 20 min.

Cooking Time: 30 min.

This recipe is **GFCF**

INGREDIENTS

- 8 oz GF Bread flour mix
- 2 tsp Turbinado sugar
- 1 tsp Baking powder
- 1 pinch Sea salt
- 2 egg Yolks
- 2 Tsp Olive oil
- 2 oz GF Beer (optional)
- 6 oz Soy, almond or coconut milk
- ½ tsp Vanilla extract
- 2 Egg whites
- 1 pinch Sea salt
- 1 pinch Cream of tartar
- 4 large Apples of your choice
- Vegetable oil for frying
- GF Powdered sugar

PROCEDURE

1. Separate the yolks from the whites. Place the yolks in a cup and the whites in a mixing bowl.
2. Place the cup with the yolks on the scale, add/weigh the olive oil, beer, alternative milk of choice and vanilla. Mix lightly together.
3. In your mixer's bowl, place the flour, sugar, baking powder and salt.
4. Using the whisk attachment, start your mixer on low speed, mixing all dry ingredients together for a few seconds. Pour in the liquids progressively and keep mixing until the dough has a semi-liquid consistency and is smooth. If you have a few lumps, increase your mixer's speed to high to break down the lumps. Pour the batter in a large bowl, cover, and let rest for 30 minutes. Wash and dry the whisk attachment.
5. Meanwhile peel and core your apples. Slice them into rounds about 1/4 of an inch thick.
6. When the batter has rested, add the pinch of salt and cream of tartar to the egg whites and whip them with the whisk attachment until light and fluffy. Do not overwhip. Fold gently into the batter.
7. Heat your oil in a large frying pan or fryer until, when you drop a little bit of batter into it, it floats right back up (350F).
8. Dip each apple slice into the batter on both sides. Drop carefully into the hot oil.

Cook for about one minute until the first side is honey colored, flip each slice and cook another minute or so. Using a skimmer, take them out and place on a plate covered with paper towels to absorb the oil.

9. When cooled, place them on the serving platter and sprinkle them with powdered sugar.

Ganses Légères à la Niçoise. *Light Niçoise-Style Beignets*

I learned to make these during my apprenticeship years at Auer in Nice. What makes them different than the beignets you find in New Orleans is the addition of orange flower water. It's easy to find these days on the internet and possibly at your nearest large health food store.

Yield: About 16 beignets

Oil Temp: 350F

Prep Time: 20 min.

Cooking Time: 20-30 min.

This recipe is **GF**. Can be made **CF**

INGREDIENTS

- 8 oz **GF Bread Flour Mix**
- ½ tsp **Baking powder**
- ¼ tsp **Sea salt**
- 4 oz **Eggs (2)**
- 1 Tbsp **Orange flower water**
- 2 Tbsp **Turbinado sugar**
- 2 oz **Butter or Coconut oil**
- 3-4 oz **Soy, coconut or almond milk**
- **Vegetable oil for frying**
- **GF powdered sugar for sprinkling**

PROCEDURE

1. Weigh all the ingredients except the milk into your mixer's bowl. Start at low speed with the paddle attachment. As the dough comes together, add the alternative milk until the dough is at the "ear lobe" consistency and smooth.

2. Store in your refrigerator for at least 1 hour until it's needed.

3. Heat 3-4 inches of oil to 350F in your fryer.

4. Roll out the dough at about 1/8 of an inch. With a pastry or pizza wheel, cut strips of dough about 2 inches wide and 4 inches long. Make a knot with each strip. Drop in the hot oil. Cook until colored on one side, then flip over and cook to finish.

5. Place on a warm platter and sprinkle with powdered sugar. Sprinkle with edible lavender flowers to add a touch of color, if you have them.

✓ Chef's Tips: If you have the time or the inclination, a nice and cool "crème Anglaise" (vanilla sauce) goes very well with these beignets.

Crêpes a l'Orange et au Grand Marnier. *Orange Grand Marnier French Crepes*

This recipe is always a winner at my yearly Mardi Gras crepe party. Here, I made it GFCF for you. This is a modern version of a recipe Mamie taught me.

Servings: 4-6

Prep and Cooking Time: 45 min.

This recipe is **GFCF**

INGREDIENTS

- **1 lb (1 pint) Soy or Almond milk**
- **8 oz Eggs (4)**
- **4 oz Margarine, melted**
- **The zest of one orange**
- **¼ cup Grand Marnier or Cointreau liquor**
- **4 oz GF Bread Flour Mix**
- **1.5 oz Turbinado sugar**
- **¼ tsp Sea salt**
- **4 oz Water to adjust thickness**

PROCEDURE

1. The reason I mentioned a modern version is because I prepare this recipe in my blender. Weigh the milk (soy or almond), eggs, melted margarine, orange zest and liquor in the blender bowl. Blend well.

2. Add the flour, sugar, and salt on top. Blend again, first at low speed, then higher until it becomes smooth. If necessary, scrape the sides of the bowl with a rubber spatula.

3. Pour into a ceramic bowl. Cover with a kitchen towel. Important: Let rest for at least 30 minutes at room temperature to allow the flour to absorb the liquid and thicken.

4. Heat an 8 or 9-inch frying pan, melt a little coconut or olive oil in it and spread thinly with a paper towel. Ladle 2 ounces of batter into the pan; rotate the batter quickly and evenly around the pan. Cook until the edges are turning light brown. With a metal spatula, pick up the crepe and flip carefully. If the batter is too thick, thin it down with water. Repeat until all the batter is used.

✓ Chef's tip: Everyone has their own favorite topping. My favorite is to sprinkle a little raw sugar and lemon juice on top and fold. Miam!

Glace au Chocolat. Chocolate « Ice Cream »

If frozen coconut "ice cream" is not available in your neighborhood, here is a simple way to feed your frozen chocolate craving without the dairy.

Servings: 4-6

This recipe is **GF.**

Can be made **CF**

INGREDIENTS

- **6 oz Dark chocolate (70%)**
- **1 Tbsp Butter or Coconut oil**
- **12 oz Vanilla Soy or Coconut yogurt**
- **1 Tbsp Soy or Coconut creamer**
- **2 Egg yolks**
- **1-2 pinches Sea salt**
- **1-2 pinches Black pepper, ground**
- **2 Egg whites**
- **1 pinch Sea salt**
- **1 pinch Cream of tartar**
- **2 oz Turbinado sugar**

PROCEDURE

1. Melt your chocolate over a bain-marie (double boiler) with the butter or coconut oil. It should be melted, but not hot.

2. While the chocolate is melting, weigh the egg whites, salt, cream of tartar and sugar in your mixer's bowl. Start whipping at medium speed with the whisk attachment to make a meringue.

3. In a separate bowl, whisk together the yogurt, creamer, yolks, salt and pepper. Pour the melted chocolate over this mixture and whisk until fully incorporated.

4. When the meringue is light and fluffy, switch to high and whip to soft peaks. Fold the meringue gently into the chocolate mixture in two batches with a rubber spatula. Pour into your favorite freezer container and wait, if you can, overnight or until frozen solid. Are you sure you can wait that long?

✓ Chef's Tips: I like to add a dollop of whipped cream or soy whip topping to make it more festive.

Gateaux et Tartes. *Cakes and Tarts*

Clafoutis aux Cerises. *Cherry Flan*

During cherry season, this is a easy and wonderful dessert. It can be savored hot or cold with a cherry "coulis" (sauce).

Servings: 6 -8

Oven Temp: 350F

Prep Time: 20 min.

Baking Time: 40 min.

This recipe is **GFCF**

INGREDIENTS

- **1 oz White rice flour**
- **½ oz Almond flour**
- **¼ tsp Sea salt**
- **8 oz Eggs (4)**
- **2 oz Honey (local if possible)**
- **1 lb (1 pint) Soy, coconut or almond milk**
- **1 to 1.5 lbs Red cherries, pitted**

PROCEDURE

1. Preheat your oven to 350F.
2. In a mixing bowl, mix the rice flour, almond flour and salt with the honey and one egg and a little milk to form a smooth and homogenous paste. Add the other eggs one at a time, then the milk of your choice until the batter is liquid and free from lumps.
3. Oil a round ceramic or glass baking dish. Place as many pitted cherries as you want into the dish. Pour the batter over the cherries.
4. Bake on the middle rack at 350F for about 40 minutes until the top of your "clafoutis" is golden brown and a knife's blade comes out clean.

Gâteau au Chocolat Sans Farine. *Flourless Chocolate Cake*

This is the infamous cake a few ladies called me "the devil" for creating. Although it is not a Devil's Cake, it sure is very temping. I'll let you decide. Caution: although it appears to be a simple recipe, its execution is very delicate. I had to test multiple versions to get it right. You've been warned.

Servings: 4-6

Yield: One 9" Cake

Oven Temp: 325F

Prep Time: 20 min.

Baking Time: 60-70 min.

Cooling Time: Overnight

This recipe is **GF**. Can be made **GFCF**

INGREDIENTS

Step one:

- 1 lb Callebaut dark chocolate, coarsely chopped
- 8 oz (2 sticks) plus 1/2 tablespoon Unsalted butter or Non-hydrogenated soy margarine, cut into 1/2-inch cubes
- 2 oz Kahlua liquor (or 1 Tbsp of coffee extract)

Step two:

PROCEDURE

Cake

1. Preheat oven to 325F.
2. Using the 1/2 tablespoon of butter or margarine, grease a 9-inch spring form pan and line the bottom with a parchment round. Cover pan underneath and along sides with a single, large, continuous piece of aluminum foil (to keep the water out) and set in a roasting pan. Bring a medium saucepan of water to boil.
3. Combine the chocolate, butter (margarine), and Kahlua in a metal bowl set over simmering water, or in the top of a double boiler. Make sure no water gets into the chocolate mixture. Melt, stirring constantly, until smooth and creamy, about 5 minutes. Reserve. Do not warm too much, just to body temperature, or it will damage the fragile egg mousse.
4. Meanwhile weigh eggs, sugar, vanilla, and salt in your mixer's bowl. Using the whisk attachment, whip at high speed until frothy and almost doubled in volume, about 10 minutes.
5. Fold 1/3 of the egg mixture gently into the chocolate mixture using a rubber spatula. Repeat this process 2 more times – until all of egg mixture has been folded into chocolate mixture.
6. Pour the batter into the prepared spring form pan and place in the roasting pan. Pour enough boiling water into the

- 1 lb large free range eggs (about 8)
- 6 oz turbinado sugar
- 1 tsp organic vanilla
- 1/2 teaspoon sea salt

Whipped cream for decoration (or use prepared Soy Whipped Cream)

- 1 pint Heavy whipping cream
- 2 oz Turbinado sugar
- ½ tsp Vanilla extract
- Fresh strawberries or raspberries

roasting pan to come about halfway up the sides.

7. Bake until the cake has risen slightly and the edges are just beginning to set, about 45-50 minutes. Let cool in the pan. Remove spring form pan from roasting pan and cool on wire rack to room temperature. Remove foil, cover, and refrigerate overnight.

8. Remove cake from refrigerator about 30 minutes before serving. Slide a paring knife blade carefully along the inside edge of the pan. Remove spring form pan sides, invert cake onto a large plate, and peel away parchment paper from bottom. Invert the cake back on a serving platter.

Whipped Cream

1. In a cold mixer bowl, whisk the whipping cream, sugar and vanilla until it reaches firm peaks. Do not overwhip or it will turn into butter. With a pastry bag fitted with a star tip, apply whipped cream scrolls around the edge and center of the cake. Or, decorate with soy whipped cream just before serving or at the table.

2. Add freshly cut fresh strawberries or raspberries. Bon Appétit!

Gâteau Exotique Aux Carottes. *GF Exotic Carrot Cake*

This is a cake I created for my GF customers at Peoples Pharmacy and they love it. I can barely keep up with demand. I hope you will enjoy it too!

Yield: One 9" double-layer cake

Oven Temp: 350F

Prep Time: 20 min.

Baking Time: 30 min.

Cooling Time: Overnight

Cake: **GFCF**. Icing: Can be made **CF**

INGREDIENTS

- 1 lb 8 oz **Carrots, grated**
- 6 oz **Walnuts pieces**
- 4 oz **Coconut, shredded**
- 4 oz **Dried Currants**
- 4 oz **Candied Ginger, chopped**
- 8 oz **GF Pastry Flour**
- 2 tsp **Baking Powder**
- 2 tsp **Baking Soda**
- 1 tsp **Cinnamon, ground**
- 1tsp **Ginger, ground**
- ½ tsp **Sea Salt**
- ½ tsp **Allspice, ground**
- 8 oz **Whole Eggs (4)**
- 4 oz **Olive Oil**
- 6 oz **Turbinado Sugar**
- 4 oz **Apple Sauce**

PROCEDURE

1. Preheat your oven at 350F

2. Weigh carrots. Grate them in the food processor fitted with a medium grating plate.

3. Place mixing bowl on the scale. Add grated carrots, walnuts, coconut, currants and candied ginger. Mix together with the paddle attachment for a minute to blend well. Let sit to allow the moisture of the grated carrots to be absorbed by the dried fruits.

4. Meanwhile, prepare your pans. Take 2 -9" spring form pans. Spray them with olive oil spray. Cut two pieces of wax or baking paper to fit the pans' bottoms. Place them carefully at the bottom of each pan. Spray the paper as well. Place the two pans on two separate baking sheets.

5. In a separate bowl, weigh all the dry ingredients and mix together with a hand whisk. Set aside.

6. Add the eggs, olive oil, sugar, apple sauce and vanilla to the fruit mix. Blend well. Add the flour a little at a time and continue to blend until all the flour is absorbed.

7. Weigh out 2 lbs 6 oz of batter per pan. Bake at 350F for 15 minutes. Turn and switch cakes around to insure even

- 2 tsp Vanilla Extract

Cream Cheese Icing for one cake

- 8 oz Butter
- 8 oz GF Powdered Sugar
- 1 lb 8 oz Cream Cheese
- 2 tsp Vanilla Extract

Dairy-Free Cream Cheese icing for one cake

- 8 oz GF Powdered Sugar
- 8oz dairy-free soy margarine (non-hydrogenated)
- 24 oz (3-8 oz) dairy-free Cream Cheese, such as Tofutti
- 2 tsp Vanilla extract

baking. Bake another 15 minutes or until a small knife's blade comes out clean.

8. Refrigerate overnight or at least 2 hours before icing.

9. When ready to ice the cake, prepare the cream cheese icing: in the mixing bowl, weigh the powdered sugar, then add the butter cut in small pieces. Using the paddle attachment, start mixing at slow speed. When butter and sugar are mixed together, switch to high speed and cream well. Add the room-temperature cream cheese a little at a time until all ingredients are well blended together. Mix in vanilla extract.

10. **Dairy-free icing.** Use the same procedure but let it "set" before you ice the cake.

11. Ice and decorate the cake your favorite way. This cake should serve at least 12 people with generous slices.

Gâteau au Chocolat à la Farine de Noix de Coco et à la Ganache. *Gluten-Free Coconut Flour Chocolate Cake with Ganache Filling and Icing*

I really like the flavor combination of coconut and chocolate. I hope you do to.

Yield: One 8x2 or 9x2 cake

Oven Temp: 350F

Prep Time: 30 min.

Baking Time: 30-35 min.

Cooling Time: 2 hours

This recipe is **GF**. Can be made **CF**

INGREDIENTS

- 8 oz Butter or non-hydrogenated margarine, softened
- 12 oz Turbinado or raw sugar
- 1 lb Eggs (about 8)
- 6 oz Coconut flour
- 2 oz Unsweetened cocoa powder
- 1 ½ tsp Baking soda
- ½ tsp Baking powder
- 1 tsp Sea salt
- 4 oz Half-half or Soy creamer or Coconut creamer
- 1 tsp Vanilla extract
- Coconut oil for the pan

PROCEDURE

1. Pre-heat your oven to 350 degrees.
2. Grease two 8- or 9- inch spring form pans with coconut oil and dust with coconut flour.
3. Weigh butter (or margarine) and sugar in your mixer's bowl. With the paddle attachment, beat them together for about 3 minutes at medium speed.
4. Add eggs in one at a time until each egg is absorbed. Add the vanilla and mix.
5. Weigh the dry ingredients in a separate bowl. Stop the mixer. Add a portion of the dry ingredients. Mix in. Then add a little of the wet ingredients and mix in. Always start with the dry ingredients and finish with the dry ingredients so the mixture never has a chance to separate.
6. Once all the ingredients are mixed in, beat another 2-3 minutes on medium-high speed to allow all the ingredients to mix properly.
7. Spoon the batter into the two prepared cake pans. Smooth out the batter tops.
8. Bake at 350F for 30-35 minutes on the middle rack, or until a small knife's blade inserted into the center of the cake comes out clean.
9. Place pans on wire rack and cool for 10 minutes before removing from pans.
10. Refrigerate the cake layers completely before icing.
11. Use your favorite frosting to frost the cake or use the chocolate "ganache" below.

Ganache au Chocolat Noir. *Dark Chocolate Ganache*

In French slang, a "ganache" was the name given to an old decrepit horse. Then the meaning shifted to mean "stupid". One day, a young pastry apprentice made the mistake of pouring boiling cream on chocolate got called by his chef a "ganache", an idiot. Since then, this creamy, melt-in-the-mouth chocolate cream has been used as the interior filling for chocolate truffles and candies as well as icing for cakes.

Yield: good for 1-9" two layers cake

Prep Time: 15 min.

Cooling time: 1 hour

This recipe is **GF.**

Can be made **CF**

INGREDIENTS

- **1 lb Dark chocolate (Callebaut or Lindt 70% cocoa content minimum)**
- **8 oz Half-and-half cream, or Soy or Coconut creamer**
- **4 oz Butter or non-hydrogenated margarine at room temperature**

PROCEDURE

1. Break or chop the chocolate in small pieces.

2. Bring the half and half or creamer to a boil.

3. Pour the boiling cream or creamer on top of the chocolate. Let the mix sit for a minute to allow the cream to melt the chocolate. Whisk together until the mixture is smooth.

4. Add the soft butter or margarine. Incorporate. Let cool to icing consistency.

5. Fill and ice your chocolate coconut cake with this yummy chocolate not-so-stupid-after-all "Ganache".

Gâteau Leger au Champagne et Cointreau. *Champagne-Cointreau Chiffon Cake*

I created this cake while at Barr Mansion in Austin. This is the GF version. In case you are worried about giving this cake to children, the alcohol in the Champagne and Cointreau evaporates during baking. Only the flavors stay.

Yield: Two 8" or 9" cake layers

Prep Time: 20 min.

Baking time: 45-50 min.

Freezing time: 1-2 hours

Oven Temp: 350F

This recipe **GFCF**

INGREDIENTS

Step 1:

- 8 oz GF Pastry Flour Mix
- 8 oz Turbinado sugar
- 1 Tbsp Baking powder
- ½ tsp Sea salt

Step 2:

- 4 oz Dry champagne
- 2 oz Cointreau liquor
- 2 oz Concentrated orange juice
- 3 oz Olive oil
- 4 oz Egg yolks (about 6)

Step 3:

- 8 oz Egg whites (about 6)

PROCEDURE

1. Preheat your oven to 350F.

2. Prepare your pans. Grease them with soft coconut oil or olive oil spray. Sprinkle them with white rice flour. Tap out the excess. Or, cut 2 pieces of baking paper to the size of the pan bottom. Spray, stick and spray again.

3. Weigh and sift all ingredients in Step 1 into a large mixing bowl.

4. Weigh all wet ingredients in Step 2 into a large measuring cup.

5. Weigh egg whites, salt, cream of tartar and sugar into your mixer's bowl. Start whipping them with the whisk attachment at medium speed.

6. Meanwhile mix the wet ingredients into the large bowl of dry ingredients with a hand whisk. Make sure there are no lumps left.

7. When the egg whites are light and foamy, increase the mixer's speed to high until your meringue is at the soft peak point. Turn mixer off.

8. Fold half of the meringue into the batter in the large bowl gently with a rubber spatula to lighten the mix. Add the rest of

- ¼ tsp **Sea salt**
- 1 knife tip **Cream of tartar**
- 2 oz **Turbinado sugar**

the meringue and fold carefully.

9. Spread evenly into the two prepared pans. Bake right away on the middle rack for about 45-50 minutes or until s small knife's blade come out clean.

10. Cool down. De-pan and freeze the cake layers. The reason for freezing it is that it is a very soft sponge cake and it will be too difficult to ice if it's only refrigerated.

Glaçage a l'Orange. *Orange Frosting*

Yield: This recipe is enough to ice this size cake.

This recipe is **GFCF**

INGREDIENTS

- **14 to 16 oz GF powdered sugar, sifted if clumpy**
- **4 oz Cold coconut oil cut in small pieces**
- **4 oz Cold non-hydrogenated margarine cut in small pieces**
- **2 oz Orange juice concentrate**
- **½ tsp Orange extract**
- **Candied Orange slices (optional)**

PROCEDURE

1. Weigh the sifted powdered sugar into your mixer's bowl. Cut the cold coconut oil and margarine in small pieces.

2. With the paddle attachment on, start the mixer on slow speed and mix until the frosting gets together. Switch to medium speed and cream well. Add the concentrated orange juice and extract a little at a time until you reach the desired consistency.

3. Switch tool to a whisk and whip well on high speed until light and fluffy. If frosting is getting too soft, place it in your refrigerator until it firms up.

4. Ice your cake as you usually would. Decorate with candied orange slices.

Poire Bourdaloue. *Pear Tart with Almond Cream*

This flavor combination is a match made in pie heaven, and a French classic. Here is my GFCF Version.

Oven Temp: 350F

Prep Time: 40 min.

Baking Time: 30 min.

Yield: 1 lb. Good for 1-10" fluted tart shell with removable bottom

This recipe is **GF**. Can be made **CF**

INGREDIENTS

Tart Dough

- **4 oz Unsalted Butter or Earth Balance Margarine**
- **2 oz Turbinado Sugar**
- **¼ tsp Sea Salt**
- **2 oz Egg (1)**
- **1 tsp Lemon Juice**
- **½ tsp Vanilla extract**
- **6 oz GF Pastry Flour Mix**
- **1.5 oz White rice flour**

Almond Cream

- **8 oz Almond Paste**
- **4 oz Butter or non-hydrogenated margarine**

PROCEDURE

Pate Sucrée Sans Gluten. *GF Tart Dough*

1. Cut butter in small pieces. Add sugar and salt. Cream together in the mixer's bowl with the paddle attachment until light and fluffy.
2. Weigh the egg and lemon juice. Beat together. Add to mix a little at a time.
3. Weigh and mix the dry ingredients. Add dry ingredients into the bowl all at once. Give a short mix until the dough comes together.
4. Gather into a ball. Flatten and wrap in plastic film. Refrigerate for at least two hours.
5. Later, place your 10" tart pan on a baking pan. Dust your working space with a little of the GF Pastry Flour Mix and roll the dough until its about two inches wider than the pan's diameter. Pick up the rolled out dough gently by wrapping it over the rolling pin. Roll it out over the pan. Push the edges gently into the pan. Cut out the extra dough. Cool down for a few minutes while you're preparing the almond cream (frangipane).

Crème Frangipane (aux Amandes). *Almond Cream*

1. Weigh the almond paste and butter (margarine) in the mixer's bowl. Start the mixer at low speed with the paddle attachment. When the two ingredients come together, switch to medium speed and cream well.

- 4 oz Eggs (2)
- ½ tsp Lemon Juice
- 3 oz Corn or potato starch

To Finish the Tart

- 1 tart shell
- Almond cream
- 1 large can Pears in syrup, drained
- Apricot glaze

To poach the pears

- 6 Pears of your choice
- 2 qt water
- 2 lbs turbinado sugar
- 2 tsp Vanilla extract

2. In a measuring cup, lightly beat the eggs and the lemon juice together.
3. Add the egg and lemon juice mix to the almond paste a little at a time. Keep on creaming until all of it is absorbed.
4. Add the corn starch and mix carefully at low speed.

Pour Finir la Tarte. *To Finish the Tart*

1. Preheat your oven at 350F.
2. Take your tart shell out of the fridge. Spread the almond cream over the bottom of the tart shell. Place your pears over the cream, keeping the narrow end towards the center. Finish with a final pear at the center.
3. Bake on the middle rack for about 30 minutes or until the cream is golden brown. Cool down. Glaze with the apricot glaze. Miam!

Pour pocher vos poires. **To poach your pears**

1. In a 4 quart pot, bring to simmer the water, sugar and vanilla extract. Lower the heat to simmer.
2. Meanwhile, peal and core your pears. Cut in halves.
3. Place the pear halves in one layer in the simmering syrup and cook gently for 20-30 minutes until the pears are tender.

✓ Chef's Tips: You can prepare this tart with many different fruits, in-season if possible.

ACKNOWLEDGMENTS

At first, this book presented me with a new challenge: how to approach a health condition I did not personally suffer from. As this book neared completion, I learned that I do, in fact, have a gluten allergy. Now that I know I am affected as well, my understanding has become much deeper of the challenges gluten and dairy-allergic people are faced with on a daily basis.

On this journey, I was helped tremendously by a small group of enthusiastic friends and professionals eager to help me spread the good news: yes, you can live without gluten and dairy, and live well. Not only that, but it is possible to eat a healthy and even gourmet diet, with beautiful, fresh and flavorful food. I would like to thank the following people for their constant inspiration, as well as their professional and volunteer assistance:

My grand-mother **"Mamie"** for teaching me by example that healthy food should come from one's kitchen garden, freshly picked and prepared quickly but with love, and that it does not have to be complicated to taste wonderful.

My mother, **Bernadette Moulin-Braux,** who encouraged me to discover and apply my culinary and baking abilities. My mother-in-law, **Helene Jaboulay**, for opening my eyes to what Mediterranean cuisine is all about. She always amazed me with her ability to feed her family with simple but flavorful home-cooked "cuisine du Sud".

Janet Zand for being my first supporter, even before I started writing the first word. She has been my model and inspiration all along. Thank you Janet.

My very creative team: My caring and understanding editor, **Kathleen Thornberry** for her loving work on my "charabia" or Frenglish gibberish. When it comes to food and health, we are kindred spirits and this project would have been almost impossible without her astute suggestions and reinterpretation of my "Frenchisms", while preserving the spirit of my writing. **Athena Danoy** for capturing that special spark in me in her portrait. **Nathan Stueve** for designing a beautiful and practical web site and an original book cover. Their creative efforts supported my vision for this book. I literally could not have done it without them.

My esteemed predecessors and guiding mentors: **Hippocrates** 460-377 B.C., the father of us all in the "food as a healing medium" movement, who affirmed, "Let thy food be thy medicine and thy medicine be thy food". And I cannot forget my daily inspiration for writing this book: **Jonny Bowden, Ph. D.** and **George Mateljan**. My Chef's hat off to both of you for proving that we can still hack it, even if we're not in our 30's.

Bill Swail for providing me the safety and security I needed during the writing of this book. Also for supporting this new effort with his astute marketing advice.

Kecia Johndrow and **Dianne Doggett** for helping with the section on Autism, making sure I did not write anything out of line. This section has been reviewed by very qualified moms.

Liz Mullen and **Beth McCall** for being my frontline celiac enthusiastic and knowledgeable reviewers, and for their careful perusal of different sections of my "compuscript".

Trish Bales, Julia Bower, Jessica Meyer, Lynda Jones, Beth McCall, Liz Mullen and **Patrick Sandoval** for helping me with the spelling and punctuation-checking of the Hidden Sources of Gluten and Dairy, Shopping List and Main Body of the book.

Tim and Barbara Cook for their spiritual guidance and encouragements.

Almost last but by no means least, my son **Gilles Braux** for inspiring me to be the best I can, just by being and staying himself no matter what. I hope that this and my other books will show him the way to healthy living.

And finally, my **GFCF Friends** and **GFCF Champions** that have been supporting me throughout in my belief that fresh and good-tasting food is the source of good health. Thanks for all you're doing.

And finally but very important to this book, the people that opened their hearts and shared with us their gut-wrenching experiences (in order of appearance in the book):

Paula Tuttle – Austin, TX

Liz V. Mullen – Dallas, TX

Annie Hebert Phenix – Durango, CO

www.mimistoast.blogspot.com and annie@phenixdogs.com

Jeff Williams – Austin, TX

Karen Morgan – Austin, TX. Founder and Owner of Blackbird Bakery. **www.blackbird-bakery.com**

Maggie Tate – Austin, TX

Dawn Aubrey – Austin, TX. Certified Clinical Nutritionist. Certified Lifestyle Educator.

Jocelyne Vince – Austin, TX

Kelly Feole – Austin, TX. Fashion Designer and Co-Founder of Feosh Designs

Kim Stanford – Austin, TX. Co-Author of "Gluten Freedom"

Charlotte Skiles , MS, NC, ACN – Austin, TX
Consultant & Clinical Herbalist
Eat in Peace Wellness Consulting
512-587-0338 cell
512-233-2755 fax
www.charlotteskiles.com

Jessica Meyer, BS, MS – Austin, TX
Nutritionist. Gluten-Free Private Chef at: http://atxglutenfree.wordpress.com

Trish Bales - Austin, TX. Chez Vous Personal Chef Services at www.chezvousbytrish.com and www.glutenfreejourney.com

Kecia Johndrow – Austin, TX. Vice President. National Autism Association of Central Texas at http://www.naacentraltexas.org

Meagan McGovern – Austin, TX

Nicole Dawkins – Austin, TX

Thank you all from the bottom of my GF heart.

Love and GFCF Dark Chocolate. Chef Alain Braux.

Do you want to know more about Chef Braux?

If you want to:

- Consult privately with me,
- Want me to create a customized diet for your specific food allergies situation,
- Want to find out about my cooking and baking classes,
- Want me to create cooking and baking classes for your Cooking School,
- Have questions about this book,
- Have questions about my upcoming book "How to Live Gluten and Dairy-free with French Gourmet Food",
- Want to hire me as a Health Food and Gluten-free consultant for your restaurant,
- Want to interview me for a featured article,
- Would like to invite me as a Health Speaker at your event,
- Or for any other health-related opportunities.

Feel free to check my constantly updated web site: **www.alainbraux.com**

You can also contact me through my web site Contact page or send me an email to: alainbraux@gmail.com

Thank you again for reading my book and "see" you soon in my next book.

Sincerely,

Chef Alain Braux

CEPC, CMB, B.S. in Holistic Nutrition, Macrobiotic Counselor.